Oxford Studies in European Law

Series Editors: Paul Craig and Gráinne de Búrca

EU CONSUMER LAW AND HUMAN RIGHTS

OXFORD STUDIES IN EUROPEAN LAW

The aim of this series is to publish important and original research on EU law. The focus is on scholarly monographs, with a particular emphasis on those which are interdisciplinary in nature. Edited collections of essays will also be included where they are appropriate. The series is wide in scope and aims to cover studies of particular areas of substantive and of institutional law, historical works, theoretical studies, and analyses of current debates, as well as questions of perennial interest such as the relationship between national and EU law and the novel forms of governance emerging in and beyond Europe. The fact that many of the works are interdisciplinary will make the series of interest to all those concerned with the governance and operation of the EU.

OTHER TITLES IN THIS SERIES

The Coherence of EU Free Movement Law
Constitutional Responsibility and the Court of Justice
Niamh Nic Shuibhne

European Law and New HealthTechnologies
Edited by Mark L Flear, Anne-Maree Farrell, Tamara K Hervey, and Thérèse Murphy

The Legal Effect of EU Agreements
Mario Mendez

The Enforcement of EU Law
The Role of the European Commission
Stine Andersen

European Agencies
Law and Practices of Accountability
Madalina Busuioc

The Foundations of European Union
The Objective and Principles of Article 102
Renato Nazzini

The Emergence of EU Contract Law
Exploring Europeanization
Lucinda Miller

Participation in EU Rule-making
A Rights-Based Approach
Joana Mendes

Regulating Cartels in Europe Second Edition
Christopher Harding, Julian Joshua

Religion and the Public Order of the European Union
Ronan McCrea

Governing Social Inclusion
Europeanization through Policy Coordination
Kenneth A Armstrong

Judicial Control in the European Union
Reforming Jurisdiction in the Intergovernmental Pillars
Alicia Hinarejos

EU Counter-Terrorist Policies and Fundamental Rights
The Case of Individual Sanctions
Christina Eckes

From Dual to Cooperative Federalism
The Changing Structure of European Law
Robert Schütze

EU Consumer Law and Human Rights

IRIS BENÖHR

OXFORD
UNIVERSITY PRESS

OXFORD
UNIVERSITY PRESS

Great Clarendon Street, Oxford, OX2 6DP,
United Kingdom

Oxford University Press is a department of the University of Oxford.
It furthers the University's objective of excellence in research, scholarship,
and education by publishing worldwide. Oxford is a registered trade mark of
Oxford University Press in the UK and in certain other countries

First Edition published in 2013
Corrected 2016

Published in the United States of America by Oxford University Press
198 Madison Avenue, New York, NY 10016, United States of America

British Library Cataloguing in Publication Data
Data available

Library of Congress Control Number: 2013946940

ISBN 978–0–19–965197–9

PREFACE

The EEC was shaped initially by the divide between market making, which was the primary objective of the single market project, and issues of social protection that were left largely to Member States. This divide has weakened considerably over time. The EC has gained competence in the latter area, as exemplified by inclusion in the Maastricht Treaty of consumer protection.

This initiative was given greater precision by the Treaty of Amsterdam, and the relevant provision is now Article 169 TFEU, which provides in essence that in order to promote the interests of consumers and to ensure a high level of consumer protection, the EU shall contribute to protecting the health, safety and economic interests of consumers, as well as to promoting their right to information, education and to organize themselves in order to safeguard their interests. The EU with 28 Member States is a very sizeable market, and hence the changes in consumer law resulting from technological innovation, and new modes of distribution are especially significant. Within the EU, consumer law is driven by twin imperatives, these being market efficiency and harmonization on the one hand, and recognition of the need to protect the consumer as a social policy objective on the other.

Iris Benöhr's book is therefore timely and considers in depth the relationship between consumer law, the EU constitutional framework, human rights and the changing role of the state in the Union. She considers how social justice and cultural diversity in consumer regulation can be included in the EU integration process, and what institutional instruments can effectively protect consumers, while promoting active participation, inclusion and confidence in the cross-border market. The linkage between fundamental rights and consumer protection is assessed both generally and in three specific areas of consumer law, these being consumer credit regulation, electronic communication and access to justice.

The book will be of interest to all those concerned with the relationship between market integration and consumer protection, and more broadly with the interaction between economic policy, social policy and fundamental rights in the EU.

Paul Craig and Gráinne de Búrca

ACKNOWLEDGMENTS

This book was completed while I was a British Academy Postdoctoral Fellow at the Centre for Socio-Legal Studies, Faculty of Law, University of Oxford. It is based on my doctoral thesis, defended at the European University Institute in Florence. I am very grateful to both institutions for their support, while I also thank the University of Lausanne, the Institute of European and Comparative Law of the University of Oxford, and the University of Wisconsin-Madison, USA, for welcoming me as a visiting researcher and for providing inspiration at different stages of the journey that led to this book.

This book would have not been possible without the support of several people. I am grateful to my PhD supervisors Christian Joerges and Hans-W. Micklitz for their valuable advice and guidance. I am indebted to my mentor Stephen Weatherill for his comments which were important to finalize this monograph, and to Roland Bieber, for his helpful suggestions on earlier drafts.

Others too have provided valuable advice, assistance, or comments. Among them, I would like to thank Denis Galligan, Ulf Bernitz, Norbert Reich, Christopher Hodges, Bruno de Witte, William Whitford, Marie-Ange Moreau, Neil K. Komesar, Bettina Lange, Adrian Duke, and the anonymous referees for OUP.

This book is dedicated to my parents, Christine and Michael Benöhr, and to my grandparents, Robert and Simone Muller, who have been supportive and encouraging during my studies. I am also particularly indebted to my husband Marco Galbiati for his patience and encouragement throughout the writing of this book.

Iris Benöhr
University of Oxford

CONTENTS

TABLE OF CASES

European Court of Justice

European Court of Human Rights

Rest of the World

TABLE OF LEGISLATION

EU Instruments

EU Communications

Council of Europe Documents

'Consumers by definition include us all. They are the largest economic group in the economy, affecting and affected by almost every public and private economic decision. Two-thirds of all spending in the economy is by consumers. But they are the only important group in the economy who are not effectively organized, whose views are often not heard.'

President John F. Kennedy, speech to Congress in 1962

1

Introduction

This book examines the impact of the Lisbon Treaty and the Charter of Fundamental Rights on consumer protection. Traditionally, EU consumer law has mostly been applied in a narrow sense, as an instrument to achieve market integration. However, the Lisbon Treaty, which entered into force on 1 December 2009, grants binding legal force to the EU Charter of Fundamental Rights, which acknowledges for the first time a broader human rights and 'solidarity' dimension to consumer protection. The Charter introduces far-reaching social and economic rights and provides new rights, such as the protection of personal data, which may well have significant implications for consumer protection. Furthermore, by requiring the European Union to become a party to the European Convention on Human Rights, the Lisbon Treaty explicitly assigns to human rights a more central role in the EU legal system.

Fundamental rights have already produced important effects in the jurisprudence of the European Court of Justice (ECJ). Recent ground-breaking and sometimes controversial judgments have highlighted the role that fundamental rights can play in consumer-related cases, dealing with questions of effective judicial protection, data protection, and the freedom to receive or impart information.[1]

The novel legal framework suggests that the EU institutions and Member States will give more importance to fundamental rights. However, a closer

[1] E.g. Joined Cases C-317/08 to C-320/08, *Alassini and others v Telecom Italia* [2010] ECR I-2213; Case C-70/10, *Scarlet Extended SA v Société belge des auteurs, compositeurs et éditeurs SCRL (SABAM)* 24 November 2011, report not yet published; regarding non-discrimination see Case C-236/09, *Association Belge des Consommateurs Test-Achats ASBL and Others v Conseil des ministres* [2011] ECR I-00773.

look reveals that the application of the Charter is limited and remains abstract in practice.

In the light of these developments, a number of important questions emerge: what is the significance of the EU Charter for the protection of individual consumers and collective social and economic interests? Will the new fundamental rights regime have a practical impact on EU consumer law and policy, both in terms of its substance and in terms of the process by which it is formed? Can the new legal framework overcome pressing challenges in the internal market, such as increasing over-indebtedness, and a lack of consumer confidence in cross-border purchases? Above all, is the binding Charter a new step for the EU towards forming a community of values and solidarity which transcends economic integration, or is it only a symbolic declaration?

To put these questions into perspective, it is useful to briefly describe the historical background of consumer protection. Consumer law has changed significantly in recent decades and now plays a central role in both EU market integration and social welfare. Its roots can be traced back to President John F. Kennedy's famous speech in 1962, which proposed the establishment of four basic consumer rights. This became necessary as product scandals, such as those following the discovery of birth defects caused by the drug Thalidomide, demonstrated that a market without regulation could harm consumers. After years of growth in global trade and expansion in the variety of goods and services, consumer law has developed into a distinct subject in national regulations, and has gained recognition at an international level.

In the EU, consumer protection was introduced in order to improve market integration, with the adoption of an action programme in 1975.[2] The European Community was initially conceived as a means of integrating the economies of the Member States, and was aimed almost exclusively at enhancing transnational market performance. The EU's approach to integration was influenced by the ordo-liberalist perspective, according to which markets are made at the transnational level, while the Member States control redistribution and formulate social policy.[3] Eventually, the Treaty of Maastricht of 1992 integrated the protection of the consumer into its objectives in Articles 3(s)

[2] Council Resolution of 14 April 1975 on a preliminary programme of the European Economic Community for a consumer protection and information policy, OJ 1975 C 92/1.

[3] See Ch. Joerges, 'What is Left of the European Economic Constitution?', EUI WP Law 2004/13, pp. 7 and 14-17.

and 129(a). Article 129(a) stated that the Community should contribute to the attainment of a high level of consumer protection, by adopting measures within the framework of the internal market, and by supporting national policies on consumer protection. In 1997, the Treaty of Amsterdam strengthened consumer protection, by stipulating in Article 153 (now Article 169 TFEU) that the Community should promote a number of consumer rights, such as the rights to information and education.

During the last 30 years, consumer law has undergone a considerable transformation both in the European Union and in the Member States due to market expansion and technological innovation. Today, the European Union, with its 28 Member States, has become one of the largest markets in the world, comprising more than 480 million consumers. The mode of exchanging products and services has changed, with modern forms of distribution and electronic cross-border purchases. EU consumer law is entering a new phase and is facing two interdependent trends. On one side, consumer protection is influenced by the EU's market efficiency and harmonization objectives. On the other, it is recognized as a fundamental social policy objective and consumers are generally becoming more politically active, for example by expressing ethical values when purchasing products or services.

In this context, consumer protection has become increasingly linked to fundamental rights, with consumers seen as vulnerable individuals who require protection by the state, but also as potentially active promoters of human rights values through ethical purchasing behaviour.[4] At the same time, the rise in consumerism has also led to externalities including environmental degradation, which pose new challenges for the concept of sustainable consumption and may negatively affect fundamental policy objectives.[5]

While the enlarged market enhances competition by favouring an increase in consumer choice and lowering prices, it also generates additional transaction complexity and creates new challenges for consumers. The growing number of cross-border exchanges in anonymous markets heightens the risk of abuse, creates new health hazards, and may render access to both information and justice more difficult. At the same time, increased information asymmetries have caused market failures to be more frequent and grave.

[4] See A. Fagan, 'Buying Rights: Consuming Ethically and Human Rights', in J. Dine & A. Fagan (eds), *Human Rights and Capitalism: A Multidisciplinary Perspective on Globalisation* (Cheltenham: Edward Elgar Publishing, 2006), p. 115.

[5] K. Tonner, 'Sustainable Consumption, Consumer Policy and the Law', in C. Verdure (ed.), 'Environmental Law and Consumer Protection', (2011) 1 *Eur J Consumer Law*, p. 9.

The inability of the market to deliver socially desirable outcomes has become manifest in the damage to health caused by unsafe products and in several other economically important cases of market failure; in particular, in the financial sector and in liberalized services, such as telecommunications and transport. Some claim that market failures are also at the root of modern social problems, such as over-indebtedness of consumers.

These episodes represent 'market failures' for several reasons: first, they depart from socially desirable market outcomes, as they impose social 'costs' which evidently outweigh the 'benefits' reaped by a few, sometimes fraudulent firms, so that the overall balance for society is negative. Secondly, in the absence of a sanction they introduce distortions into the market, as some companies may gain a competitive advantage over other companies which, in contrast, adopt more 'correct' behaviour. Finally, these episodes have instilled a high degree of suspicion in consumers towards certain markets (in particular, cross-border markets), thwarting the realization of the benefits of an integrated EU economy.[6]

Market expansion, along with financial and technological innovation, is thus generating new challenges for consumer protection. The EU has responded to these challenges by strengthening its consumer policy and by creating an autonomous consumer protection competence at the EU level. The Treaties of Maastricht and Amsterdam endowed the EU with the competence to regulate consumer matters. An analysis of this competence, however, reveals limitations which stem from an approach based upon a narrow concept of the consumer. Indeed, the notion of the consumer introduced by the European Court of Justice is often 'instrumental' to the functioning of the market.[7] The same narrow approach is evident in the law-making process of the EU, which usually approves new legislation on the basis of Article 114 TFEU (ex Article 95 EC). This norm allows harmonization measures only when they have a beneficial impact on the efficiency of the market. Alternatively, Article 169(2)(b) TFEU (ex Article 153 EC), which allows consumer protection independently of market rationales, has hardly ever been applied in order to make legislative initiatives.

[6] This has been illustrated in European market studies, which have highlighted that the consumer lacks confidence and does not participate actively in cross-border purchases; see European Commission, Eurobarometer 2006 Special Report 252, 'Consumer Protection in the Internal Market', pp. 44-79.

[7] See e.g. Case C-183/00, *Gonzalez Sanchez* [2002] ECR I-3901, Case C-52/00, *Commission v France* [2002] ECR I-3827, and Case C-154/00, *Commission v Greece* [2002] ECR I-3879.

The limitations stemming from this conception of the consumer are now more visible than in the past. Initially, the EU's focus on economic integration was less problematic, because national regulators could often adopt higher standards of consumer protection if necessary. However, the growing impact of EU law through full harmonization has altered the structural equilibrium between EU and national consumer competences. Some argue that this has led to a social deficit, because, inter alia, with the current EU policy direction towards the full harmonization of consumer law, Member States are increasingly unable to provide more stringent protective standards for consumers.[8] The influence of the primary goal (namely, economic integration) might de facto prevail over high-standard national consumer law and does not fully take account of different legal cultures. Thus, the question arises of how certain values can be maintained in an expanding market with growing competition and less control. How can consumers be taken account of as human beings? Finally, why should the EU be better placed to decide on consumer standards than the Member States?

These challenges have been met by a revitalized discourse about human rights and consumer law, sustained by the re-emergence of social movements and crowned at an EU level by the inclusion of consumer protection in the Charter of Fundamental Rights. The Charter was created with a detailed catalogue of fundamental rights, encompassing core values that are common to the Member States and defining a society founded on pluralism, non-discrimination, justice, and solidarity. Consumer protection is included in chapter IV of the Charter on 'Solidarity', recognized as a fundamental policy objective.

Such high-level recognition of consumer protection is a clear departure from the traditional approach discussed earlier in the chapter. Furthermore, the Charter and the Lisbon Treaty introduce a number of new provisions that are relevant for consumer protection. However, some doubts exist as to whether the Charter will be able to complement the existing approach effectively.[9] Can the Lisbon Treaty and the Charter lead the way in broadening the traditional consumer model of market integration? Importantly, what is the role of the

[8] See e.g.: S. Weatherill, *European Consumer Law and Policy*, (Cheltenham: Edward Elgar Publishing, 2005); H.-W. Micklitz, 'European Consumer Law', in E. Jones, A. Menon & S. Weatherill (eds.), *The Oxford Handbook of the European Union* (Oxford: OUP, 2012).

[9] M. Hesselink, 'European Contract Law: A Matter of Consumer Protection, Citizenship, or Justice?', (2007) 3 *Eur. Rev. Private Law*, pp. 323 *et seq*.

ECJ in this regard and how will economic freedoms and fundamental social rights be balanced in practice?

To date, few theoretical enquiries exist into the relationship between consumer law, the EU constitutional framework and human rights. This book addresses this gap by analyzing the implications of the Lisbon Treaty and the Charter of Fundamental Rights on consumer protection. It provides a novel perspective on consumer law, centered on human rights and inspired by economic, social and legal theories.

The links between fundamental rights and different theoretical approaches, and their bearing on consumer protection, will be systematically assessed in three core areas of consumer law: consumer credit regulation, electronic communication, and access to justice. An analysis of consumer credit regulation will show how financial capability can be achieved in practice, illustrating the impact of fundamental rights, and other EU laws and principles on the provision of fair contractual conditions. In the second area, regarding electronic communication services, the book will examine the key role played by the fundamental right to data protection and the freedom to receive or impart information, which have to be balanced against other fundamental rights, such as the right to property. Moreover, the provision of electronic communication services will be shown to be an effective tool for consumer participation in society. Finally, moving to the third area, this work will consider the role of alternative dispute resolution, collective actions, and litigation funding in strengthening the fundamental right of access to justice. These case studies are of particular importance because they touch upon typical problems engendered by enlarged markets and privatization and offer fresh insights into how to empower and protect consumers.

Conceptually, this book is divided in two parts, comprising eight chapters. The first part (Chapters 1–4) analyzes the content and limitations of the current European framework, proposing a new theoretical approach to consumer law. In the second part (Chapters 5–7), this approach is explored in three relevant areas, as detailed below.

Chapters 1–2 sketch the development of consumer law and analyze the legal framework and policy approach of the EU in this area. Chapter 3 explores the progressive convergence of consumer protection and fundamental rights, examining the possible implications of consumer protection as a human right. Chapter 4 proposes a new theoretical approach to consumer law and human rights, which can be promoted by fundamental rights and may reconcile economic integration and social principles. Chapters 5 to 7 make the proposed consumer approach operational in three key areas of consumer law: consumer credit, services of general interest (electronic communication in particular), and finally access to justice. The concluding Chapter 8 summarizes and proposes new directions for consumer law and policy in the EU.

2

Consumer Law and the Market

1. Introduction

In the eighteenth century, consumer law was almost non-existent and had to be created through civil society movements.[1] It was only after World War II that consumer protection developed in its own right as a separate branch of rules and principles. This evolution was part of a profound change in the attitude of individuals and governments, caused by an increase in goods and services in larger markets that, without adequate regulation, could be hazardous for consumers.[2] In more recent times, with the creation and enlargement of the common market, consumer law has become a driving force in the European integration process.

From the outset, the European Community was based upon a neo-liberal philosophy.[3] While consumer protection had first appeared at the national level, in the Community it was mainly used as an instrument to drive market integration. As a result, from the 1970s onwards, many scholars started to argue for an improvement in the legal position of consumers through the adoption of specific laws or a comprehensive consumer code.[4]

Eventually, consumer protection was included in the Single European Act (1986), instigated by the drive towards a single market (Article 100a). The Treaty of Maastricht (1992) provided the European Community with the express

[1] F. Trentmann, 'Knowing Consumers—Histories, Identities, Practices: An Introduction', in F. Trentmann (ed), *The Making of the Consumer: Knowledge, Power and Identity in the Modern World* (Oxford-New York: Berg, 2006), pp. 6–9.

[2] M. Everson & Ch. Joerges, 'Consumer Citizenship in Postnational Constellations?' EUI WP Law 2006/47, Florence, p. 8.

[3] W. van Gerven, *The European Union: A Polity of States and Peoples* (Oxford: Hart Publishing, 2005), p. 200.

[4] J. Calais-Auloy, *Propositions pour un nouveau droit de la consommation* (Paris: Documentation française, 1985).

competence to protect consumers in Article 129a, whereas the subsequent Treaty of Amsterdam (1997) gave the European Community the potential to promote specific consumer rights, including the right to information and education (Article 153).

Since the Commission's Consumer Policy Strategy 2002-2006,[5] the EU has pursued a full-harmonization approach to consumer law. As it does not allow more stringent national consumer protection, such an approach might diminish both legal diversity and higher standards of protection in force in some Member States. In addition, EU measures have mostly been adopted as a tool of market integration, and seldom for consumer protection per se. Consequently, rising tensions have become apparent between national measures of consumer protection and EU actions to improve market integration.

In the light of this development, a number of questions arise. What is the division of competences between the EU and the Member States? Should consumer law in the EU be limited to a market-forming role, or should it include wider citizens' concerns? What legal instruments can promote consumer welfare in a broad sense and not only in terms of expanded markets and economic integration?

In order to address some of these questions, this chapter will explore the development of EU consumer law and will assess the application and the limitations of the Treaties and their impact on Member States. Section 2 gives a historical overview of consumer law, explaining how it evolved in both national and international law. Section 3 describes the evolution of consumer law at the EU level and analyzes the Union's competence in this field. Finally, section 4 explores the current policy trend towards full harmonization of consumer law in the EU and the need for a new legal approach.

2. Historical Evolution of Consumer Law and Policy

Laws protecting the buyer against fraud have existed for a long time in society.[6] However, consumer protection as a systematic policy goal is a

[5] Communication from the Commission of 7 May 2002—'Consumer Policy Strategy 2000–2006', COM (2002) 208 final—OJ 2002 C137/2.

[6] For instance, rules on weights and measures existed to protect the buyers from fraud; see G. Howells & T. Wilhelmsson, 'EC Consumer Law', in G. Howells (ed.), *European Business Law* (Aldershot: Dartmouth, 1996), pp. 273 *et seq*; regarding protection from excessive pricing see B.W. Harvey, & D.L. Parry, *The Law of Consumer Protection and Fair Trading*, 5th edn (London: Butterworths, 1996), pp. 1–3.

recent phenomenon which began, globally, only in the middle of the twentieth century.

Three stages can be distinguished in the evolution of national and international consumer protection. In the first stage, before and during the nineteenth century, there was no effort to protect consumers as a particular group within the market.[7] During the second stage, the political awareness of consumers increased internationally in the 1960s because of mass production and health scandals, which clearly highlighted the need for regulation, and resulted in civil movements for consumer protection.[8] Finally, in the third stage which began at the end of the 1970s, the consumer has been protected by legal norms in European Member States and at the Community and international level.

2.1. *The lack of a consumer law category*

Initially, consumer law was not recognized as a separate legal category, because the buyer was not believed to be in need of special legal protection.[9] When the majority of people still subsisted on agricultural goods, only basic transactions were concluded in order to purchase goods which could not easily be produced on the family farm. This changed in ancient Rome, where a number of contractual laws were introduced which formed the basis of future consumer laws. For instance, Roman law provided for an action against the seller in order to protect buyers from any hidden defects in goods purchased. Furthermore, Roman law introduced the principle that the seller had to be in good faith in seeking not to cause damage to the buyer.[10]

In the medieval age, the legal institutions to protect the buyer could again be found in the *jus commune* of the time. However, according to a German saying 'buy with open eyes', the purchaser had to assess the good carefully before the transaction, because it was difficult to withdraw from the contract in the case of a defect.[11] At that time, there was no significant need for

[7] See more on the evolution of consumer law at national level in Everson & Joerges, 'Consumer Citizenship in Postnational Constellations?' (n 2), pp. 3 *et seq*.

[8] This period started with President John F. Kennedy's speech in 1962, which outlined four basic consumer rights, later translated into the Consumer Bill of Rights.

[9] See Everson & Joerges (n 2) pp. 4–7.

[10] See more in V. Truchet, 'Le concept du consommateur informé en droit européen', in R. Bieber (ed.), *Swiss Papers on European Integration* (Bern-Zurich: Stämpfli-Schulthess, 2000), p. 7.

[11] Truchet, 'Le concept du consommateur informé en droit européen' (n 10), p. 7.

consumer protection because markets were relatively small and the good reputation of the seller and the personal relationship between tradespersons were deemed sufficient to protect buyers from any potential abuse or harm.[12]

This relationship-oriented exchange disappeared, however, with the Industrial Revolution, owing to progress in transport and infrastructure, which facilitated exchange between diverse cities and states. As a result, the market expanded from a regional, to a national and world-wide exchange. With the arrival of mass production, producers and distributors became anonymous entities for the buyer and trade became more complex. Consequently, regulation was necessary to organize the relationship between consumers and sellers in order to prevent market abuses.

In the nineteenth century, in line with Adam Smith's 'invisible hand', it was assumed that the market was sufficient to ensure consumer welfare.[13] As a result, specific protection of the weaker contractual party was considered unnecessary and a focus on contractual autonomy was predominant.[14] This slowly changed with emerging consumer mobilization, which first became visible in Britain, aimed at overcoming the information deficit through the development of consumer protection measures.[15] Driven by consumer movements, this trend was followed in a number of countries, eventually leading to an international recognition of consumer law.[16]

2.2. *Political recognition of the consumer at the international level*

Consumer protection attracted political attention in the early 1960s. This sudden interest was due to health scandals that painfully demonstrated that an unbalanced power relationship between purchasers and producers could result in serious damage to consumers, and opened the door to the creation of a proper consumer protection policy.

[12] Truchet (n 10), p. 7.

[13] M. Everson, 'Legal Construction of the Consumer', in F. Trentmann (ed.), *The Making of the Consumer: vol 1, Knowledge, Power and Identity in the Modern World* (Oxford-New York: Berg, 2006), pp. 100–1.

[14] Everson, 'Legal Construction of the Consumer' (n 13), pp. 100–3.

[15] In 1962 the 'Molony Report' of the Committee on Consumer Protection was issued in the UK; see more in I. Ramsay, *Consumer Law and Policy: Text and Materials on Regulating Consumer Markets* (Oxford: Hart Publishing, 2012), pp. 3–6.

[16] F. Trentmann (ed.), *The Making of the Consumer: vol 1, Knowledge, Power and Identity in the Modern World* (Oxford-New York: Berg, 2006).

The historical moment associated with the birth of consumer policy was President John F. Kennedy's speech to Congress in 1962.[17] This speech was made in response to public anger about the thalidomide scandal, which showed that the safety interest of consumers had been seriously neglected. Therefore, pressure was exerted for more regulatory control in order to protect the consumer. In his speech, Kennedy stressed the need for a distinct legal protection of the consumer, which required new legislative and administrative measures. The ensuing Consumer Bill of Rights highlighted the importance of protecting the consumer per se, enumerating four different rights: the right to safety, the right to be informed, the right to choose, and the right to be heard. Following this, the consumer movement crossed the Atlantic and, from the 1970s onwards, various European countries adopted protective consumer regulations.[18]

Several international organizations were similarly developing the idea of consumer protection as an independent legal concept.[19] On 9 April 1985, the Assembly of the United Nations adopted Resolution 39/248, which established general principles for consumer protection, endorsing Kennedy's Consumer Bill of Rights.[20] This resolution did not have a compulsory value but it represented a landmark: with it, a universally recognized institution enounced general principles and guidelines, inviting governments to propose policies for consumer protection. The general principles section of the resolution enumerates a number of goals that the guidelines intend to meet:

(a) the protection of consumers from hazards to their health and safety;
(b) the promotion and protection of the economic interests of consumers;
(c) access of consumers to adequate information;
(d) consumer education;

[17] John F. Kennedy's speech, Public Papers of the United States, Public Messages, Speeches and Statements of the President, 1 January to 31 December, 1962, pp. 235–43.

[18] For a historical overview, see F. Trentmann, 'Knowing Consumer-Histories, Identities, Practices', in F. Trentmann (ed.), *The Making of the Consumer: vol 1, Knowledge, Power and Identity in the Modern World* (Oxford-New York: Berg, 2006), pp. 2–8; see also H.-G. Haupt, *Konsum und Handel: Europa im 19. und 20. Jahrhundert* (Göttingen: Vandenhoeck & Ruprecht, 2003).

[19] Besides the UN and the Council of Europe, the WHO, FAO, and the OECD also contributed to the development of consumer protection standards; see T. Bourgoignie, 'Consumer Law and the European Community: Issues and Prospects', in T. Bourgoignie & D. Trubek (eds), *Consumer Law, Common Markets and Federalism in Europe and the United States* (Vol. 3: Integration through Law Series) (Berlin: de Gruyter, 1987), pp. 91 *et seq*.

[20] United Nations General Assembly on 16 April 1985, A/RES/39/248; see also the UN website: <http://www.un.org/documents/ga/res/39/a39r248.htm>.

(e) availability of effective consumer redress; and
(f) freedom to form consumer organizations and the opportunity of such organizations to present their views in decision-making processes.[21]

At the European level, the Council of Europe also contributed at an early stage to the protection of consumer standards. The Consultative Assembly of the Council adopted a Consumer Protection Charter in Resolution 543 of 17 May 1973, which, while lacking a binding character, represented a clear political recognition of consumer protection.[22] This helped to raise awareness of consumer matters and provided an impetus for its Member States to introduce protective measures. Moreover, the Council of Europe adopted a number of Conventions, some of which had a direct impact on the European Community and national consumer regulation, such as the European Convention on Products Liability in regard to Personal Injury and Death of 27 January 1977[23] and the European Convention on Transfrontier Television of 15 March 1989.[24]

2.3. *Different national models of consumer protection*

At the national level, consumer law developed in the 1960s and 1970s and expanded in the 1980s, before it developed as part of the European Community policy.[25] The gradual recognition of consumer protection at the national level as a distinct policy goal changed the focus of the welfare state, which was now adopting a more protective role with regard to consumers, by establishing a broader set of economic and social rights.[26]

[21] See section II, 3 of the UN Resolution 16 April 1985, A/RES/39/248. For more information on the UN Guidelines, see ch. 3.

[22] Recommendation 705 (1973) on consumer protection by the Council of Europe (Parliamentary Assembly) (17 May 1973): <http://assembly.coe.int/Main.asp?link=/Documents/Adopted Text/ta73/EREC705.htm>; see also Bourgoignie, 'Consumer Law and the European Community' (n 19), p. 93.

[23] Council of Europe, ETS no. 91, Strasbourg, 27.1.1977, see the text at: <http://conventions.coe.int/Treaty/en/Treaties/Html/091.htm>; see also the explanations on the European Commission's website: <http://ec.europa.eu/consumers/cons_issue/council_en.htm>.

[24] Council of Europe, ETS no. 132, Strasbourg, 5.5.1989; text amended by the Protocol (ETS no. 171), entered into force on 1 March 2002.

[25] See N. Reich & H.-W. Micklitz, *Consumer Legislation in the EC Countries: A Comparative Analysis* (New York: Van Nostrand Reinhold, 1980); H.-W. Micklitz, 'De la nécessité d'une nouvelle conception pour le développement du droit de la consommation dans la Communauté européenne', in *Mélanges en l'honneur de Jean Calais-Auloy* (Paris: Dalloz, 2004), pp. 729 *et seq*.

[26] Everson & Joerges (n 2), p. 8.

Although there was a common movement towards consumer protection, in the 1970s, the approaches in the Member States varied considerably, influenced by diverse cultural backgrounds. According to Micklitz, four different models could be distinguished at that time: the common law, the Mediterranean, the German, and the Scandinavian approaches.[27]

The consumer law in common law countries was rather political or pragmatic. Regulation was constrained to certain consumer areas, such as product liability and competition, and relied on self-regulation.[28] Consumer groups had little power and the state was responsible for implementing consumer rules.

In the Mediterranean countries, consumer law alternated between laissez-faire and interventionism, depending on prevailing political influences.[29] For instance, in France the implementation of consumer protection was organized in a centralized manner. Consumer groups exerted strong influence to increase protection, resulting in a consumer code, and supported consumer law implementation.[30] Consumer law prevailed as a separate branch of law, and was inspired by a social approach, according to which the state had to intervene beyond competition law, in order to protect consumers and guarantee fair market behaviour.[31]

In comparison, in Germany, consumer law was incorporated into civil law and was not consolidated in a separate consumer code.[32] Its implementation was guaranteed both by the court and by important consumer interest groups.[33]

Finally, in Scandinavia, state agencies had, and continue to have an important role in protecting consumers and are supported by interest groups.[34] In particular, an ombudsman system promotes consumer interests and helps consumers to solve disputes.

[27] Micklitz, 'De la nécessité d'une nouvelle conception pour le développement du droit de la consommation dans la Communauté européenne' (n 25), pp. 729 *et seq.*

[28] Micklitz (n 25), pp. 729 *et seq.*

[29] Micklitz (n 25).

[30] G. Trumbull, *Consumer Capitalism: Politics, Product Markets, and Firm Strategy in France and Germany* (Ithaca NY-London: Cornell University Press, 2006), p. 10.

[31] J. Stuyck, 'European Consumer Law after the Treaty of Amsterdam: Consumer Policy in or Beyond the Internal Market?', (2000) 37 *CML Rev.*, p. 369.

[32] J. Drexl, *Die wirtschaftliche Selbstbestimmung des Vebrauchers: Eine Studie zum Privat- und Wirtschaftsrecht unter Berücksichtigung gemeinschaftsrechtlicher Bezüge* (Tübingen: Mohr Siebeck, 1998, pp. 72–75.

[33] See also Micklitz (n 25), pp. 729 *et seq*; Reich & Micklitz, *Consumer Legislation in the EC Countries* (n 25).

[34] In Denmark the Danish Competition and Consumer Authority is responsible for consumer protection and acts as a secretariat for the Consumer Ombudsman (http://en.kfst.dk/); Micklitz (n 25), pp. 730 *et seq.*

In summary, some of these models adopted a liberal approach to consumer law instruments, stressing the importance of information and competition. Others, more socially focused, emphasized the importance of state intervention by mandatory rules, and explicitly recognized collective consumer interests. However, all of these models illustrated a general acceptance of consumers as a separate legal class of economic actors.

Besides innovations at the national level, Europe saw an important evolution in consumer law at the European Union level. Looking at the current situation, two important questions arise here: first, given that consumer law in a large number of Member States is relatively well developed, how should competences be distributed between the individual states and the Union? Secondly, how can legal diversity, economic freedom, and social interests be balanced at the European level? These questions will be addressed in the following chapters.

2.4. *The notion of the average consumer in EU law*

Within the contemporary EU, it is generally accepted that the consumer needs special legal protection, in particular to ensure product safety and to rebalance inequalities between consumers and companies in market knowledge and bargaining power.[35] It is, however, difficult to determine both what level and what kind of protection is adequate for the consumer in the increasing multilevel cross-border market.[36] A reason for this is that groups of consumers are not homogeneous, as they have different expectations, depending on their tastes, cultural backgrounds, and social position.[37]

A number of scholars argue that European consumer law is still lacking a conclusive and coherent core.[38] It is commonly recognized that EU law and the law of the Member States do not have a unique definition of the consumer.

[35] For a detailed analysis see H.-W. Micklitz , N. Reich , & P. Rott , *Understanding EU Consumer Law* (Antwerp: Intersentia, 2009).

[36] See e.g. V. Mak, 'Two levels, one standard? The multi-level regulation of consumer protection in Europe' in J. Devenney and M. Kenny (eds), *European Consumer Protection: Theory and Practice* (Cambridge: CUP, 2012), pp. 21 *et seq.*

[37] See e.g. T. Wilhelmsson, 'The Average European Consumer: A Legal Fiction', in T. Wilhelmsson, E. Paunio. A. Pohjolainen (eds), *Private Law and the Many Cultures of Europe* (Alphen aan den Rijn: Kluwer Law International, 2007), pp. 243–68.

[38] W. Faber, 'Elemente verschiedener Verbraucherbegriffe in EG-Richtlinien, zwischenstaatlichen Übereinkommen und nationalem Zivil- und Kollisionsrecht', (1998) *ZeuP*, p. 854; more generally see: N. Reich, 'A European Concept of Consumer Rights: Some Reflections on Rethinking Community Consumer Law', in *Liber Amicorum Bernd Stauder*, *Consumer Law* (Baden-Baden: Nomos, 2006), pp. 431 *et seq.*

Despite this, it is possible to identify common elements across several consumer directives which may be used to delineate a common notion of the consumer.[39] Furthermore the ECJ case law has provided a more concrete idea of the consumer: the consumer is a natural person, who, in transactions, is acting for purposes which can be regarded as being outside his or her trade or profession.[40] This distinguishes the consumer from a company and from an employee.

In turn, the EU legislators and judges apply a broad definition of the professional person or entity that sells products or services to consumers. The professional is a person who acts within the framework of his or her commercial or professional activity. It thus seems that all businesses are included from the moment they act in their usual activity, independently of their dimensions or the nature of their activity. The professional has to respect, among other things, both the health and safety, and the economic interests of the consumer, and engage in fair market behaviour.[41]

Furthermore, the ECJ follows an approach which depends on the aim of the legislative act, and generally applies a restrictive interpretation of the consumer model. The ECJ constantly refers to 'the average consumer',[42] who is reasonably well informed and reasonably observant and circumspect.[43] However, in some cases, the ECJ has also recognized the 'vulnerable consumer', who requires a higher level of protection in particular circumstances. For example, in *Buet* the Court upheld a French law prohibiting doorstep selling of educational materials, although it constituted an obstacle to free movement of goods.[44]

In order to understand the interrelation between consumer law in the EU and in its Member States, the next section explores the competence of the EU to regulate consumer law.

[39] For instance, the directives on contracts concluded away from business premises, consumer credit, unfair contract terms, and time-sharing; Stuyck, 'European Consumer Law after the Treaty of Amsterdam' (n 31), p. 376.

[40] See e.g. Case C-269/95, *Francesco Benincasa v Dentalkit Srl* [1997] ECR I-3767, paras 17–19 of the judgment.

[41] D. Fasquelle & P. Meunier, *Le droit communautaire de la consommation: Bilan et perspectives* (Paris: Documentation Française, 2002), p. 12.

[42] Regarding the application of this concept in unfair commercial practices see R. Incardona & C. Poncibò, 'The Average Consumer, the Unfair Commercial Practices Directive and the Cognitive Revolution', (2007) 30 *J Consumer Policy*, pp. 21–38.

[43] See e.g. Case C-210/96, *Gut Springenheide GmbH, Rudolf Tusky v Oberkreisdirektor des Kreises Steinfurt* [1998] ECR I-4657, para. 37.

[44] Case C-382/87 *Buet and Educational Business Services (EBS) v Ministère Public* [1989] ECR 1235, para. 13.

3. The European Union's Competence in Consumer Law

While the European Community initially paid little attention to consumer protection, its position has changed considerably in recent decades. The evolution of consumer law can be broadly divided into three periods.[45] The first period lasted until the introduction of the Single European Act, and was mainly based upon the idea of the national welfare state and European market integration. Thus, consumer protection at the European level remained very limited until the 1970s. In the second phase, which extended up to the early 1990s, consumer rights were linked to the internal market and the European Community acquired a formal competence to legislate on consumer issues. The third phase, still underway, includes two tendencies: full harmonization of consumer law by the EU on the one hand, and further recognition of consumer protection following the Charter of Fundamental Rights, on the other.

The next section will explore the increasing competences of the EU in consumer law.

3.1. *The Treaty of Rome*

In 1957, the Treaty of Rome was signed, establishing the European Economic Community (EEC), which aimed mainly at economic integration. Consumer issues were mentioned only in a few Articles and purely in relation to other policies, namely, the agricultural and competition policies. The improvement of the common market through fundamental freedoms, such as free movement of goods, people, and services, was the absolute priority.[46] The drafters of the Treaty implicitly assumed that consumer protection would automatically result from the development of the internal market.[47] Therefore, an explicit and articulate consumer policy was not considered to be necessary and remained absent.

Consumer protection partially began in the 1970s, prompted by international developments and by the increasing market integration which revealed

[45] See e.g. Everson & Joerges (n 2), p. 10.

[46] N. Reich, 'Der Verbraucher im Binnenmarkt', in N. Reich & H.-W. Micklitz, *Europäisches Verbraucherrecht* (Baden-Baden: Nomos, 2003), p. 14; L. Krämer, *EEC Consumer Law* (Brussels: Story-Scientia, Centre de droit de la Consommation, Louvain-la-Neuve, 1986), pp. 7 *et seq*.

[47] See S. Weatherill, *EU Consumer Law and Policy* (Cheltenham: Edward Elgar Publishing, 2005), p. 4.

a need for regulatory standards common to all the Member States.[48] Two main legislative and jurisprudential trends became apparent: positive integration of consumer policy through both soft law and hard law mechanisms, and negative integration driven by the European Court of Justice.[49]

Positive integration of consumer policy developed through soft law mechanisms in the form of communications and programmes. At the Paris Summit, in October 1972, for the first time an effort was made to improve consumer law at the Community level. Subsequently, in 1975[50] and 1981,[51] the European Council of Ministers approved two programmes on consumer protection in order to respond to public concern about market risks. These programmes, focusing on health protection and on the quality of goods and services, demonstrated the first sign of political readiness to accept the consumer as a separate category of law.[52] Although without binding effect, these programmes did incidentally serve as an inspirational basis for the ECJ to analyze binding provisions and were used by the Commission as an instrument for the European integration process.[53]

Besides this 'soft law' approach, 'hard law' harmonization measures were also applied to develop consumer law. As the Community lacked legislative competence in regard to consumer law, measures were based upon Article 100 EEC (later 94 and 95 EC). According to this Article, the Council could adopt directives and harmonize the legislation of the Member States when the latter was in conflic with the development of the internal market. These legislative acts could only be made through unanimity-voting by the Member States, and required a direct link with the common market. As a result, consumer protection goals were seen and presented as a means of overcoming

[48] T. Bourgoignie, 'Consumer Law and the European Community: Issues and Prospects', (n 19) pp. 97 *et seq.*

[49] P. Craig & G. de Búrca, *EU Law: Text, Cases and Materials*, 3rd edn (Oxford: OUP, 2003), pp. 114 *et seq.*

[50] EEC Council Resolution on a 'Preliminary Programme for a Consumer Protection and Information Policy', OJ 1975, C 92/1.

[51] OJ 1981, C 133/1; another Council Resolution was adopted on 23 June 1986, OJ 1986, C167/1; see also N. Reich, 'Protection for Consumers' Economic Interests by the EC', (1992) 14 *Sydney L. Rev.*, p. 23.

[52] Another 'soft law' mechanism was the Commission's White Paper on the Completion of the Internal Market, COM(85) 310 final of 14 June 1985; see Weatherill, *EU Consumer Law and Policy* (n 47), pp. 7–10.

[53] Case C-362/88, *GB-INNO-BM v Confédération du commerce luxembourgeois* [1990] ECR I-667; see also Weatherill (n 47), pp. 7–8.

the distortion of competition and the obstacles to the completion of the common market. Numerous legislative consumer acts were adopted following this strategy; among them the directive on misleading advertising and the directive on product liability.[54]

Via these means, the Community was able to develop its consumer policy, thereby expanding its limited competences. However, an explicit consumer policy was not possible under the existing legal framework. As Weatherill points out, this approach was typical of the initial Community consumer policy, and has changed little in practice today.[55] These beginnings are important to understand the economic integration focus that is continuously attached to consumer law.

A second feature of the European system is that its consumer law has developed in an indirect manner through negative integration by the ECJ. This process of deregulation of national provisions meant that the ECJ abolished actions by Member States that would impede cross-border trade in the market. The prohibition of discriminatory behaviour, the four freedoms, and competition law provisions, were the instruments for this approach[56] which served to eliminate national protective barriers and, at the same time, constituted a source of new individual rights.[57]

This negative integration approach is well demonstrated by the seminal *Cassis de Dijon* case of 1979.[58] Rewe-Zentral AG, a French company, was not authorized to import the liqueur called 'Cassis de Dijon' into Germany. The German Federal Monopoly Administration for Spirits refused to grant a licence on the basis of a German law, which forbade liqueurs that contain less than 25 per cent of alcohol content.[59] Rewe-Zentral AG argued that the German measure was contrary to Article 30 EEC, as the measure was equivalent to a quantitative restriction on importation. In contrast, the German government claimed, among other things, that the fixing of a lower limit for the alcohol content of certain liqueurs was designed to protect the consumer

[54] See e.g. Directive 84/450 of 10 September 1984 on misleading advertising, OJ 1984 L 250/17, amended by Directive 98/55 of 17 July 1998, OJ 1997 L 290/18, and Directive 85/374 of 27 July 1985 on product liability, OJ 1985 L 210/29.

[55] Weatherill (n 47), p. 4.

[56] See H. Unberath & A. Johnston, 'The Double-Headed Approach of the ECJ Concerning Consumer Protection', (2007) *44 CML Rev.*, pp. 1237–84.

[57] O. Gerstenberg & G. de Búrca, 'The Denationalization of Constitutional Law', (2006) 47 *Harv. Int'l L. J.*, p. 223.

[58] Case C-120/78, *Rewe Zentrale AG v Bundesmonopolverwaltung für Branntwein* [1979] ECR 649.

[59] 'Cassis de Dijon' contained only 15 to 20% of alcohol content.

against unfair practices by producers and was applied both to domestic and to imported products.

The ECJ held that barriers to trade which result from differences between national laws could only be permitted in exceptional cases 'in so far as those provisions may be recognized as being necessary in order to satisfy mandatory requirements relating in particular to the effectiveness of fiscal supervision, the protection of public health, the fairness of commercial transactions and the defence of the consumer'.[60] However, these conditions were not met in the specific case, as in particular less restrictive measures would have been more proportionate to guarantee the fairness of commercial transactions, by requiring the display of the alcohol content on the packaging of products. Therefore, the ECJ decided that the German measure constituted an obstacle to trade that was unlawful.

This case was based upon the principle of mutual recognition, according to which 'a Member State may not, in principle, prohibit the sale in its territory of a product lawfully produced and marketed in another Member State even if the product is produced according to technical or quality requirements which differ from those imposed on its domestic products'.[61]

The mutual recognition approach of the ECJ improved market functioning and enlarged the choice of consumers.[62] However, it raised concerns over a potential regulatory race to the bottom, especially among countries with high consumer standards: high standards would impose extra costs on national producers, while at the same time not fully benefiting the consumers, as the importation of lower-standard products had to be accepted under certain conditions.[63]

3.2. *The Single European Act*

With the entry into force of the Single European Act (SEA) in 1987,[64] the Community explicitly recognized consumer protection as an autonomous policy aim within the internal market. According to Article 100a SEA, the Commission must guarantee a high level of consumer protection. In

[60] Case 120/78, *Rewe Zentrale AG v Bundesmonopolverwaltung für Branntwein* [1979] ECR 649, para. 8.

[61] Communication from the Commission concerning the consequences of the judgment given by the ECJ on 20 February 1979 in Case 120/78 (*Cassis de Dijon*), OJ C 256/2, 3.10.80.

[62] See Weatherill (n 47), p. 50.

[63] P. Marleix, 'Que peuvent espérer en 1981 les consommateurs', (1981) *Les cahiers de l'AFOC*.

[64] OJ L 169, 29.06.1987.

addition, the Single European Act introduced qualified-majority voting for the adoption of Community actions proposed by the Commission in the European Council. This simplified the adoption of measures to approximate the legislation of the Member States and improve market functioning.

However, the Single European Act did not provide a specific legal basis for secondary consumer legislation.[65] As a result, numerous consumer directives were still adopted indirectly, under the general motivation of establishing and developing the internal market.[66] The aim was to create a basic level of protective provisions, to enhance consumer confidence in cross-border trade thereby increasing market integration.[67]

The ECJ played an important role in enhancing consumer information and choice in the integrated market through its case law. In *GB-INNO-BM* the ECJ was faced with the question of whether national legislation which restricted certain forms of advertising and means of sales promotion may be unlawful under Community law.[68] The Court held that a national provision forbidding comparative advertising of temporary sales with previous prices was not justified on the grounds of general economic interests of consumers. The provision was deemed contrary to Article 30 EEC, as this Article could not be interpreted as meaning that a national law which denies the consumer access to information may be justified by consumer protection.[69] This ruling thus reinforced the consumer right to be informed, while also limiting the regulatory powers of the Member States.[70]

However, in other cases, the ECJ has upheld national measures that were adopted to protect vulnerable consumers, such as in *Buet*.[71] In this case, a

[65] European Consumer Law Group, 'Consumer Protection in the EEC After Ratification of the Single Act', (1978) 10 *J. Consumer Policy*, pp. 319 *et seq*.

[66] For instance, Directives on Consumer Credit (87/102, OJ L 42/48, 12.2.1987), Doorstop Selling (85/577, OJ L 372/31, 31.12.1985), Package Travel (90/314, OJ L 158/59, 23.6.1990), Product Liability (85/374, OJ L 210/29, 7.8.1985), Unfair Terms in Consumer Contracts (93/13, OJ L 95/29, 21.4.1993). See Weatherill (n 47), p.13.

[67] Stuyck (n 31), p. 379.

[68] Case C-362/88, *GB-INNO-BM SA v Confédération du commerce luxembourgeois (CCL)* [1990] ECR I-667; see also Case C-126/91, *Schutzverband gegen Unwesen in der Wirtschaft v Y. Rocher GmbH* [1993] ECR I-2361.

[69] Case C-362/88, *GB-INNO-BM SA v CCL* [1990] ECR I-667, para. 19.

[70] In another case, the Court also held that the recipients of services (tourists, persons receiving medical treatment, and persons travelling for educational reasons) have the freedom to go to another Member State to receive services without being hindered by restrictions, see Cases C-286/82 & 26/83 *Luisi and Carbone v Ministero del Tesoro* [1984] ECR 377.

[71] Case C-382/87, *Buet v Ministère Public* [1989] ECR 1235; see also more recently Case C-441/04, *A-Punkt Schmuckhandels GmbH v Claudia Schmidt* [2006] ECR I-2093.

French consumer law on canvassing and doorstep selling prohibited canvassing for the purpose of selling educational material to consumers.[72] The ECJ held that although this measure constituted a barrier to imports it could be justified by the need to protect particularly vulnerable consumers from the purchase of unsuitable teaching material, which 'could compromise the consumer's chances of obtaining further training and thus consolidating his position on the labour market'.[73]

In summation, the ECJ helped to define the notion and rights of the consumer in the common market. Moreover, the case law highlighted the need to delicately balance two objectives: market integration and enlargement of consumer choice on the one hand, and the preservation of protective standards offered by national laws on the other.[74] At the same time, a coherent promotion of consumer interest per se was lacking at the policy level, in particular owing to the absence of a specific competence of the Community to legislate in consumer matters.[75] This changed to a certain degree with the Treaty of Maastricht.

3.3. *The Treaty of Maastricht*

With the entry into force of the Treaty of Maastricht in 1993, a stronger commitment beyond market goals became apparent in the EU, made manifest by the insertion in the Treaty of explicit consumer protection objectives and new citizenship rights.[76] Article 3(s) of the European Community (EC) Treaty stated that 'a contribution to the strengthening of consumer protection' should be part of the activities of the Community.

Furthermore, the Treaty added, for the first time, a formal competence for the European Community to legislate on consumer issues. According to Article 129(a)(1) EC, the 'Community shall contribute to the attainment of a high level of consumer protection'. In this context, the Community could either adopt measures pursuant to Article 100(a) EC to facilitate the completion of the internal market (Article 129(a)(1)(a) EC), or take a 'specific action which supports and supplements the policy pursued by the Member States to

[72] Case C-382/87, *Buet v Ministère Public* [1989] ECR 1235, para. 3.

[73] Case C-382/87, *Buet v Ministère Public* [1989] ECR 1235, para. 8; see also C. Barnard, *The Substantive Law of the EU, The Four Freedoms* (Oxford: OUP, 2007), pp. 118–19.

[74] Weatherill (n 47), p. 39.

[75] H.-W. Micklitz & S. Weatherill, 'Consumer Policy in the European Community: Before and After Maastricht', (1993) 16 *J. Consumer Policy*, pp. 292 and 294 *et seq.*

[76] J.H.H. Weiler, 'To be a European Citizen, Eros and Civilization', in J.H.H. Weiler, *The Constitution of Europe, Do the New Clothes Have an Emperor? and other Essays on European Integration* (Cambridge: CUP, 1999), p. 332.

protect the health, safety and economic interests of consumers and to provide adequate information' (Article 129(a)(1)(b) EC). Such a formal legal basis was important because the Community was only empowered to act according to Article 3(b)(1) EC, within the limits of the competences provided by the Treaty.

The Community could now officially intervene according to Article 129(a)(1)(b) EC to improve consumer protection, independently from measures taken in connection with the internal market.[77] Practice revealed, however, the relatively low significance of the new legal basis for the development of consumer law.[78] Only in rare cases have specific actions been based on Article 129(a)(1)(b) EC, such as Directive 98/6/EC on consumer protection in the indication of the prices of products offered to consumers.[79] The majority of directives continued instead to be adopted on the basis of the 'market integration' provision (Article 100(a) EC).[80] As we will see later in this book,[81] even after the Lisbon Treaty, consumer measures often still refer back to internal market justifications for harmonization directives.

Another important effect of the Maastricht Treaty was the institutionalization of a minimum-harmonization approach for specific Community actions. Article 129(a)(3) EC stated that actions adopted to support and supplement national policies according to Article 129(a)(1)(b) EC do not prevent Member States from maintaining or introducing more stringent protective measures.[82] However, these consumer measures had to be compatible with the Treaty, and the Member States were obliged to notify the Commission of them.

Consumer policy was also influenced by Article 3(b)(2) EC, which formally introduced the subsidiarity principle by stating that in areas of shared competence 'the Community shall take action, in accordance with the principle of subsidiarity, only if and in so far as the objectives of the proposed action cannot be sufficiently achieved by the Member States and can (. . .) be better achieved by the Community'. This principle aimed to clarify the division of competences and to control the increase in the Community's harmonization measures, because it gradually restrained the powers of the Member States.

77 Micklitz & Weatherill, 'Consumer Policy in the European Community' (n 75), p. 298.

78 Stuyck (n 31), p. 380.

79 Directive 98/6/EC of 16 February 1998, OJ 1998 L 80/27.

80 See also T. Bourgoignie, 'European Community Consumer Law and Policy: from Rome to Amsterdam', (1998), *Consumer L. J.*, pp. 443–62, at 447.

81 See e.g. subsection 4.4. of this chapter.

82 Micklitz & Weatherill (n 75), p. 300.

However, the vagueness of this principle left considerable room for interpretation on the determination of an adequate level of Community action, generating a level of legal insecurity.[83] However, as noted by Weatherill, eventually this principle had rather little effect on consumer law, as the EU continued to adopt consumer measures upon the basis of Article 100(a) EC in the context of the completion of the internal market.[84]

Besides the general modifications introduced by the Maastricht Treaty, the ECJ also showed a change of direction in its case law. In *Keck and Mithouard* the Court had to decide on the legality under EC law of a French law prohibiting the resale of products at a loss.[85] The Court clarified and refined its earlier case-law by stating that national provisions restricting certain selling arrangements were not such as to hinder trade between Member States, on the condition that 'those provisions apply to all relevant traders operating within the national territory and so long as they affect in the same manner, in law and in fact, the marketing of domestic products and of those from other Member States'.[86] As an effect of this judgment, Member States gained, under specific conditions, a greater degree of autonomy to adopt and maintain national measures.

Yet, although Member States had, to a certain extent, gained more freedom, their discretionary power remained restricted, as highlighted in *Clinique*.[87] This case concerned the question whether a prohibition could be imposed in Germany on the importation and marketing of a cosmetic cream named 'Clinique', on the basis that this product name may mislead consumers into believing that it had medicinal properties. The ECJ considered that such a prohibition was not required to protect consumers, because the medical connotations of the product name were not sufficient to mislead consumers. In particular, the product was not presented as a medicinal product and a comparison in other countries showed that consumers had not been misled by such a name. Therefore, the Court decided that a prohibition to import and market the cosmetic product in the German market, because of its name, was not justified.

[83] Weatherill (n 47), p. 19; for a general analysis see L. Grard, 'La subsidiarité et le droit communautaire de la consommation', in D. Fasquelle & P. Meunier (eds), *Le droit communautaire de la consommation: bilan et perspectives* (Paris: documentation française, coll. CEDECE, 2002), p. 147.

[84] Weatherill (n 47), pp. 20–3.

[85] Cases C-267/91 and C-268/91, *Keck and Mithouard* [1993] ECR I-6093.

[86] Cases C-267/91 and C-268/91, *Keck and Mithouard* [1993] ECR I-6093, para. 16; see a detailed analysis of the case law that followed in Unberath & Johnston, 'The Double-Headed Approach of the ECJ Concerning Consumer Protection' (n 56), pp. 1245–48.

[87] Case C-315/92, *Verband sozialer Wettbewerb v Clinique Laboratoires* [1994] ECR I-317.

In more recent case law the ECJ has further defined the consumer notion and has paid increased attention to national approaches to consumer protection. On the one hand, the ECJ has often held that it is necessary to take into account the presumed expectations of an 'average consumer', who is 'reasonably well informed and reasonably observant and circumspect'.[88] On the other, in some cases, the ECJ has attached particular importance to even rather subtle differences between Member States. For instance, in *Estée Lauder v Lancaster*,[89] the ECJ stated that 'it must be determined whether social, cultural or linguistic factors' may justify a different national concept of a product, and hence a particular consumer protection level. In this case, the ECJ maintained that a particular, national 'understanding' of a cosmetic advertisement and social interest can justify a specific local protection of the consumer.[90]

In conclusion, the Treaty of Maastricht constituted an important milestone because it conferred a legal competence to the EU in consumer protection. However, in practice, this changed little in legislative terms, because the EU continued to adopt consumer directives under Article 100(a) EC, which required a market-making objective.

3.4. *The Treaty of Amsterdam and the Tobacco Advertising case*

Since the mid-1990s, policy-makers have begun trying to pursue consumer protection as a distinct EU goal. Product scandals during this period, such as 'Bovine Spongiform Encephalopathy' (BSE), hormone-treated beef, and toys treated with phthalates, provided an opportunity for the EU to define a pro-consumer agenda. The Treaty of Amsterdam responded to such needs for stronger consumer protection, by enlarging the competence of the Union in consumer law.[91]

Article 153(1) EC stated that the Community 'shall ensure a high level of consumer protection' by contributing 'to protecting the health, safety and

[88] See e.g. Case C-210/96, *Gut Springenheide and Tusky* [1998] ECR I-4657, para. 31; for a critical view of the notion of the average consumer, see Incardona & Poncibò, 'The Average Consumer, the Unfair Commercial Practices Directive, and the Cognitive Revolution' (n 42), pp. 21–38.

[89] Case C-220/98, *Estée Lauder Cosmetics GmbH & Co. OHG v Lancaster Group GmbH* [2000] ECR I-117, para. 27.

[90] Case C-220/98, *Estée Lauder Cosmetics GmbH & Co. OHG v Lancaster Group GmbH* [2000] ECR I-117, para. 29.

[91] These changes have resulted from a compromise between the proposals of Scandinavian countries for broader community powers, and, in particular, German and British opposition; see N. Reich, 'Verbraucherpolitik und Verbraucherschutz im Vertrag von Amsterdam', (1999) *Verbraucher und Recht*, p. 3.

economic interests of consumers' and 'promoting their right to information, education and to organise themselves in order to safeguard their interests'. The right to information, education, and organization were new consumer rights, which did not exist in the Treaty of Maastricht.[92]

The improvement of information was already mentioned before the Amsterdam Treaty, but merely as an objective of which care was to be taken, without stating its relevance as a fully fledged right.[93] Following the Treaty of Amsterdam, the right to information has been reinforced and has been included in recent directives, such as the new Consumer Credit Agreement Directive (2008/48) of 2008.[94] Furthermore, the new right to education proved crucial to improve decision-making by the consumer and prevent manipulation through advertising, enabling the Community to take measures to educate the consumer, supporting, supplementing, and monitoring the policy pursued by the Member States in this respect. On the other hand, the right of consumers to organize themselves, which is linked to the freedom of association, has been implemented through the Cross-border Injunctions Directive (98/27).[95]

Article 153(2) EC obliged the European institutions to take account of consumer protection interests in the definition and implementation of other EU policies. However, according to some scholars, the practical impact of this provision has remained limited.[96]

Article 153(3) EC provided two different legislative competences for the EU, which already existed in the Treaty of Maastricht. Thus, the Community could take either '(a) measures adopted pursuant to Article 95 in the context of the completion of the internal market', or '(b) measures which support supplement and monitor the policy pursued by the Member States'. The first type of measures allowed the EC to harmonize the laws of Member States to improve market functioning. This implied that directives should be adopted

[92] See more in Stuyck (n 31) pp. 384–92.

[93] This right has been recognized by the ECJ in the previously discussed Case C-362/88, *GB Inno BM v CCL* [1990] ECR I-667.

[94] Directive 2008/48/EC of 23 April 2008 on credit agreements for consumers, OJ L 133/66, 22.5.2008; see more on this directive in ch. 5.

[95] Directive 98/27/EC on injunctions for the protection of consumers' interests adopted in 1998, OJ L 166, 11.6.1998 (modified subsequently and codified by Directive 2009/22/EC of 23 April 2009 on injunctions for the protection of consumers' interests, OJ L 110/30, 1.5.2009), see ch. 7 in this book.

[96] See e.g. Reich, 'Verbraucherpolitik und Verbraucherschutz im Vertrag von Amsterdam' (n 91), p. 9; Stuyck (n 31), p. 386.

only if there was a need to harmonize the law in order to establish or improve the functioning of the internal market. The internal market was defined in Article 14 EC as an 'area without internal frontiers in which the free movement of goods, persons, services and capital is ensured'. Consequently, consumer protection measures could be adopted by the EU on this legal basis if national provisions differed so as to require an approximation of law, and if there was a sufficient link with a market-integration objective. In contrast, the second type of measures could be used by the Community for consumer protection initiatives independently of a market integration objective. Regarding these measures Member States kept the right of the Treaty of Maastricht to introduce 'more stringent' consumer protection rules (Article 153(5) EC). In practice, however, Article 153(3)(b) has seldom been used by the Community to adopt consumer protection measures; instead, consumer legislation continued to be created under the market-making basis of Article 95 EC. Indeed, the Commission has proposed numerous directives upon the basis of Article 95 EC (now Article 114 TFEU) by making the formal argument of market integration objectives. Among these, the directives on consumer credit (87/102),[97] doorstep selling (85/577), package travel (90/314),[98] unfair terms in consumer contracts (93/13),[99] and the protection of consumers in respect of distance contracts (97/7)[100] have been adopted. However, in certain cases, such as in the Doorstep Selling Directive, the consumer protection aim prevailed over the market integration objective.[101]

This growing harmonization trend, based upon Article 95 EC, caused some Member States to fear for their national powers.[102] Indeed, under the Amsterdam Treaty, the EU had only limited powers to adopt measures, as Article 5 EC required that the Community act within the limits of the powers conferred upon it by this Treaty. In addition, the principle of subsidiarity established in the Treaty of Maastricht had not been altered. This meant that, regarding areas of shared competences, the EU was only allowed to take measures 'in so far as the objectives of the proposed action cannot be sufficiently achieved by the Member States and can (…) be better achieved by the Community'. In addition, the measures by the Community were not permitted to go beyond what is necessary to achieve the Treaty's objective (Article 5(3) EC).

97 Directive 87/102 of 12 February 1987, OJ 1987 L 42/48.
98 Directive 90/314 of 23 June 1990, OJ 1990 L 158/59.
99 Directive 93/13 of 21 April 1993, OJ 1993 L 95/29.
100 Directive 97/7 of 4 June 1997, OJ 1997 L 144/19.
101 Weatherill (n 47) pp. 71–72.
102 Weatherill (n 47) pp. 72 *et seq.*

Therefore, in the late 90s, Member States were becoming increasingly less tolerant towards the growing competence of the EU. This was for example reflected in the 'Tobacco Advertising' judgment,[103] where Germany sought the annulment of Directive 98/43/EC which banned the advertising and sponsorship of tobacco products.[104] This directive had been adopted under Article 100(a) EC (later Article 95 EC) presented as a measure of harmonization to improve internal market functioning. However, Germany argued inter alia before the ECJ that the legal basis applied for this directive was incorrect, because this measure did not actually contribute to the improvement of the internal market, and its true objective was to protect public health.[105]

The ECJ annulled the directive, because of its invalid legal basis. According to the Court, Article 95 EC does not give a general power to the Community to regulate the internal market. This would also be incompatible with Article 5 EC that provides that 'the powers of the Community are limited to those specifically conferred on it'.[106] However, the ECJ specified that the fact that harmonizing measures have a positive effect on health does not exclude Article 95 EC as a legal basis. In order to assess its validity, it is 'necessary to verify whether the directive actually contributes to eliminating obstacles to the free movement of goods and to the freedom to provide services, and to removing distortions of competition'.[107] In the Court's view the ban on advertising imposed by the directive was too broad.

While in principle, the prohibition on advertising of tobacco products for the written media might be based on Article 95, with the aim of improving the free movement of press products, numerous other prohibitions, for example regarding advertising on posters, parasols, and ashtrays did not help to facilitate trade in the product concerned. Therefore, the Court considered that an outright prohibition of advertising was disproportionate and the measure was not apt to eliminate appreciable distortion of competition.[108]

This case had an important impact on EU law-making on the basis of Article 95 EC. The Commission has become more aware of its limited competence

[103] Case C-376/98, *Germany v Parliament and Council* [2000] ECR I-08419; S. Weatherill, 'The Constitutional Competence of the EU to deliver Social Justice', (2006) 2 *Eur. Rev. Contract Law*, p. 140.

[104] Directive 98/43/EC relating to the advertising and sponsorship of tobacco products, OJ 1998 L213/9, 30.7.98.

[105] Case C-376/98, *Germany v Parliament and Council* [2000] ECR I-08419, paras 11–35.

[106] Case C-376/98, *Germany v Parliament and Council* [2000] ECR I-08419, para. 83.

[107] Case C-376/98, *Germany v Parliament and Council* [2000] ECR I-08419, para. 95.

[108] Case C-376/98, *Germany v Parliament and Council* [2000] ECR I-08419, paras 111–12.

and has dedicated more effort to carefully justify new actions by establishing a stronger link to market-functioning objectives. Accordingly, after the annulment of the Tobacco Advertising Directive 98/43, a more restrictive measure was adopted by the EU in 2003[109] and this time the Commission shaped the directive so as to expressly underline the market-integration aim that was previously missing.

Although the more recent case law of the ECJ has revealed a rather permissive approach to new EU legislation,[110] a number of former consumer directives based on Article 95 EC have become constitutionally vulnerable according to Weatherill, because of their weak links to the required market-building objectives.[111] This in turn has created uncertainty over the effective division of competences between the EU and Member States in developing consumer protection.[112] All these issues, according to some scholars, would require an open debate on Treaty reform for a clearer competence in consumer law.[113]

In conclusion, since the *Tobacco Advertising* case, it has become more difficult to adopt harmonization measures for consumer protection based on Article 95 EC (now Article 114 TFEU), unless they contain an explicit market-integration objective. While adding yet another focus on market integration, this was not the last piece of an already complex mosaic. The Lisbon Treaty and, eventually, the Charter of Fundamental Rights, provide new elements to consumer law, which will be analyzed in the following section and chapters of this book.

[109] See the second directive on tobacco advertising adopted in light of the judicial annulment of the first: Directive 2003/33/EC of May 2003, OJ 2003, L 152/16. This directive was again tested before the Court of Justice in *Tobacco Advertising II*, Case C-380/03, *Germany v Parliament and Council* [2006] ECR I-11573; in this case, however, the Court concluded that the use of Art. 95 EC was valid.

[110] E.g. Case C-377/98, *Netherlands v Parliament and Council* [2001] ECR I-7079, Case C-491/01, *Imperial Tobacco* [2001] ECR I-11543, or Case 210/03, *Swedish Match* [2004] ECR I-11893.

[111] See more in S. Weatherill, 'The Commission's Options for Developing EC Consumer Protection and Contract Law: Assessing the Constitutional Basis', (2002) 13 *Eur. Bus. L. Rev.*, p. 497.

[112] In recent decisions, such as Case C-491/01, *Imperial Tobacco* and Case C-210/03, *Swedish Match*, these issues were not resolved; see Weatherill, 'The Constitutional Competence of the EU to Deliver Social Justice' (n 103), pp. 141 and 146.

[113] See the reform proposed in the Treaty revision by H.-W. Micklitz, N. Reich, & S. Weatherill, 'EU Treaty Revision and Consumer Protection', (2004) 27 *J. Consumer Policy*, pp. 367–99.

4. Consumer Policy and the Lisbon Treaty

In the last decade EU consumer law has been marked by three important changes: a modification in the EU harmonization strategy, the adoption of the Charter of Fundamental Rights, and the Lisbon Treaty.

For a long time, the Union has harmonized consumer law at a minimum level, allowing the Member States to determine higher standards of protection.[114] This changed in early 2000, when the Commission began promoting a full-harmonization approach, precluding higher protective rules by Member States in the harmonized field.[115]

In 2000 the Charter of Fundamental Rights of the European Union was adopted, elevating consumer protection to a fundamental rights objective of the EU.[116] Furthermore, the Lisbon Treaty of 2009, while strengthening the role of human rights in the EU, introduced new rights, such as the right to citizens' initiative, which will have implications in several legal areas.

How are these new developments going to interact and influence consumer protection? To answer this question, the following subsection starts by describing the harmonization phenomenon and its potential impact on Member States' consumer laws.

4.1. *The full-harmonization trend*

The full-harmonization trend was initiated by the Consumer Policy Strategy 2002–2006, which stated the objective to progressively adapt existing consumer directives from minimum-harmonization to full-harmonization measures.[117] The Distance Marketing of Consumer Financial Services Directive,[118] issued in 2002, was the first measure adopting the maximum-harmonization principle, and was followed by the Unfair Commercial Practices Directive in 2005.[119] The EU Consumer Policy Strategy 2007–2013 then reaffirmed the intentions of its 2002–2006 predecessor, stating that 'if legislative proposals are identified as the appropriate response, targeted

[114] E.g. Directive 93/13 on unfair terms in consumer contracts, OJ 1993 L 95/29 contained such a minimum rule.

[115] Weatherill (n 47), p. 2.

[116] The Charter will be further discussed in ch. 3 of this book.

[117] Communication from the Commission of 7 May 2002—'Consumer Policy Strategy 2000–2006', COM (2002) 208 final—OJ 2002 C137/2.

[118] Directive 2002/65/EC of 9 October 2002, OJ 2002, L 271/16.

[119] Directive 2005/29/EC of 11 June 2005 concerning unfair commercial practices in the internal market, OJ L 149/22.

full harmonization of consumer protection rules at an appropriately high level will tend to be the Commission's approach'.[120] The Consumer Credit Agreement Directive of 2008[121] and the Timeshare Directive of 2009[122] followed this approach, further reflecting the paradigm shift from minimum to full harmonization. More recently, on 8 October 2008, the European Commission adopted a controversial proposal for a directive on consumer rights, which intended to fully harmonize various directives on contract law.[123] The resulting draft directive revised and merged four existing EU consumer directives—Unfair Contract Terms,[124] Sales and Guarantees,[125] Distance Selling,[126] and Doorstep Selling[127]—into one single instrument. While the original directives followed the principle of minimum harmonization, the new draft directive on consumer rights proposed a fully targeted harmonization.[128] Directive 2011/83/EU on consumer rights was eventually adopted in November 2011,[129] applying a full-harmonization approach. It is, however, smaller in scope than originally proposed, as it only replaces two legislative acts: Directive 97/7/EC on the protection of consumers in respect of distance contracts, and Directive 85/577/EEC, which protects consumers in contracts negotiated away from business premises.[130] The new directive fully

[120] EU Consumer Policy Strategy 2007–2013, COM(2007), 13.3.2007 (OJ C 279/E).

[121] Directive 2008/48/EC of 2008 on credit agreements for consumers, OJ 2008 L 122/66.

[122] Directive 2008/122/EC of 2009 on certain aspects of timeshare and long-term holiday products, 2009 OJ L 33/10.

[123] Proposal for a Directive on Consumer Rights, COM(2008) 614 final, 2008/0196 (COD) (2008); see also the 2003 Action Plan on a more coherent European contract law COM(2003) 68 final OJ 2003, C 63/01 and Green Paper on the Review of the Consumer Acquis, Brussels, COM (2006) 744 final.

[124] Directive 93/13/EEC of 21 April 1993 on unfair terms in consumer contracts, OJ L 95/29.

[125] Directive 1999/44/EC of 7 July 1999 on sale of consumer goods, OJ L 171/12.

[126] Directive 97/7/EC of 4 June 1997 on consumer protection regarding distance contracts, OJ L 144/19.

[127] Directive 85/577/EEC of 31 December 1985 to protect consumers in respect of contracts negotiated away from business premises, OJ L 372/31.

[128] For a critical assessment, see M. Loos, 'Consumer Sales Law in the Proposal for a Consumer Rights Directive', (2000) 1 *Eur. Rev. Private Law*, pp. 15–55; H.-W. Micklitz & N. Reich, 'Crónica de una Muerte Anunciada: The Commission Proposal for a "Directive on Consumer Rights"', (2009) 46 *CML Rev.*, pp. 471–519.

[129] Directive 2011/83/EU of 25 October 2011 on consumer rights, amending Council Directive 93/13/EEC and Directive 1999/44/EC and repealing Council Directive 85/577/EEC and Directive 97/7/EC OJ L 304/64, 22.11.2011.

[130] In contrast, Directive 1999/44/EC on certain aspects of the sale of consumer goods and associated guarantees as well as Directive 93/13/EEC on unfair terms in consumer contracts remain in force.

harmonizes key provisions on distance contracts, including pre-contractual information and rights of withdrawal. Here too, full harmonization is explicit: Article 4 stipulates that 'Member States shall not maintain or introduce, in their national law, provisions diverging from those laid down in this directive, including more or less stringent provisions to ensure a different level of consumer protection'.

The main argument in favour of full harmonization is that it fosters economic integration and promotes the consumers' interest in cross-border purchases. Common rules can encourage companies to access cross-border markets, which may result in greater competition and ultimately reduce prices and broaden the choice of products and services.

Full harmonization though, and especially the idea that this is the best way to strengthen consumers' confidence in the market, as they would only face one set of standards, has been critically questioned by scholars.[131] On the one hand, harmonized rules do not automatically result in consumer confidence to undertake cross-border purchases. The importance of harmonization in itself to boost cross-border purchases may be smaller than assumed at first sight. Consumers may prefer to continue to shop within their country, owing to commercial customs, language, and the convenience of shopping at a well-known local seller.

On the other hand, it is not clear to what extent the potential financial gains would compensate for the fact that protection standards were lowered in some Member States. From the perspective of consumer protection, minimum harmonization offered security in the event that EU laws did not provide a sufficiently high level of protection. Minimum harmonization also drew a demarcation line of competences which left ample room for Member States to provide more stringent protection for national consumers, if they wished to do so.

The following subsection analyses the impact of the full-harmonization interpretation of directives taken by the ECJ on national consumer protection frameworks.

4.2. *The implications for national systems*

In 2002 the jurisprudence of the ECJ clarified the implications of 'complete' harmonization directives for consumer protection at the national level. In at least three cases on product liability, the ECJ found that higher protection

[131] Micklitz & Reich, 'Crónica de una Muerte Anunciada' (n 128), pp. 471–519; Weatherill (n 103), pp. 155–6; for a new understanding of full harmonization, see V. Mak, 'Full Harmonization in European Private Law: A Two-Track Concept', (2012) 1 *Eur. Rev. Private Law*, pp. 213–36.

rules governing product liability in member countries were inconsistent with the less stringent terms of the EU Product Liability Directive, and thus decided against their applicability.[132] Possibly the most famous of these cases is *González Sánchez v Medicina Asturiana*,[133] which concerned the interpretation of the Product Liability Directive of 1985.[134]

María González Sánchez, a Spanish citizen, received a blood transfusion in a medical establishment belonging to Medicina Asturiana, in the course of which she was allegedly infected by the Hepatitis C virus. Therefore, she sought compensation from Medicina Asturiana for the damage suffered. The competent Spanish court found that national consumers benefited from more extensive rights under the original Spanish Law No. 26/84 before the Product Liability Directive was transposed into domestic law (Law No. 22/94). This raised questions regarding the interpretation of Article 13 of the directive, which expressly provides that it 'shall not affect any rights which an injured person may have according to the rules of the law of contractual or non-contractual liability or a special liability system existing at the moment when this Directive is notified'. Therefore, the case was referred to the ECJ for a preliminary ruling on the question of whether Article 13 of the directive must be 'interpreted as precluding the restriction or limitation, as a result of transposition of the Directive, of rights granted to consumers under the legislation of the Member State'.[135] The ECJ held that the margin of discretion available to national systems depends, among other things, on the purpose of the Product Liability Directive, which is 'to ensure undistorted competition between traders, to facilitate the free movement of goods and to avoid differences in levels of consumer protection'.[136] The Court further noted that this directive did not contain a provision expressly authorizing the Member States to maintain a higher level of consumer protection. It also found that Article 13 should be understood as only referring to specific liability systems limited to a particular sector or production. Therefore, the ECJ concluded, this provision could not be interpreted as giving Member States the possibility of

[132] Case C-183/00, *María Victoria González Sánchez v Medicina Austuriana* [2002] ECR I-3901, other relevant cases are Case C-52/00, *Commission v France* [2002] ECR I-3856 and Case C-154/00, *Commission v Greece* [2002] ECR I-3879.

[133] Case C-183/00, *María Victoria González Sánchez v Medicina Austuriana* [2002] ECR I-3901.

[134] Directive 85/374/EEC, OJ 1985 L 210/29.

[135] Case C-183/00, *María Victoria González Sánchez v Medicina Austuriana* [2002] ECR I-3901, para. 13.

[136] Case 183/00, *María Victoria González Sánchez v Medicina Austuriana* [2002] ECR I-3901, paras 25–6.

maintaining a general system of product liability different from that provided for in the directive, by offering greater protection to consumers.[137]

This judgment was criticized by several scholars who argued that the directive, despite not including an explicit minimum-harmonization clause, should have been interpreted in this sense, given the low level of protection level it offered.[138] In addition, the Council of the European Union has openly criticized the ECJ's narrow interpretation in this case, and has highlighted the Court's obligation to effectively protect consumers.[139] A number of national legislators were also hesitant to lower the level of protection regarding product liability offered by their own domestic provisions in the interest of greater market integration.[140] This could be seen in France and in Greece, which were confronted with a Treaty infringement, because they did not want to lower their level of protection and thus did not comply with the directive.[141] In the respective cases, the ECJ applied a similar reasoning as in *González Sánchez* and expressly stated that the Product Liability Directive seeks to achieve, in the matters regulated by it, complete harmonization of national laws.[142] Member States can therefore not apply a general system of product liability that diverges from the harmonized field by going beyond the basic standard set by the directive. However, the ECJ held in *Société Moteurs Leroy Somer* that Directive 85/374 does not cover compensation for damage to an

[137] Case C-183/00, *María Victoria González Sánchez v Medicina Austuriana* [2002] ECR I-3901, paras 30–3.

[138] See e.g. G. Howells, 'Is the General Product Safety Directive a Maximum Harmonization Directive?', in L. Thévenoz & N. Reich (eds), *Liber amicorum Bernd Stauder, Droit de la Consommation* (Baden-Baden/Geneva: Nomos/Schulthess, 2006), p. 147; M. Reimann, 'Product Liability in a Global Context: the Hollow Victory of the European Model', (2003) 11 *Eur. Rev. Private Law*, p. 128.

[139] The Council of Ministers proposed to amend the directive to permit more stringent national treatment; see OJ 2003 C 26/1.

[140] France did not implement the Product Liability Directive for a long time, as there was a strong opposition against the lowering of the liability that the EU solution provided. See Trumbull, *Consumer Capitalism: Politics, Product Markets, and Firm Strategy in France and Germany* (n 30), p. 151.

[141] Cases C-52/00, *Commission v France* [2002] ECR I-3827 and C-154/00, *Commission v Greece* [2002] ECR I-3879.

[142] Cases C-52/00, *Commission v France* [2002] ECR I-3827, para. 24 and C-154/00, *Commission v Greece* [2002] ECR I-3879, paras 10–20; see also the more recent case regarding the reference for a preliminary ruling from the 'Vestre Landsret' (Denmark), Case C-402/03, *Skov Æg v Bilka Lavprisvarehus A/S and Bilka Lavprisvarehus A/S v Jette Mikkelsen and Michael Due Nielsen* [2006] ECR I-199 and the critical assessment by C. Twigg-Flesner, 'An English Perspective on Producers' Liability', in M. Ebers, A. Janssen, & O. Meyer (eds), *European Perspectives on Producers' Liability* (Munich: Sellier, 2009), p. 272.

item of property *intended for professional use* and employed for that purpose.[143] Therefore Member States can provide in that specific respect for a different system of liability. This leads to the paradoxical result that French law can provide a higher protection for business users than for consumers.[144]

As these cases have shown, full-harmonization measures can result in a lowering of standards of consumer protection in a number of Member States. More importantly from a constitutional point of view, complete harmonization also de facto implies a transfer of legislative powers from national states to the EU, because it constrains the ability of Member States to protect consumers according to their own legal systems.[145] Whether such a transfer of power is desirable is debatable: indeed, there is at least a presumption that Member States are better informed about their own citizens' needs as consumers than a more distant EU institution and are thus well placed to determine the adequate standard of protection. This conclusion is reinforced if one observes, as discussed previously, that the EU has traditionally focused on market-promoting objectives, rather than on consumer protection as an independent matter.[146] Finally, full harmonization would reduce legal diversity, which may stifle the process of legal evolution, which is also made possible by learning from different regulatory solutions in Member States.

These potential drawbacks of full harmonization, criticized in the literature,[147] do not imply that this approach should be completely abandoned. Full-harmonization measures do have some advantages, primarily in simplifying the legal environment and thus removing barriers to trade.[148] Thus, the optimal balance between consumer protection and market development could be reached via a mix of full and minimum harmonization. Consumer

[143] Case C-285/08, *Société Moteurs Leroy Somer v Société Dalkia France, Société Ace Europe* [2009] ECR I-4733.

[144] See R. Sefton-Green, 'Multiculturalism, Europhilia and Harmonization: Harmony or Disharmony?' *Utrecht L. Rev.*, (2010) 6(3).

[145] S. Weatherill, 'Pre-emption, Harmonization and the Distribution of Competences', in C. Barnard & J. Scott (eds), *The Law of the Single European Market* (Oxford: Hart Publishing, 2002), p. 52; see also Weatherill (n 103), p. 139.

[146] G. Howells & T. Wilhelmsson, 'EC Consumer Law: Has it Come of Age?', (2003) 4 *Eur. L. Rev*, p. 370. For the specific field of product safety, see also C. Hodges, *European Regulation of Consumer Product Safety* (Oxford-New York: OUP, 2003), p. 76.

[147] See e.g. T. Wilhelmsson, 'Full Harmonization of Consumer Contract Law?', (2008) *ZeuP*, p. 225; Micklitz & Reich (n 128), pp. 477–8; M.-E. Arbour, 'Compensation for Damage Caused by Defective Drugs: European Private Law between Safety Requirements and Free-Market Values', (2004) 10 *Eur. L. J.*, p. 8.

[148] See also H. Schulte-Nölke, C. Twigg-Flesner, & M. Ebers (eds), *EC Consumer Law Compendium* (Munich: Sellier, 2008), p. 797; Micklitz & Reich (n 128), p. 478.

law in the EU should, in general, be based upon a minimum-harmonization approach and only be regulated exceptionally at a full-harmonization level,[149] the reason being that a minimum-harmonization approach at the EU level is often more favourable for consumers, as it would fit the diverse protective requirements that consumers have in different Member States and allow a higher level protection at national level, if required. This approach would also be more suitable to maintain a multi-level system[150] and adapt to the fact that there is not one unique harmonizer, but a process involving many actors with different objectives.[151]

4.3. *The citizen consumer and the Charter of Fundamental Rights*

Extensive application of the full-harmonization approach described in the previous sections brought into question the overall consumer policy of the EU. Consumer law has deeper implications for the life of individuals than mere price-measurable, market effects—to the point that a particular consumer law system implicitly defines, to a certain extent, the way a society regards its people.[152]

In this light, the uniformity implied by full harmonization has been seen as a worrying change in the way the EU envisions itself and its own citizens.[153] At stake are not only elements for the correction of market failures, but also the achievement of social and economic justice.

Member States have built, through slow and country-specific paths, elaborate and diverse models of consumer law, including the protection in various ways of vulnerable and uninformed consumers. Such a complex and delicate system can be limited by the pre-emptive effect of increasingly fully harmonized directives, which pursue 'the establishment and functioning of the internal market' (Article 114 TFEU)[154] and reflect an

[149] This could, for instance, be the case concerning pre-contractual information duties or information about withdrawal from contracts; see also the opinion of G. Alpa, 'New Perspectives in the Protection of Consumers' (2005) 16 *Eur. Bus. L. Rev.*, p. 733.

[150] H. Collins, 'European Private Law and Cultural Identity of States', (1995) 3 *Eur. Rev. Private Law*, p. 353.

[151] M. Dougan, *National Remedies before the Court of Justice: Issues of Harmonization and Differentiation* (Oxford: Hart Publishing, 2005), p. 3.

[152] G. Howells & S. Weatherill, *Consumer Protection Law*, 2nd edn (Aldershot: Ashgate Publishing, 2005), pp. 7–14.

[153] Howells & Weatherill, *Consumer Protection Law* (n 152).

[154] T. Wilhelmsson, *Social Contract Law and European Integration* (Brookfield VT: Dartmouth, 1995); L. Krämer, 'The European Union, Consumption and Consumer Law', in L. Thévenoz & N. Reich (eds), *Liber amicorum Bernd Stauder: Consumer Law* (Geneva: Schulthess, 2006).

EU focus on economic efficiency, rather than on diversity and benevolent protection.[155]

While some maintain that the antagonism between the internal market and consumer policy is exaggerated, and that the ECJ and legislative changes have taken account of consumer interests,[156] a large group of scholars continue to deplore the lack of a social dimension in the EU. For instance, Micklitz regrets the market implementation focus in consumer law, and argues in favour of a concurrent national and European protection policy and of a broader consumer concept.[157] Weatherill concurs with this view, pointing out a conflict between the EU political environment and groups that aim at improving social justice.[158] Finally, Alpa affirms the need for measures which go beyond economic interest and protect consumers per se.[159]

These concerns have been supported by the idea of a 'citizen consumer' endowed with basic rights—a concept which has found increasing popularity among scholars and EU policy-makers.

On the one hand, in the literature, the notion of the 'citizen consumer' has been introduced to escape the narrowness of a market-making approach and to promote a broader consumer concept.[160] Reich argues that consumer law as defence of citizen rights should also take account of political, social, and cultural aspects that are related to consumers.[161]

On the other hand, EU policy-makers have increasingly referred to 'consumer citizens' in their effort to reduce the distance between institutions and citizens and to regain popularity, particularly after the rejection of the European Constitutional Treaty. The notion of the consumer citizen was thus included in various speeches by President Barroso, and in Europe's citizens actions plan, which also aim to improve consumer welfare.[162]

155 Weatherill (n 103), pp. 136–158.

156 Stuyck (n 31), p. 389.

157 Micklitz (n 25), pp. 725 *et seq.*

158 See Weatherill (n 103), pp. 136–158.

159 Alpa, 'New Perspectives in the Protection of Consumers' (n 149), p. 722.

160 'Consumer citizenship' has mainly been debated in political science, but has spilled over into law; see N. Reich, *Bürgerrechte in der Europäischen Union: subjektive Rechte von Unionsbürgern und Drittstaatsangehörigen unter besonderer Berücksichtigung der Rechtslage nach der Rechtsprechung des EuGH und dem Vertrag von Amsterdam* (Baden-Baden: Nomos, 1999), p. 26.

161 Reich, *Bürgerrechte in der Europäischen Union* (n 160), p. 263.

162 See the Communication from the Commission: 'Delivering an area of freedom, security and justice for Europe's citizens — Action Plan Implementing the Stockholm Programme' COM(2010) 171. See also M. Hesselink, 'Are we Human Beings or Mere Consumers?', (2006) 12 (38) *European Voice*.

Moreover, in an effort to come closer to its citizen-consumers, the EU established a Commissioner from 2007 to 10 who was solely responsible for consumer policy.

More generally and importantly, the EU adopted the Charter of Fundamental Rights, which was signed on 7 December 2000 and became binding in 2009, with the entry into force of the Lisbon Treaty.[163] For the first time in the EU, the Charter sets out in a single text a whole range of fundamental civil, political, economic, and social rights for the Union's citizens and residents. In particular, Article 38 in the 'Solidarity' chapter states that 'Union policies shall ensure a high level of consumer protection', recognizing consumer protection as a fundamental policy objective. While this norm aims at improving public confidence both in the market and in the institutions of the EU it also indicates that consumer protection is now regarded as a fundamental social goal in the Union.[164]

Although the integration of consumer protection in the Charter has been important symbolically, a closer look raises questions with regard to its broader implications, namely: what will be the practical impact of these high-level statements? How are the innovations, brought about by the Charter, going to interact with the recent trend towards full harmonization? Importantly, what is the role of the Lisbon Treaty in this picture? These questions will be analyzed in the next subsection and in the following chapters.

4.4. *The Lisbon Treaty*

The Lisbon Treaty was signed in 2007 and entered into force on 1 December 2009 to reform the foundations of the European Union following the two waves of enlargement. It replaced the draft Constitutional Treaty,[165] which was rejected in 2005, and amended the Treaty on European Union (TEU) and the Treaty establishing the European Community, renaming the latter, Treaty on the Functioning of the European Union (TFEU).[166] The Lisbon Treaty introduced structural and institutional changes and strengthend the

[163] Charter of Fundamental Rights of the European Union [2000] OJ C/364/1, proclaimed at Nice on 7 December 2000; see more on the Charter in J.-F. Renucci, *Droit européen des droits de l'homme*, 3rd edn (Paris: LGDJ, 2002), p. 450.

[164] Hesselink, 'Are we Human Beings or Mere Consumers?' (n 162).

[165] The Lisbon Treaty contains a modified part of the rejected draft Constitution; see P. Craig, *The Lisbon Treaty, Law Politics and Treaty Reform* (Oxford: OUP, 2010).

[166] Consolidated versions of the Treaty on European Union and the Treaty on the Functioning of the European Union, OJ C 83, 30.3.2010.

role of fundamental rights.[167] While some Treaty provisions bring modest substantive innovation, others may influence consumer protection in new ways, in particular regarding regulatory participation, access to justice, and fundamental rights protection. A number of key aspects of the Lisbon Treaty which are relevant to consumer protection are described here, whereas broader changes will be considered in more detail in the following chapters.

Since the Lisbon Treaty reforms, the division of competences between the European Union and Member States has become to a certain extent more transparent. The TFEU sets out three main categories of competences: exclusive, shared, and supporting competences (Articles 2 to 6 TFEU). Furthermore, it contains a non-exhaustive description of the areas covered by each category, including consumer protection as a shared competence between the EU and Member States (Article 4(2)(f) TFEU). According to Article 2(2) TFEU this means that both the EU and the Member States are authorized to adopt legally binding acts in that area. However, the Member States may only exercise their competences provided that the EU has not exercised its competence or has decided to cease exercising them.[168] In addition, Article 5 TEU sets out three fundamental principles applicable to the exercise of EU competences. According to the *principle of conferral:* 'the Union shall act only within the limits of the competences conferred upon it by the Member States in the Treaties to attain the objectives set out therein' (Article 5(2)). All other competences remain with the Member States. Pursuant to the *principle of subsidiarity*, for shared competences, 'the Union shall act only if and in so far as the objectives of the proposed action cannot be sufficiently achieved by the Member States (…)'(Article 5(3)). Finally, under the *principle of proportionality* 'the content and form of Union action shall not exceed what is necessary to achieve the objectives of the Treaties' (Article 5(4)).[169] These provisions are more detailed than pre-Lisbon and intend to clarify the distribution of competences, which has been relatively vague and

[167] For a comprehensive legal analysis of the Lisbon Treaty see Craig, *The Lisbon Treaty, Law Politics and Treaty Reform* (n 165); A. Biondi, P. Eeckhout, & S. Ripley (eds), *EU Law after Lisbon* (Oxford: OUP, 2012).

[168] Protocol No. 25 to the Lisbon Treaty further defines the exercise of shared competences, by stipulating that when the Union has taken action, 'the scope of this exercise of competence only covers those elements governed by the Union act in question'. Therefore, it does not cover the whole area, leaving the possibility for Member States to intervene.

[169] Protocol no. 2 provides more details on the application of the principles of subsidiarity and proportionality in the Lisbon Treaty; see also the description at: <http://europa.eu/legislation_summaries/institutional_affairs/treaties/lisbon_treaty/ai0020_en.htm>.

contentious in the past.[170] While they do not involve any notable transfer of competence and still leave scope for interpretative questions, they provide some guidance, potentially contributing to an easier control and exercise of these competences.

Furthermore, the Treaty states for the first time in the field of health protection in Article 168(c) TFEU (ex Article 152 EC) that the EU can adopt measures setting high standards of quality and safety for medicinal products and devices. While this provision primarily concerns health protection measures, it is arguably also essential for consumer safety, to protect them from hazardous drugs and harmful medical devices.

Another set of Treaty provisions expressly mentioning consumer protection do not, at first sight, seem to bring major substantive innovations. Nonetheless a change in the placement of the consumer protection provision in the Treaty and its recognition in the binding Charter may entail a distinct qualitative improvement. Article 12 TFEU, as under the pre-Lisbon provision (ex Article 153(2) EC), states that 'Consumer protection requirements shall be taken into account in defining and implementing other Union policies and activities'. However, in contrast with the earlier version, this provision now appears at the beginning of the Treaty under Title II together with other 'provisions having general application', which might improve the visibility of this objective. In addition, Article 38 of the Charter of Fundamental Rights provides further support in this regard as it stipulates that Union policies shall ensure a high level of consumer protection.

The inclusion of consumer protection in such a list of transversal provisions and in the Charter may facilitate the systematic consideration of this objective before an EU measure is adopted and possibly contributes to a more consistent integration of consumer interests within different EU policy fields. Such integration is already most evident in specific areas of competition policy,[171] where consumer interests are applied as the ultimate standard to assess whether the practice of a dominant undertaking is legitimate under competition law.[172] For example, a dominant market position of a business

[170] For a detailed analysis, see S. Weatherill, 'The Limits of Legislative Harmonization Ten Years after *Tobacco Advertising*: How the Court's Case Law has become a "Drafting Guide"', (2011) 12(3) *German L. J.*, pp. 827 *et seq.*

[171] See also the recent case by the General Court in T-224/10, *Association belge des consommateurs test-achats ASBL v European Commission* 12 October 2011, not yet reported, paras 43–4.

[172] Article 102 TFEU (ex Art. 82 EC).

may be accepted if the overall balance in terms of consumer interests is positive.[173]

A core provision of consumer protection comes under Title XV and its Article 169(1) TFEU and remained substantially unchanged, besides the renumbering. It states, like Article 153 EC previously, that the Community has the power to 'contribute to protecting the health, safety and economic interests of consumers, as well as to promoting their right to information, education and to organise themselves in order to safeguard their interests'. Article 169(2) TFEU then specifies that these goals can be achieved either by '(a) measures adopted pursuant to Article 114 TFEU in the context of the completion of the internal market'; or '(b) measures which support, supplement and monitor the policy pursued by the Member States'.[174] Here no modification in wording or strategy is apparent. The term 'supplement' national policies provides the Commission, in theory, with the opportunity to create new consumer provisions that protect consumers per se, without the need for a market-integration justification, provided that Member States have already acted in this field.[175] However, as explored earlier in this chapter, in practice, Community legislation in relation to consumer protection has been based almost exclusively upon Article 169(2)(a) and Article 114 TFEU (ex Article 95 EC), which continues to be the case.[176] Although Article 114(3) TFEU requires that a directive has to comply with a high level of consumer protection, the main requirement remains that of promoting economic efficiency. This harmonization approach based on market-focused rationales is problematic, owing to potential tensions between economic efficiency objectives and consumer protection per se in some areas, and may lead to a lowering of standards in specific countries.[177] This requires an open debate and new

[173] European Commission, 'Antitrust: Consumer Welfare at the Heart of the Commission Fight against Abuses by Dominant Undertakings', in IP/08/1877, 03/12/2008. The guidance paper on Art. 82 sets out the Commission's determination to prioritize cases where the exclusionary conduct of a dominant undertaking is liable to have harmful effects on consumers.

[174] In addition, Art. 169(3) TFEU repeats the provision already existent in the previous Treaties that measures adopted under para. 2(b) should not prevent Member States introducing more stringent protective measures.

[175] Stuyck (n 31), p. 387.

[176] See e.g. the recent 2011 legislative proposals on consumer ADR and ODR, which are based on Art. 114 TFEU described in ch. 7 of this book.

[177] C.U. Schmid, 'The Instrumentalist Conception of the Acquis Communautaire in Consumer Law and its Implications on a European Contract Law Code', (2005) 2(1) *Eur. Rev. Contract Law*, pp. 211–27; for a general assessment of harmonization in private law, see W. van Gerven, 'Harmonization of Private law: Do we Need it?', (2004) 41 *CML Rev.*, p. 505; S. Weatherill, 'Why Object to the Harmonization of Private Law by the EC?', (2002) 39 *CML Rev.*, p. 12; Weatherill (n 103).

strategies on how consumer protection can be promoted when it pursues broader objectives, for instance of a social nature, that may be unrelated to, or clash with, market-integration goals.

Later on, we will examine in more depth the issue of whether the Lisbon Treaty, along with the Charter of Fundamental Rights, may contribute to a more comprehensive form of consumer protection. For now, we anticipate that the Treaty will strengthen the role of fundamental rights, with important implications for the discussion in the following chapters. Article 6(1) TEU states that the EU 'recognises the rights, freedoms and principles set out in the Charter of Fundamental Rights'. More importantly this provision also expressly stipulates that the Charter 'shall have the same legal value as the Treaties'.[178] Therefore, with the adoption of the Treaty of Lisbon, the Charter has now become legally binding for EU institutions and for most Member States applying EU law, acquiring an equal status with EU Treaties.[179] At the same time, the Charter is not designed to extend the competence of the EU as circumscribed in the Treaties (Article 6(1) TEU). Another significant innovation in terms of human rights is provided by Article 6(2) TEU, which stipulates that the EU shall accede to the European Convention for the Protection of Human Rights and Fundamental Freedoms, without affecting the Union's competences established in the Treaties. The wider implication of the Charter of Fundamental Rights and of the Lisbon Treaty for consumer law will be assessed in the following chapters.[180]

5. Conclusions

Despite important recent innovations, EU consumer law needs to develop further into a coherent and comprehensive framework. As the EU evolves, it is acquiring additional competences in consumer law. However, it only has the competence set out in the Treaties, and cannot go beyond these boundaries.

As described in this chapter, market-integration objectives have played a central role in the development of EU consumer law, and have paved the

[178] For the online version of the Treaty of Lisbon, see the Council website: <http://register.consilium.europa.eu/pdf/en/08/st06/st06655.en08.pdf>.

[179] Poland and the UK opted out of the Charter; see also the opt-out Protocol on the application of the Charter of Fundamental Rights to Poland and the UK, OJ 9.5.2008 C 115/313–14.

[180] See in particular ch. 3 and chs 5, 6, 7, and 8 of this book.

way for a narrow, 'instrumentalist' approach to the definition of the EU consumer. Legislative initiatives purely aimed at consumer protection, without a market-integration goal, remain limited at the Union level.

In some respects, the harmonization approach of the Union has been a success, as it established a common standard of consumer protection. However, the full harmonization trend of the EU raises questions about the adequacy of this approach in achieving high levels of consumer protection. In particular, as highlighted in this chapter, a full-harmonization approach to consumer law, based on market-integration objectives, might limit more stringent national provisions in some countries. Furthermore, there is now a strong academic demand for a new consumer concept which coherently integrates a social dimension in EU consumer law and policy.

The next chapters will analyze the impact of human and fundamental rights on consumer protection. The Charter of Fundamental Rights includes for the first time consumer protection as a fundamental policy objective in its 'Solidarity' chapter (Article 38). In addition, a range of other and fundamental rights may have a direct influence on consumer protection as the recent case law has shown. The following chapter will thus examine intersections between human rights and consumer protection.

3

The Evolution of Consumer Protection and Human Rights

1. Introduction

Recent years have seen a progressive convergence of fundamental rights and consumer protection in EU law. Fundamental rights are having an increasing impact on consumer protection, playing a growing role in EU and Member States' law.[1]

The recognition of consumer protection at the fundamental rights level is a relatively new phenomenon in the EU. Consumer protection is included in the 'Solidarity' chapter of the EU Charter of Fundamental Rights, along with other social provisions such as the right to preventive healthcare, environmental protection, and access to services of general interest. These provisions affirm a social European model formulated in response to a perceived need to create a stronger link between the EU and its citizens.[2] Despite their high-level status, the question arises as to whether these new provisions will be effective in offering better legal protection.

The idea that social rights should have the same status as civil and political rights has not always been recognized in practice and thus the inclusion of social provisions in the Charter has sparked academic and political debate. There is also a more practical question of how relevant the Charter will be in strengthening fundamental rights.[3] For some, the recognition of the

[1] Some Member States show a similar trend, by including high-level consumer protection provisions in their constitutions, described later in this chapter. This chapter draws on previous work of the author published in I. Benöhr & H.-W. Micklitz, 'Consumer Protection and Human Rights', in G. Howells, I. Ramsay, & T. Wilhelmsson (eds), *Handbook of Research on International Consumer Law* (Cheltenham: Edward Elgar Publishing, 2010).

[2] Report of the Expert Group on Fundamental Rights, *Affirming Fundamental Rights in the European Union* (Luxembourg: Office for Official Publications of the European Communities, 1999), p. 13.

[3] S. Fredman, 'Transformation or Dilution: Fundamental Rights in the EU Social Space', (2006) 12 *Eur. L. J.*, pp. 41–60.

fundamental rights in the Charter amounts simply to a formal acceptance of the legal instruments already in place. For others, the Charter is seen as providing a propulsive force for future policies and legislation, and thus is expected to have important practical effects.

This chapter explores the conceptualization of consumer protection as a human right, and analyzes the impact of human and fundamental rights on consumer protection. First, it describes the influence of international human rights on consumer law. Secondly, it analyzes the scope and the limitation of consumer protection under the Charter of Fundamental Rights. Finally, the significance of constitutional consumer protection will be assessed in the light of cases in specific countries.

2. The International Law Context

During the last 40 years we have experienced a marked increase in cross-border trade and new technologies leading, among other things, to more consumer choice, but also to new risks and growing power of large companies. As a result of these phenomena, consumer law has developed to provide protection and ensure transparency in the market. More recently, consumer protection is also increasingly assessed as a matter of human rights protection.[4] This raises the question of whether consumer protection may become a category of human rights and what would be the benefit of such an international recognition.

2.1. *Consumer protection as a new generation of human rights?*

Human rights, whose birth is traditionally traced back to the French Revolution, developed in waves over time, giving rise to three 'generations' of rights.[5] The first generation comprises civil and political rights, such as the right to life and the right to liberty and security, and includes the rights developed in the United Kingdom and France during the seventeenth and eighteenth centuries. These rights are sometimes also categorized as

[4] S. Deutch, 'Are Consumer Rights Human Rights?', (1994) 32(3) *Osgoode Hall L. J.*, pp. 551–2; C. Harding, U. Kohl, & N. Salmon, *Human Rights in the Market Place: The Exploitation of Rights Protection by Economic Actors* (Aldershot: Ashgate Publishing, 2008), pp. 53–80 and pp. 125–66.

[5] K. Vasak, 'Human Rights: A Thirty-Year Struggle: the Sustained Efforts to Give Force of Law to the Universal Declaration of Human Rights', *UNESCO Courier* 30:11 (Paris: UNESCO, November 1977).

'negative' rights 'which require only forbearance on the part of others' as opposed to 'positive' rights, 'which require others to provide goods, services or opportunities'.[6] The first-generation rights have been enshrined in the Universal Declaration of Human Rights 1948[7] and the United Nations International Covenant on Civil and Political Rights (1966).[8]

The second-generation rights, which were influenced by the revolutions of the early twentieth century and consolidated after the Second World War, were of an economic, social, and cultural nature. These human rights were seen as an instrument, or a necessary condition, to preserve liberty and autonomy in the market.[9] Typical socio-economic rights, such as the guarantee of a minimum living standard, education, and health, were seen as prerequisites for full participation in an autonomous life. These rights are often described as positive rights, characterized by intervention, rather than the abstention, of the state, and were acknowledged in the Universal Declaration of Human Rights 1948 and in the International Covenant on Economic, Social and Cultural Rights of the UN in 1966.[10]

The third generation consists of rights which have not been recognized as international human rights yet, but which were, nevertheless, approved by various organizations of the United Nations. They include the right to development and to peace, environmental rights, and cultural rights.

There has always been a division between the first generation of 'classical' human rights, and the second- and third-generation rights founded upon the welfare state and the protection of the individual. The first generation of rights have benefited from a growing recognition in the free democracies and are directly applicable to individuals. In contrast, the second and third generations of human rights often play a subordinate role and remain contested.[11]

[6] See J. Donnelly, who convincingly argues that a clear categorization based on positive and negative rights to distinguish between civil and political rights and economic and social rights cannot be drawn; J. Donnelly, *Universal Human Rights in Theory and Practice* (Ithaca, NY: Cornell University Press, 2003), p. 30.

[7] The Declaration was proclaimed by the United Nations General Assembly in Paris on 10 December 1948, General Assembly resolution 217 A (III).

[8] Adopted by the United Nations General Assembly resolution 2200A (XXI) of 16 December 1966, entry into force 23 March 1976.

[9] P. Badura, 'Das Prinzip der sozialen Grundrechte und seine Verwirklichung im Recht der Bundesrepublik Deutschland', (1975) 14 *Der Staat*, p. 17, at 20.

[10] Adopted and opened for signature by General Assembly resolution 2200A (XXI) of 16 December 1966.

[11] A. Eide & A. Rosas, 'Economic, Social and Cultural Rights: A Universal Challenge', in A. Eide, C. Krause, & A. Rosas (eds), *Economic, Social and Cultural Rights: A Textbook* (Dordrecht: Martinus

Numerous attempts have been made to define the notion and characteristics of human rights. According to Cranston, human rights are genuinely universal moral rights, of paramount importance and of which no one may be deprived without a grave affront to justice.[12] Deutch refers to this definition and argues that, consumer rights have the potential to become human rights because they contain a number of the characteristics of human rights.[13] In particular, key elements are the wide recognition and universality of these rights, the promotion of human dignity and well-being, and the protection of individuals against more powerful entities such as governments.

According to such a broad description, consumer rights may be regarded as universal rights. First, the rising international recognition of consumer rights and safety standards in international guidelines or treaties shows the universal acceptance of such rights (at least in general terms). Consumer rights also apply to all individuals, as every person is a consumer. Secondly, consumer rights to safe products and access to justice are granted to maintain human dignity and well-being, thus possessing the second characteristics pointed out by Deutch. Thirdly, these rights may protect from arbitrary infringements by governments or other powerful entities. As Deutch argues,[14] with the internationalization of trade the large corporations have become increasingly powerful, and consumers cannot bargain on equal terms under fair market conditions, thereby undermining the consumer's autonomy.[15] Defending individuals against more powerful counterparties, consumers' rights may also possess the third characteristic of human rights. At the same time, as trade has become international, the problem of hazardous goods and defective products is no longer a purely national concern, so that coherent consumer protection standards have to be developed at an international level.

This discussion suggests that consumer protection may develop as a new extension or 'generation' of international human rights law, emerging in response to globalization and recent technological evolution. However, as we will see later, the conceptualization of consumer protection as a human rights objective remains controversial. The next section will explore existing

Nijhoff, 1995), p. 15; J. Kenner, 'Economic and Social Rights in the EU Legal Order', in T. Hervey & J. Kenner, *Economic and Social Rights under the EU Charter of Fundamental Rights: A Legal Perspective* (Oxford: Hart Publishing, 2003), p. 2.

[12] M. Cranston, *What are Human Rights?* (London: Bodley Head, 1973), pp. 54–68.

[13] See Deutch, 'Are Consumer Rights Human Rights?' (n 4), pp. 551–2.

[14] Deutch (n 4), pp. 552–3.

[15] See also Harding, Kohl, & Salmon, *Human Rights in the Market Place* (n 4).

international conventions and guidelines, to understand the current legal status of consumer law in the human rights and international law field.

2.2. *Implicit consumer protection in human rights agreements*

Before an explicit mention was made of consumer law at the international level, several human rights agreements already implicitly protected consumers.[16] In 1966, the United Nations General Assembly adopted the International Covenant on Economic, Social and Cultural Rights (ICESCR),[17] which is compulsory at the international level and has been in force since 1976. At the regional level, the Council of Europe established two treaties, the European Convention on Human Rights (ECHR) in 1950[18] and the European Social Charter (ESC) in 1961,[19] which can be seen as the social counterpart of the ECHR.

Some of the economic and social rights in the ICESCR can be conceived of as consumer protection. The right to an adequate standard of living, established in Article 11(1), includes the right to adequate food, clothing, housing, and to a continuous improvement of living conditions. Adequate food and improvement of living conditions also means safety, information, and arguably fair prices, which can be achieved through consumer protection legislation. The right to physical and mental health in Article 12 of the ICESCR includes the improvement of environmental and industrial hygiene, and the prevention of diseases. As the protection of the individual from hazardous products is equally an aim of consumer law, this provision implicitly also protects consumers.

The same can be deduced for the ECHR and the ESC. Article 6 of the ECHR enshrines the human right to a fair trial, including access to justice within a reasonable time for each citizen. This provision already plays an important role in procedural consumer law as a basis to ensure effective judicial protection.[20]

[16] See also Deutch (n 4), pp. 558 *et seq*.

[17] The Covenant was adopted and opened for signature, ratification, and accession by General Assembly resolution 2200A (XXI) of 16 December 1966, entry into force 3 January 1976, in accordance with Art. 27.

[18] For the full text see the European Treaty Series no. 5 at the Council of Europe website: <http://www.conventions.coe.int/Treaty/en/Treaties/Word/005.doc>.

[19] European Social Charter, CETS no. 035, opening for signature: Turin 1961, entry into force: 1965. Full text at: <http://conventions.coe.int/Treaty/Commun/QueVoulezVous.asp?NT=035&CM=1&CL=ENG>.

[20] See e.g. Joined Cases C-317/08 to C-320/08, *Alassini and others v Telecom Italia* [2010] ECR I-2213 and ch. 7 in this book.

Article 10 of the ECHR includes the right to freedom of expression, which may also protect the right of consumers or consumer organizations to form opinions and to receive and divulge information. Interestingly, the objective of consumer information and protection became an important element of assessment by the European Court of Human Rights in connection with the freedom of expression of authors or publishing firms regarding publications on consumer-related matters.[21] For example, in *Hertel v Switzerland* the European Court of Human Rights held that the freedom of expression could not be restricted although this impinged inter alia on competition law. In other cases, it acknowledged a restriction under certain conditions, in particular, where the 'commercial expression' by an organization might mislead consumers through its marketing practices.[22]

Another ECHR provision of particular interest for consumer protection is Article 11 on the right to freedom of assembly and association. This provision may serve as a guarantee for consumer organizations to establish themselves freely and hold meetings to promote consumer interests. Finally, the provision on health protection, in Article 11 of the ESC, may also be a source of consumer law, protecting the individual against defective products or harmful services.

In conclusion, although none of the documents mention consumers explicitly, they may well address consumer protection issues in an indirect way. In particular, Article 6 of the ECHR has already played a significant role in cases regarding consumer access to justice.

2.3. *The United Nations Guidelines for Consumer Protection*

The United Nations Guidelines for Consumer Protection (UNGCP) were adopted by the UN General Assembly on 9 April 1985 in its resolution 39/248.[23] The Guidelines identify seven areas in which governments have to enhance their consumer policy according to their economic and social circumstances. These areas are physical safety; the promotion and protection of consumers' economic interests; standards for the safety and quality of consumer goods and services; distribution facilities for essential consumer goods

[21] ECtHR, *Hertel v Switzerland*, App. no. 25181/94, Judgment of 25 August 1998; ECtHR, *Markt Intern Verlag GMBH and Klaus Beermann v Germany*, App. no. 10572/83, Judgment of 25 October 1989.

[22] See e.g. ECtHR, *X and Church of Scientology v Sweden*, App. no. 7805/77, Judgment of 5 May 1979.

[23] See <http://www.un.org/esa/sustdev/publications/consumption_en.pdf>.

and services; improved consumer redress; consumer education and information; and measures relating to specific areas, such as food, water, and pharmaceuticals. More recently, the UN Guidelines were extended in 1999 to insert sustainable consumption as a principle of consumer policy.[24] Being relatively new, sustainability may be regarded as a third-generation right aiming to improve the ecological system of the world. The inclusion of this sustainability aspect reveals a new conception of consumer empowerment: the consumer not only has the right to be protected, but must also assume a certain responsibilities for promoting a clean and healthy environment.[25]

Especially directed at developing countries, the Guidelines established a list of basic objectives to promote consumer legislation and policies. The reason for developing them was 'that consumers often face imbalances in economic terms, education levels, and bargaining power'. In particular, the Guidelines aim to ensure consumer access to non-hazardous products, and to promote just, equitable, and sustainable economic and social development.[26]

While not a binding instrument, the Guidelines were the first measure that promoted consumer protection explicitly on an international scale.[27] The international consensus on the Guidelines for consumer protection can be seen as a general acceptance of consumer protection as a 'universal' right; moreover, it provides additional support for considering consumer rights as human rights.[28] Although the Guidelines are clearly not mandatory, and there is no enforcement mechanism for them, they may develop in customary law and further promote binding laws in the future.

2.4. *Debates on human rights*

Human rights have become very popular in international discourse and are used to promote and protect a wider range of policy objectives. Despite this increasing prominence, the gradual proliferation of new human rights claims in law and politics has led to some scepticism and to suggestions for stronger

[24] This new version was included by the Economic and Social Council in July 1999 and adopted by the General Assembly in its decision 54/449.

[25] See more on the 'greening' of international consumer rights in H.-W. Micklitz, 'International Regulation on Health, Safety, and the Environment—Trends and Challenges', (2000) *J. Consumer Policy*, pp. 2–24.

[26] ECOSOC, *Consumer Protection*, Report of the Secretary General, E/1995/70.

[27] Although the Guidelines sparked some controversy at the beginning, they have been positively assessed in recent literature. For an initial critique, see M. Wiedenbaum, 'The Case Against the United Nations Guidelines for Consumer Protection', (1987) 10 *J. Consumer Policy*, p. 425, at 432; in contrast for more recent positive assessment, see Deutch (n 4), pp. 551–2.

[28] Deutch (n 4), pp. 551–2.

quality controls of these rights.[29] In particular, economic and social rights that emerged relatively recently in comparison to civil and political rights, have remained contested on the ground of feasibility and dependence on political will.[30] While almost all states recognize economic and social rights in ordinary law, establishing amongst other things some form of consumer protection, their acceptance as human rights is controversial.

Those who argue that economic and social rights should *not* be given the status of international human rights put forward a number of arguments to support their claim, some of which are discussed here. First, they argue, these rights are less 'fundamental' than, for example, the rights to life, freedom, and physical integrity.[31] Secondly, and consequentially, the proliferation of human rights would lead to a dilution of existing rights and might conflict with other interests. Furthermore, some scholars maintain that second- and third-generation human rights are resource-dependent and costly, imposing high financial burdens which only wealthy states can afford.[32] The inclusion of such rights would result in the promise of a certain standard of living, which economic circumstances might make impossible to sustain.[33] Instead, the argument goes, the proclamation of new rights can be justified only when the need is sufficiently great, and the chance of acceptance and sustainability is strong.

Other scholars, however, argue that welfare state rights such as consumer rights should be protected as fundamental rights in modern law systems.[34] On the one hand, it is argued, these rights are sufficiently important to be granted the highest possible level of protection.[35] This challenges the idea

[29] See P. Alston, 'Conjuring up New Human Rights: a Proposal for Quality Control', (1984) 78 *American J. Int'l Law*, pp. 607; J. Raz, 'Human Rights without Foundations', in S. Besson & J. Tasioulas (eds), *The Philosophy of International Law* (Oxford: OUP, 2010), pp. 321–38.

[30] For a general description see Fredman, 'Transformation or Dilution' (n 3), pp. 41–60.

[31] P. Alston, 'Human Rights and Basic Needs: A Critical Assessment', (1979) 12 *Hum. Rts. J.*, pp. 39 and 45; P. Alston & H.J. Steiner, *International Human Rights in Context: Law, Politics, Morals: Text and Materials*, 2nd edn (Oxford: OUP, 2000), p. 237.

[32] Alston & Steiner, *International Human Rights in Context* (n 31), p. 16; see also in general M. Cranston, 'Are There Any Human Rights?' (1983) 112(4), *Daedalus*, 1–17. For similar debates in the field of constitutional law, see G. Bognetti, 'Social Rights, a Necessary Component of the Constitution? The Lesson of the Italian Case', in R. Bieber & P. Widmer (eds), *The European Constitutional Area* (Zürich: Schulthess, 1995), p. 85.

[33] See e.g. the study by the European Parliament: M. Butt, J. Kübert, & C. Schultz, 'Fundamental Social Rights in Europe', Working Paper, European Parliament, DG for Research, Social Affairs Series, 11 (1999).

[34] See Deutch (n 4), p. 567.

[35] Eide & Rosas, 'Economic, Social and Cultural Rights' (n 11), p. 17.

described before that economic and social rights are only of a 'secondary' nature. As previously noted, some scholars have argued that consumers have become more exposed to risks and therefore need additional protection.[36] The broad acceptance of consumer protection by the UN member states (via the Guidelines for Consumer Protection) may be regarded as an indirect support of their stance.

On the other hand, some scholars note that economic and social rights are both similar to, and interdependent with, widely accepted first-generation fundamental rights (i.e. civil and political rights). They are similar to civil and political rights, because these too require positive implementation measures by national states—something which undermines the argument that economic and social rights would be too expensive for most countries, except the wealthiest. Moreover, these scholars argue that economic and social rights and civil and political rights are interdependent as lack of equal protection of the former may undermine the latter.[37]

When it comes to the European context, the recognition of consumer protection in the Solidarity Chapter of the Charter of Fundamental Rights may provide a counterweight to the predominantly economic- and market-based concept of integration of the EU.[38] We will not go further into this general debate here, as these issues will be explored in the following chapter.

2.5. *The impact of international law on consumer protection*

At the international level, consumer law measures are not conceived as formally binding instruments. They may, instead, be regarded as a step towards creating mandatory norms of international law and a catalyst for reform.[39] The adoption of international Consumer Guidelines by the UN shows a general acceptance of consumer protection as an international principle, and has already stimulated important changes in national laws, even at the constitutional level.[40] Indeed, following such Guidelines, several countries

[36] See Harding, Kohl, & Salmon (n 4); see also Deutch (n 4), p. 567.

[37] For a defence of social rights, see C. Fabre, *Social Rights under the Constitution: Government and the Decent Life* (Oxford: OUP, 2000), p. 17; M. Weiss, 'The Politics of the EU Charter of Fundamental Rights', in B. Hepple (ed.), *Social and Labour Rights in a Global Context* (Cambridge: CUP, 2002), pp. 73–94.

[38] For the wider debate regarding economic and social rights, see M.P. Maduro, 'L'équilibre insaisissable entre la liberté économique et les droits sociaux dans l'Union européenne', in P. Alston, *L'Union européenne et les droits de l'homme* (Brussels: Bruylant, 2001), p. 465.

[39] D. Harland, 'The United Nations Guidelines for Consumer Protection', (1987) 10 *J. Consumer Policy*, p. 251.

[40] Deutch (n 4), pp. 573–4.

have introduced laws and raised consumer protection to the constitutional level.[41] Furthermore, as shown by Consumers International, at least 26 national constitutions already contain specific provisions on consumer protection.[42] Thus, the UN Guidelines provided an important example and source of inspiration for countries wishing to include consumer rights in their legal system. Although international consumer protection is still soft law, it is undoubtedly having a considerable impact on national consumer law.

3. Consumer Protection in the EU Charter of Fundamental Rights

The 1957 Treaty of Rome did not include provisions on the protection of fundamental rights as it focused mainly on economic integration. EU fundamental rights appeared first as general principles of law, owing to the judicial activism of the European Court of Justice, and were then strengthened in the Treaty of Maastricht. Eventually, in 2000, the EU Charter of Fundamental Rights was adopted, listing the fundamental rights recognized by the European Union, and containing important provisions that could improve consumer protection.

3.1. *The creation and the aim of the Charter of Fundamental Rights*

The place given to fundamental rights in the European Union has changed considerably since the founding Treaties, which did not mention them explicitly. However, as economic integration progressed, pressure has been brought to bear on the European Community to adopt a human rights dimension to its activities.

Since 1969 the ECJ has gradually developed fundamental rights, recognizing them as general principles of Community law and actively protecting them.[43] Through its case law, the Court gradually established what effectively

[41] D. Harland, 'Implementing the Principles of the United Nations Guidelines for Consumer Protection', (1991) 33 *J. Indian Law Institute*, pp. 189 *et seq*.

[42] Countries including constitutional provisions are, for instance, Vietnam, South Africa, Turkey, Andorra, Bulgaria, Lithuania, Poland, Portugal, Spain, Switzerland, Ukraine, Argentina, Brazil, Colombia, Costa Rica, Ecuador, Paraguay, Peru, and Mexico; see more at Consumers International: <http://www.consumersinternational.org>.

[43] See e.g. Case C-29/69, *Stauder v City of Ulm* [1969] ECR 419; Case C-11/70, *Internationale Handelsgesellschaft v Einfuhr-und Vorratsstelle*, [1970] ECR 1125; see more on this in. J.H.H. Weiler &

amounts to an unwritten charter of rights for the Community.[44] This favourable human rights interpretation found formal recognition in Article F(2)[45] of the Maastricht Treaty, which explicitly mentioned that: 'The Union shall respect fundamental rights, as guaranteed by the European Convention for the Protection of Human Rights and Fundamental Freedoms signed in Rome on 4 November 1950 and as they result from the constitutional traditions common to the Member States, as general principles of Community law'. Subsequently, the Treaty of Amsterdam reaffirmed the respect for fundamental rights. Article 6(1) TEU stated that: 'The Union is founded on the principles of liberty, democracy, respect for human rights and fundamental freedoms, and the rule of law, principles which are common to the Member States'. Nevertheless, a detailed catalogue of human rights provided by a charter was still missing.[46] According to some, the creation of fundamental rights by the ECJ did not ensure sufficient transparency and was unlikely to increase public confidence in the EU.[47] A unique charter was necessary to ensure that fundamental rights were given an explicit and precise role in the EU legal system.[48]

As a first step in this direction, the European Parliament (EP) issued a 'Declaration of Fundamental Rights and Freedoms' in April 1989, as part of a 'Constitution' for the Communities.[49] This Declaration contained a comprehensive list of fundamental rights, from social rights to other 'classic' rights. Article 24 integrated several Community policies, such as the protection of the environment, of consumers, and of health. Although this document was

N. J.S. Lockhart, 'Taking Rights Seriously: The European Court and its Fundamental Rights Jurisprudence', (1995) 32 *CML Rev.*, pp. 51–94.

[44] See e.g. Case C-4/73, *Nold v European Commission* [1974] ECR 491.

[45] With the adoption of the Amsterdam Treaty this provision became Art. 6(2) TEU.

[46] G. de Búrca, 'The Drafting of the European Union Charter of Fundamental Rights', (2001) 26 *Eur. L. Rev.*, pp. 126 *et seq.*

[47] Criticism came particularly from Italy and Germany, which have a tradition of strict fundamental rights scrutiny: T. von Danwitz, 'The Charter of Fundamental Rights of the EU: Between Political Symbolism and Legal Realism', (2001) *Denver J. Int'l Law and Policy*, p. 2; A. Adinolfi, 'The Judicial Application of Community Law in Italy (1981–1997)', (1998) 35 *CML Rev.*, p. 1313, at 1323.

[48] Report of the Expert Group on Fundamental Rights, *Affirming Fundamental Rights in the European Union* (n 2).

[49] In 1977, the EP adopted the Joint Declaration on Human Rights, which was extended in 1989 by a Declaration of Fundamental Rights and Freedoms. See also R. Bieber, K. de Gucht, K. Lenaerts, & J.H.H. Weiler (eds), *Au nom des peoples européens—in the name of the peoples of Europe* (Baden-Baden: Nomos, 1996), p. 365.

adopted in neither the Treaty of Maastricht nor the Treaty of Amsterdam as intended by the European Parliament, it represented an important step, because it was an expression of the popular will of European citizens.

This attention to human rights protection was revived 10 years later at the 1990 European Council of Cologne, when the Member States decided to create a Charter of Fundamental Rights of the European Union. The Charter was eventually signed on 7 December 2000 at the European Council of Nice, and contained a catalogue of fundamental rights.[50] This catalogue was inspired by various legal sources: national constitutional traditions, the European Social Charter, the Community Charter of Fundamental Social Rights of Workers, the 1950 European Convention on Human Rights, and the case law of the ECJ.

3.2. *The functions of the Charter and its social dimension*

The Charter can have an important role in increasing legitimacy, autonomy, diversity, and solidarity. All of these aspects are crucial for EU consumer law, as underlined in the previous two chapters.

First, fundamental rights may strengthen legitimacy of the EU, by setting a catalogue of basic rights and objectives that link the Union with its citizens. This might create a stronger acceptance of the legal system if these rights can be made effective.

Secondly, fundamental rights protect individual freedoms.[51] For instance, Müller describes the function of fundamental rights as a way of securing the integrity and freedom of individuals in society against the limitations of social power.[52] Pernice goes further, maintaining that, in the present global and multi-level European system,[53] fundamental rights have a broader role than protecting individuals against the public authority.[54] A positive definition of freedom

[50] Charter of Fundamental Rights of the European Union [2000] OJ C/364/1, proclaimed in Nice on 7 December 2000; see more on the Charter in J.-F. Renucci, *Droit européen des droits de l'homme*, 3rd edn (Paris: LGDJ, 2002), p. 450.

[51] T. Marauhn, *Rekonstruktion sozialer Grundrechte als Normkategorie—zugleich eine Kritik der konventionellen Gegenüberstellung von Grundrechten und Staatszielbestimmungen* Frankfurt (Main): Habilitation manuscript, 2000, p. 262.

[52] J.P. Müller, 'Koordination des Grundrechtsschutzes in Europa—Einleitungsreferat', (2005) *ZSR*, p. 9.

[53] Political science scholars describe the EU as a multilevel system, in which competence is spread between different levels; F. Scharpf, P. Schmitter, & W. Streeck (eds), *Governance in the European Union* (London: Sage, 1996).

[54] See I. Pernice, 'Multilevel Constitutionalism in the European Union', (2002) *Eur. L. Rev.*, p. 511; this approach forms part of a broader conception which Marauhn calls a 'citizen constitution'; Marauhn, *Rekonstruktion sozialer Grundrechte als Normkategorie* (n 51), p. 265.

ensures that citizens have the possibility to actively participate in the political process to make claims against public institutions to develop policies that effectively realize fundamental rights.[55]

Thirdly, the Charter includes a minimum set of values that are of central importance for both human dignity and individual identity in the pluralistic European society. This highlights the possibility of being culturally diverse, but being treated equally, thereby promoting diversity.[56]

Finally, the Charter contains a 'Solidarity' chapter IV comprising fundamental social provisions aimed at securing the autonomy of individuals and their well-being.[57] Consumer protection is included among them, suggesting that it will be pursued as an autonomous social objective of the EU. Fundamental social provisions aim at ensuring a specified standard of living to everyone without discrimination, and are increasingly considered a necessary condition to preserve autonomy in the market.[58] For instance, Alexy considers fundamental social rights essential to ensure that the individual is able to act in an autonomous way.[59] Frankenberg explains the quest for social safety as a need for decent living conditions and protection against the life risks in society. But, above all, he links it to the foundation of a political community that allows political participation, a condition for human self-realization in any society.[60]

Besides having these functions the Charter may also have a powerful role in orienting the EU policy, in providing interpretative guidance of other provisions, and it might help to circumscribe the legal and political status of the citizen.[61] In particular, for the consumer, fundamental provisions could

[55] I. Pernice & R. Kanitz, 'Fundamental Rights and Multilevel Constitutionalism in Europe', WHI-Paper 7/04, p. 5.

[56] See I. Pernice, M. Franz, & C.W. Stephan, 'Renewing the European Social Contract: The Challenge of Institutional Reform and Enlargement in the Light of Multilevel Constitutionalism', (2001) *Kings College L. J.*, p. 61.

[57] On the role of social rights in Europe, see G. De Búrca and B. De Witte (eds), *Social Rights in Europe* (Oxford: OUP, 2005); see also Fabre, *Social Rights under the Constitution* (n 37), pp. 17–22.

[58] Marauhn (n 51), p. 175.

[59] R. Alexy, 'Diskurstheorie und Menschenrechte', in R. Alexy, *Recht, Vernunft, Diskurs. Studien zur Rechtsphilosophie* (Frankfurt am Main: Suhrkamp, 1995), p. 127, at 145; R. Alexy, *Theorie der Grundrechte*, 3rd edn (Frankfurt am Main: Suhrkamp Verlag, 1996), pp. 377 *et seq*.

[60] G. Frankenberg, 'Why Care? The Trouble with Social Rights', (1996) 17 *Cardozo L. Rev.*, p. 1369; see also R. Arango, 'Basic Social Rights, Constitutional Justice, and Democracy', (2003) 16 *Ratio Juris*, p. 151.

[61] Pernice & Kanitz, 'Fundamental Rights and Multilevel Constitutionalism in Europe' (n 55), p. 7.

lead to an improvement of 'protection and enablement', as well as granting greater voice to the consumer.[62]

3.3. *The relevant provisions in the Charter for consumer protection*

The Charter is structured in six chapters: dignity, freedoms, equality, solidarity, citizens' rights, and justice. It sets out significant socio-economic rights and some new rights and objectives which constitute an innovation for traditional human rights. Article 38 on consumer protection and Article 8 on data protection are some examples of these innovative provisions.[63]

Previously, consumer law had been regulated in primary and secondary Community law, as well as in Member States' legislation. Hence, the inclusion of consumer protection in the 'Solidarity' chapter of the Charter was controversial. The draft Charter stated that the EU policy would ensure a high level of protection on health, security, and consumer interests.[64] In the following drafts, various proposals were made, ranging from the complete elimination of consumer law from the Charter, to the proposal of a subjective right for consumer protection.[65] None of these proposals has been adopted by the European Union though, as the final text, in Article 38, states that: 'Union policies shall ensure a high level of consumer protection.'[66]

Article 38 has been based upon Article 169 TFEU (ex 153 EC), which promotes a high level of consumer protection. However, in contrast to Article 169, the consumer provision in the Charter is kept very short. Article 169 TFEU contains more detailed indications as to the way the EU can achieve consumer protection, including specific rights, such as the rights to safety and information. The inclusion of consumer protection as an objective in the Charter can be regarded as a compromise, acknowledging its importance

[62] Harding, Kohl, & Salmon (n 4).

[63] A. Kiss, 'Environmental and Consumer Protection', in S. Peers & A. Ward (eds), *The EU Charter of Fundamental Rights: Politics, Law and Policy* (Oxford: Hart Publishing, 2004); E. Poillot, *Droit européen de la consommation et uniformisation du droit des contrats* (Paris: LGDJ, 2006), p. 64.

[64] Draft Charter of Fundamental Rights of the European Union- Amendments submitted by the members of the Convention regarding social rights and the horizontal clauses (Reference doc.: CHARTE 4316/00 CONVENT no. 34, see Art. 45 regarding consumer protection May 2000.

[65] See Draft Charter of Fundamental Rights of the European Union, CHARTE 4372/00 CONVENT no. 39 Brussels, June 2000.

[66] E. Riedel, 'Verbraucherschutz, Artikel 38', in J. Meyer, *Kommentar zur Charta der Grundrechte der Europäischen Union* (Baden-Baden: Nomos, 2003), fn. 4.

as a policy goal, but without providing it the legal effect of a fundamental subjective right.[67]

Other provisions of the Charter may also help to further consumer protection in a broader sense; among them, the recognition of human dignity in Article 1, and of the 'right to the integrity of the person' in Article 3. Article 3(1) states that 'Everyone has the right to respect for his or her physical and mental integrity'. Article 3(2) specifically requires, for interventions in the health field, 'the free and informed consent of the person concerned, according to the procedures laid down by law'. In particular, this provision is relevant for consumer protection in relation to the provision of health services. It helps to ensure that no health intervention is made (for example, for preventive, diagnostic, therapeutic, or research purposes), before the person concerned has received appropriate information from a health professional.[68] The principle of informed consent requires that the individual is adequately informed about the purpose and nature of the intervention as well as on its consequences and risks. Furthermore, this implies that consent may be freely withdrawn at any time by the person concerned.[69]

Another fundamental right which is becoming increasingly important for consumers with the frequent use of Internet services for communication or online transactions is the protection of personal data, enshrined in Article 8. Article 8(2) states that 'data must be processed fairly for specified purposes and on the basis of the consent of the person concerned'. This Article is also essential for the protection of medical records or against misuse by institutions which hold personal data. However, the protection of personal data may conflict with other fundamental rights. The ECJ has already referred to this provision in several cases when it had to balance the right to privacy and information against property rights.[70]

[67] Regarding different legal approaches to consumer protection, see H.-W. Micklitz, 'Consumer Rights', in A. Cassese, A. Clapham, & J.H.H. Weiler (eds), *Human Rights and the European Community: The Substantive Law* (Baden-Baden: Nomos, 1991), pp. 53–4.

[68] This key principle of medical ethics has been enshrined in Art. 5(1) of the Biomedicine Convention.

[69] For more information see M. Nowak, 'Article 3—Right to the Integrity of the Person', in EU Network of Independent Experts on Fundamental Rights, *Commentary of the Charter of Fundamental Rights of the European Union* (2006), p. 39, published online, see: <http://infoportal.fra.europa.eu/InfoPortal/infobaseShowContent.do?btnCat_183&btnCountryBread_169>.

[70] E.g. Case C-275/06, *Productores de Música de España (Promusicae) v Telefónica de España SAU* [2008] ECR I-271, and more recent cases, which will be discussed in greater depth in ch. 6 of this book.

In addition, the freedom of expression and information in Article 11 and the freedom of assembly and of association in Article 12 of the Charter may be relevant for consumer associations to promote consumer interests. Article 11(1) states that: '(e)veryone has the right to freedom of expression. This right shall include freedom to hold opinions and to receive and impart information and ideas without interference by public authority and regardless of frontiers'. Article 12 of the Charter states that '(e)veryone has the right to freedom of peaceful assembly and to freedom of association at all levels'.

Moreover, according to Article 36 of the Charter '(t)he Union recognises and respects access to services of general economic interest as provided for in national laws and practices'. This Article provides a framework for those EU activities which may impact on social and territorial cohesion, by requiring that they respect national laws and practices on access to services of general economic interest. This may be particularly relevant for vulnerable consumer groups which could apply the former provision in conjunction with other specific rights. For example, Article 25 of the Charter states that the Union recognizes and respects the rights of the elderly to lead a dignified and independent life, and to participate in social and cultural activities. A similar clause exists in Article 26 concerning the integration of people with disabilities. These provisions could support the promotion of specific technical facilities in Member States, such as transportation or communication devices to enable elderly or disabled consumers to participate independently in daily life.[71]

Furthermore, Article 35 includes a right of access to preventive healthcare, and the right to benefit from medical treatment under the conditions established by national laws and practices.[72] Such a provision might improve consumer access to preventive healthcare services and to medical treatment.[73]

Finally, Article 47(1) provides a right to an effective remedy and to a fair trial. This means that anyone who has had an EU right violated is entitled to a fair and public hearing within a reasonable time by an independent and impartial tribunal. In addition, it also guarantees the possibility of being advised, defended, and represented, and, in particular, legal aid shall be made available

[71] See more on access to essential services in the telecommunication services in ch. 6 of this book.

[72] See T. Hervey, 'The Right to Health in European Union Law', in T.K. Hervey & J. Kenner (eds), *Economic and Social Rights under the EU Charter of Fundamental Rights: A Legal Perspective* (Oxford: Hart Publishing, 2003), pp. 193–222; for cross-border healthcare, see the recent Directive 2011/24/EU on the application of patients' rights in cross-border healthcare, OJ L 88/45, 4.4.2011.

[73] For an international example regarding the impact of the right of access to healthcare, see the case law in South Africa in subsection 4.3 of this chapter.

for financially disadvantaged individuals. This provision could be invoked to strengthen the right of access to justice for consumers in the Union.[74]

The Charter was included in the 2004 European Draft Constitution and, in particular, its Article 38 became Article II-98 of this draft. Although the European Draft Constitutional Treaty was eventually rejected, the Charter survived in its original form as a separate document and has become legally binding since the entering into force of the Lisbon Treaty.[75]

To conclude, the integration of consumer protection in the Charter shows the commitment of the European Union to promote a high level of consumer protection.[76] Consumer law has thus received recognition as a fundamental social value, which might be further strengthened by the Treaty of Lisbon. However, the Charter also has various limitations, which are discussed in the following subsections.[77]

3.4. *The scope and limited application of the Charter*

The application of the Charter is limited, as determined by the general provisions regarding the scope and interpretation of the Charter (Articles 51 and 52).

Article 51(1) states that the provisions of the Charter 'are addressed to the institutions and bodies of the Union with due regard for the principle of subsidiarity and to the Member States only when they are implementing Union law'. This means that the Charter is primarily applicable to EU institutions (e.g. the Commission or the Parliament) and bodies (i.e. authorities established by the Treaties or by secondary legislation), which are bound to 'respect the rights, observe the principles and promote the application thereof'.[78] As to the Member States, the Charter is only binding on them when they take actions

[74] See ch. 7 in this book; see also E. Storskrubb & J. Ziller, 'Access to Justice in European Comparative Law', in F. Francioni (ed.), *Access to Justice as a Human Right* (Oxford: OUP, 2007); pp. 177–203. A. Ward, 'Access to Justice', in S. Peers & A. Ward (eds), *The EU Charter of Fundamental Rights* (Oxford: Hart Publishing, 2004), pp. 123–40.

[75] On EU constitutionalism, see P. Craig, 'Constitutions, Constitutionalism and the European Union', (2001) 7 *Eur. L. J.*, pp. 125 *et seq*; J. Shaw, 'The Emergence of Post-national Constitutionalism in the European Union', (1999) 6 *J. Eur. Public Policy*, pp. 579 *et seq*; I. Pernice, 'Multi-level Constitutionalism and the Treaty of Amsterdam: Constitution-Making Revisited?', (1999) *CML Rev.*, pp. 703 *et seq*.

[76] Riedel, 'Verbraucherschutz, Artikel 38' (n 66), fn. 5.

[77] S. Weatherill, *EU Consumer Law and Policy* (Cheltenham: Edward Elgar Publishing, 2005), p. 31.

[78] Note from the Praesidium of the Convent, *Charte 4473/00* (Brussels, 11 October 2008); regarding an indirect horizontal effect of the Charter, see P. Craig, *The Lisbon Treaty, Law, Politics, and Treaty Reform* (Oxford: OUP, 2010), pp. 209 *et seq*.

within the scope of EU law. [79] This means in particular that Member States' legislators have to respect fundamental rights when implementing EU measures in national law. The national courts also have to respect these rights when interpreting EU secondary law.[80]

Article 51(2) then stipulates that the 'Charter does not extend the field of application of Union law beyond the powers of the Union or establish any new power or task for the Union, or modify powers and tasks as defined in the Treaties'. Thus, the Charter can be regarded as a means 'to consolidate and render visible' the existing fundamental rights in the EU, without however establishing new competences.[81]

According to a number of fundamental rights experts, Article 51(2) of the Charter is too restrictive.[82] Fundamental rights are general principles of EU law, which have been recognized by the ECJ. In their opinion, the fact that the Charter does not transfer new competences to the EU conflicts with the requirement of effective protection of these rights. Still, although the Charter cannot, on its own, change the distribution of competences concerning fundamental rights, it may influence the exercise of these powers in an indirect way.[83]

Finally, Article 52 provides information on the scope and interpretation of rights and principles of the Charter. In particular, paragraph 1 states that any 'limitation on the exercise of the rights and freedoms recognised by this Charter must be provided for by law'. Furthermore, according to the same paragraph, 'Subject to the principle of proportionality, limitations may be

[79] Poland and the UK have opted out of the Charter; see the opt-out Protocol on the application of the Charter of Fundamental Rights of the EU to Poland and to the UK, OJ C 115/313–14, 9.5.2008.

[80] See Case C-275/06, *Productores de Música de España (Promusicae) v Telefónica de España SAU* (2008) ECR I-00271. See more in C. Busch, 'Fundamental Rights and Private Law in the EU Member States', in C. Busch and H. Schulte-Nölke, *Fundamental Rights and Private Law* (Munich: Sellier, 2011), pp. 4–5.

[81] P. Craig and G. de Búrca, *EU Law: Text, Cases and Materials*, 4th edn (Oxford: OUP, 2008), pp. 413–14. Regarding the question of competence, see also the EU Network of Independent Experts on Fundamental Rights, *Report on the Situation of Fundamental Rights in the European Union in 2004*, January 2005, pp. 15 *et seq*.

[82] EU Network of Independent Experts on Fundamental Rights, 20 June 2006: <http://ec.europa.eu/justice_home/doc_centre/rights/charter/doc_rights_charter_en.htm#network_commentary>, pp. 389–92.

[83] O. de Schutter, 'Les droits et principes sociaux dans la Charte des droits fondamentaux de l'Union européenne', in J.-Y. Carlier & O. de Schutter (eds), *La Charte des droits fondamentaux de l'Union européenne* (Brussels: Bruylant, 2002), pp. 117–48.

made only if they are necessary and genuinely meet objectives of general interest recognised by the Union or the need to protect the rights and freedoms of others'. Paragraph 3 then stipulates that if the Charter covers rights which correspond to rights guaranteed by the ECHR, 'the meaning and scope of those rights shall be the same as those laid down by the said Convention'. This should not, however, prevent Union law from providing more extensive protection. The aim of this provision is to ensure consistency between the ECHR and Charter rights, without the EU losing the possibility of setting broader standards.

Articles 51 and 52 also deal with the difference between rights and principles, which is of particular importance for consumer protection, and which is explained in the next subsection.

3.5. *The difference between rights and principles*

Article 51(1) of the Charter imposes a distinction between subjective rights and mere principles, by stating that rights should be 'respected' whereas principles should be 'observed'. The difference between these two categories is that principles only have limited justiciability, whereas subjective rights can be claimed directly in the courts.[84]

Article 52(5) of the Charter further clarifies this distinction: 'principles may be implemented by legislative and executive acts' taken by the Union, and by acts of Member States when they are implementing Union law. 'They shall be judicially cognisable only in the interpretation of such acts and in the ruling on their legality'. This implies that for the courts they are important only when these acts are analyzed or their validity is reviewed; however, they do not provide the basis for direct claims for positive measures.[85]

Article 38 of the Charter, on consumer protection, refers to the policy level, rather than to rights.[86] This broad formulation reflects the drafter's

[84] On the differences between principles and rights, see de Schutter, 'Les droits et principes sociaux dans la Charte des droits fondamentaux de l'Union européenne' (n 83) and R. Alexy, 'Rights, Legal Reasoning, Legal Dicourse', (1992) 5(2) *Ratio Juris*, p. 145.

[85] See OJ 2007, C 303/17 on the Charter explanations provided under the Praesidium of the Convention which drafted the EU Charter (referring to e.g. the CFI case T-13/99, *Pfizer v Council*, 11 September 2002).

[86] D. McGoldrick, 'The Charter and UN Human Rights Treaties', in S. Peers & A. Ward (eds), *The European Union Charter of Fundamental Rights* (Oxford/Portland: Hart Publishing, 2004), p. 97.

aim for consumer protection to be intended as a legal principle, and not as a subjective right.[87]

The 'principle' status of consumer protection has stirred criticism with regard to the value of such provisions, as the amended Charter postulates a sort of inferiority of certain social provisions compared to civil and political rights.[88] For instance, some scholars claim that Article 38 is not sufficiently detailed to guarantee consumer protection, because it only repeats the existing Treaty provisions without providing specific rights.[89] Nevertheless, several scholars argue that legal principles could evolve and become a subjective right through the development of the case law.[90] As they point out, experience has shown that it is common for the full implications of fundamental rights to develop in a progressive way: fundamental provisions are often abstract, but they can become more specific in time, and may develop into rights by favourable court ruling.

Consequently, although there is no doubt that consumer protection has a 'principle' status in the Charter, this provision could evolve in the future. In particular, it may become more concrete if it is applied in combination with other rights of the Charter, Treaties, or constitutional provisions.[91] Article 38 of the Charter could, for instance, be applied in a cumulative manner with Article 3 of the Charter on physical integrity, with Article 12 on freedom of assembly, or with Article 8 on the right to data protection. In fact, in some national cases a cumulative application of basic provisions has resulted in successful claims for individuals.

Thus, it can be argued that the key distinction between the Charter's principles and subjective rights lies more in the manner of their justiciability, than in the possibility itself of invoking the provision before the courts.[92] The real implications of fundamental consumer protection will remain in the hands of both the European Court of Justice and the courts of the Member States.[93]

[87] See also in general T. Goldsmith, 'A Charter of Rights, Freedoms and Principles', (2001) 38 *CML Rev.*, pp. 1201 *et seq.*

[88] Weatherill (n.77) p. 31. G. de Búrca, 'Beyond the Charter: How Enlargement has enlarged the Human Rights Policy for the EU', (2004) 27 *Fordham Int'l L. J.*, pp. 679–714.

[89] C. Callies, 'Die Europäische Grundrechts-Charta', in D. Ehlers (ed.), *Europäische Grundrechte und Grundfreiheiten* (Berlin-New York: De Gruyter, 2003), p. 23.

[90] CFR-CDF, *Rapport sur la situation des droits fondamentaux dans l'Union européenne et ses Etats membres en 2003*, p. 121; de Schutter (n 83).

[91] Riedel (n 66), p. 430.

[92] de Schutter (n 83).

[93] Riedel, (n 66) fnn. 9–10.

3.6. *The implications of the Charter and the Lisbon Treaty*

The integration of consumer protection in the binding EU Charter is a significant novelty, because of its high-level legal status and supra-national scope. In fact, as described previously, neither the ECHR nor the international human rights provisions directly address this issue or expressly mention consumer protection. Therefore, the Charter can be regarded as providing a newly added value and higher profile for consumer protection.[94]

We can expect that the formal recognition of the Charter by the Lisbon Treaty will generally improve human rights protection, since the EU institutions and the Member States are now legally bound by it.[95] In practical terms, during the last five years and especially since the Charter became binding in 2009, a number of key developments at an institutional and policy level have helped to promote fundamental rights.[96] In 2007, the Agency for Fundamental Rights (FRA) was established in Vienna as an independent advisory body of the European Union,[97] which aims to assist EU institutions and Member States by providing expertise and support regarding fundamental rights.[98] Its main tasks are to monitor fundamental rights in the EU by gathering data on the situation of fundamental rights, analyzing core human rights issues, and raising awareness on this topic.[99]

Since 2010 the European Commission has intensified its efforts to check compliance of all its legislative proposals with EU fundamental rights,[100] adopting a strategy for the effective implementation of the Charter. The Commission also published an annual report in 2010 on the application of the Charter and its progress on this.[101]

[94] See also F. Benoît-Rohmer, 'Article 38, Protection des Consommateur', in EU Network of Independent Experts on Fundamental Rights, *Commentary of the Charter of Fundamental Rights of the European Union* (2006), p. 319.

[95] Except Poland and the UK which opted out of the Charter; see the opt-out Protocol on the application of the Charter of Fundamental Rights to Poland and the UK, OJ C 115/313–14, 9.5.2008.

[96] S. Douglas-Scott, 'The European Union and Human Rights after the Treaty of Lisbon', (2011) 11(4) *Hum. Rts. L. Rev.*, pp. 645–82.

[97] Council Regulation No 168/2007 of 15 February 2007 establishing a European Union agency for fundamental rights, OJ L 53/1, 22.2.2007.

[98] See the FRA's website: <http://ec.europa.eu/justice/fundamental-rights/agency/index_en.htm>.

[99] For more see P. Alston and O. de Schutter, *Monitoring Fundamental Rights in the EU: The Contribution of the Fundamental Rights Agency* (Oxford: Hart Publishing, 2005).

[100] See the European Commission's website, DG Justice: <http://ec.europa.eu/justice/fundamental-rights/index_en.htm>.

[101] <http://ec.europa.eu/justice/fundamental-rights/index_en.htm>.

The most recent annual report (2011) on the application of the Charter shows a marked increase of references to the Charter by the ECJ and by national courts makings requests for preliminary rulings.[102] The report also deals on several occasions with the issue of consumer protection.

In the field of consumer protection, the Charter could have three major effects,[103] influencing consumer protection in respect of: (1) legislative actions; (2) contractual relationships; and (3) possible exceptions to the free movement provisions.[104]

First, the Charter could give a new direction to legislative actions both at the European and at national level. Under EU law, fundamental rights must be respected when adopting and implementing EU provisions and the national law of the Member States must be interpreted and applied in a way which is compatible with them. Thus, the provision regarding consumer protection may be used to influence the interpretation of specific legislation or to abrogate incompatible legislation.[105] EU institutions are obliged to promote the Charter without an extension of their powers, and Member States have to respect these rights. When the European Union adopts new consumer laws, a high level of protection has to be respected according to the fundamental rights principle contained in the Charter. For example, the recent Directive 2011/83/EU on consumer rights[106] expressly states in its recital 66 that it 'respects the fundamental rights and observes the principles recognised in particular by the Charter of Fundamental Rights of the European Union'. Consequently, consumer law should not only be revised for improved coherence, but also has to comply with fundamental rights standards and principles.

Secondly, contractual relationships between private parties, such as a consumer and a company, might be directly affected. A contract can be tested through a fundamental rights review of EU legislation and of national laws

[102] The number of references by the ECJ and by national courts addressing questions to the ECJ has grown by almost 50% in comparison to the previous year; see European Commission, *2011 Report on the Application of* the *EU Charter of Fundamental Rights*, COM(2012) 169, p. 24.

[103] O. Cherednychenko, 'Fundamental Rights and Contract Law', (2006) *Eur. Rev. Contract Law*, pp. 500 *et seq.*

[104] Additional results could be: (1) creating additional legislation on consumer protection; (2) promoting the enforcement of existing laws and regulations; (3) influencing governments and the judiciary to intervene.

[105] H. Collins, (2005) 'European Social Policy and Contract Law', (2005) 11 *Eur. Rev. Contract Law*, p. 115, at 117.

[106] Directive 2011/83/EU on consumer rights, OJ L 304/64, 22.11.2011.

adopted to implement directives. Such a contractual review might challenge the validity of certain contractual terms and strengthen the position of the consumer as the weaker contractual party.

Finally, the Charter may help to justify an exception to the free movement of goods and services for reasons of general interest, such as the protection of consumer health or human dignity.[107] In recent case law, the ECJ has recognized that fundamental rights may serve as a justification for the Member States' restriction of free movement rights. This may result in the prohibition of a commercial activity in a Member State despite the cross-border element. For example, in *Omega*[108] the German authorities banned the computer game 'Laserdrom' as it involved simulated killings. The Court held that the objective of the protection of human dignity could justify the restriction of the freedom to provide services.

As the Treaty of Lisbon has only been in force since December 2009, the long-term impact of the binding Charter remains to be seen.[109] The ECJ increasingly refers to the Charter besides the ECHR, using it as a primary source of human rights in its judgments.[110] A growing number of these ECJ cases also directly or indirectly affect consumer-related matters.[111] These will be discussed in detail in the following chapters.

The Charter can help to confirm and strengthen applicable rights. This is particularly true for the application of consumer provisions in combination with other rights, such as the right to dignity, healthcare, or the right to autonomy.

[107] T. Wilhelmsson, 'The Ethical Pluralism of Late Modern Europe and Codification of European Contract Law' in J Smits (ed.), *The Need for a European Contract Law: Empirical and Legal Perspectives* (Groningen: Europea Law Publishing, 2005), p. 143; de Schutter (n 83).

[108] Case C-36/02, *Omega Spielhallen- und Automatenaufstellungs-GmbH v Oberbürgermeisterin der Bundesstadt Bonn* [2004] ECR I-9609; see also Case C-112/00, *Schmidberger Internationale Transporte und Planzüge v Republik Österreich* [2002] ECR I-5659.

[109] Even before the Charter became a binding document it was being interpreted extensively. For instance, in the *BECTU* case, Advocate General Tizzano of the ECJ stated that the Charter cannot be ignored as a 'substantive point of reference for all those involved (...) in the Community context'. Opinion of Advocate General Tizzano, in Case C-173/99, *BECTU v Secretary of State for Trade and Industry*, 8 February 2001; see also Joined Cases C-402/05P & C-415/05P, *Kadi and Al Barakaat v Council* [2008] ECR I-6351.

[110] E.g. Case C-236/09, *Association Belge des Consommateurs Test-Achats et al. v Council*, 1 March 2011; Joined Cases C-297/10; and C-298/10, *Hennigs v Eisenbahn-Bundesamt, Land Berlin v Mai*, 8 September 2011; and Case C-447/09, *Prigge*, 13 September 2011.

[111] See e.g. Case C-236/09, *Association Belge des Consommateurs Test-Achats ASBL and Others v Conseil des ministres*, 1 March 2011.

A number of constitutional cases in Member States illustrate the role that basic constitutional rights and principles can have in protecting the weaker contractual party. The next sections will illustrate some of these cases.

4. The Influence of Constitutional Rights and Principles

Consumer protection is finding an increasingly important place in the constitutions of European countries.[112] This section analyzes the scope and implication of constitutional consumer protection, exploring a number of relevant cases.

4.1. *Constitutional consumer law models in selected countries*

A constitutional comparison reveals different approaches to the incorporation of consumer rights into national legal systems, as constitutions always reflect a country's traditions and economic and political experience. For Europe, a broad distinction can be made between three systems: a protective model, a moderate model, and a liberal model, although they all overlap to some extent.[113]

The protective model is characterized by the fact that extensive fundamental social rights have been included in the national constitution. These rights are ultimately treated as an instruction to the state to initiate measures that enable the citizen to exercise the rights concerned.[114] The authors of such constitutions have tried to cover every sphere of life and to provide comprehensive protection for their citizens. Member States such as Italy, Portugal, and Spain have consumer or health protection provisions in their constitutions.

Article 51 of the 1978 Spanish Constitution[115] serves as an illustration of the acknowledgement of basic consumer protection. Consumer protection comes under Chapter 3 of the Constitution, concerning principles governing economic and social policy. Article 51(1) states: 'The public authorities

[112] M. Hesselink, 'Are we Human Beings or Mere Consumers?', (2006) 12(38) *European Voice*.

[113] Butt, Kübert, & Schultz (n 33), pp. 32–3.

[114] Butt, Kübert, & Schultz (n 33), pp. 32–3.

[115] Constitución Española 1978.

shall guarantee the protection of consumers and users and shall, by means of effective measures, safeguard their safety, health, and legitimate economic interests.' Article 51(2) continues: 'The public authorities shall promote the information and education of consumers and users, foster their organisations, and hear them on those matters affecting their members.' Thus, this Article aims at improving consumer protection by requiring the public authorities to further the education, information, and health protection of consumers. Based upon the Constitution, the Law for the Defence of Consumers and Users was published on 24 July 1984.[116]

In Portugal, Article 60 of the Constitution of the Portuguese Republic provides detailed consumer provisions.[117] Article 60(1) states that: 'Consumers have the right to the good quality of the goods and services consumed, to training and information, to the protection of health, safety and their economic interests, and to reparation for damages.' Furthermore, according to Article 60(3): 'Consumers' associations and consumer cooperatives have the right, as laid down by law, to receive support from the state and to be consulted in relation to consumer-protection issues.' This Article forms part of Title III of the Constitution, which is entitled 'Economic, Social and Cultural Rights and Duties', and uses terms similar to the 1966 ICESCR.[118] These constitutional provisions were the basis of the Consumer Protection Law of Portugal in 1981.[119]

Poland has also integrated consumer protection into Article 76 of its Constitution. As a result, the state has to protect consumer interests and the Constitutional Court can test the compliance of laws with the principles of consumer protection.[120] Similarly, Article 46 of Lithuania's Constitution states that 'the state shall defend the interests of the consumer'. The reason for including this constitutional provision was to render consumer policy less vulnerable to short-term economic considerations and to unfair market

[116] See more in M. Ángel Larrosa Amante, *Derecho de Consumo, Protección Legal del Consumidor* (Madrid: El Derecho, 2011), p. 16.

[117] Constitution of the Portuguese Republic (seventh revision 2005).

[118] V. de Andrade & J. Carlos, *Os Direitos Fundamentais na Constituição Portuguesa de 1976*, 3rd edn (Coimbra: Almedina, 2004), pp. 62–6.

[119] For the impact of fundamental rights on consumers see D. Barbieri, 'The Binding of Individuals to Fundamental Consumer Rights in the Portuguese Legal System: Can/Should it be Thought of in Terms of Direct Horizontal Effect?', (2008) 16 *Eur. Rev. Private Law*, pp. 665 *et seq.*

[120] However, according to Letowska, judges are still reluctant to apply this new constitutional consumer provision; E. Letowska, 'The Constitutional Aspect of Consumer Protection in Poland', in L. Thévenoz & N. Reich (eds), *Liber amicorum Bernd Stauder, Consumer Law* (Baden-Baden-Zurich: Nomos-Schulthess, 2006), pp. 227 *et seq.*

practices. Early experience in Central European countries demonstrates the important role that basic rights are playing in the current practice of constitutional courts.[121] This is particularly true with regard to the protection of the economic interests of consumers, for which the highest courts rely upon basic rights to break down established legal formalism in national private legal orders. These rights are used to give national private legal orders a more value-orientated social outlook.

The 'moderate' model applies particularly to countries such as Germany. This model combines liberal tendencies with social principles. For example, the German Constitution (named 'Basic Law': *Grundgesetz* (GG)) does not contain an explicit list with fundamental social rights including consumer protection, but enshrined a general and abstract welfare state clause (Articles 20(1) and 28(1)).[122] In particular, Article 20 entitled 'Constitutional principles' states at paragraph 1 that: 'The Federal Republic of Germany is a democratic and social federal state.'[123] The 'social state' principle (*Sozialstaatsprinzip)* enshrined in this provision has to be respected by the public authorities in any actions that they take. In the following subsection we will see the possible effect that such a principle may have in contractual matters. A number of Central and Eastern European countries have also integrated social objectives in their constitutions. For instance Article 10 of the Estonian Constitution refers to 'social justice' as a basic principle that needs to be respected.[124] This application of principles reflects the constitutional traditions of specific Member States, which distinguish between rights and social principles.[125]

Finally, the United Kingdom and Austria have been described as a liberal model.[126] In the UK, there is no formal constitution and the liberal economic ideal favours a limited approach to regulation. Like the USA, the United Kingdom prefers a market-oriented solution with light state regulation. From the wide-ranging social safeguards in Austria and the UK, however, it

[121] W. Sadurski, '"Solange, Chapter 3": Constitutional Courts in Central Europe—Democracy—European Union', (2008) *Eur. L. J.*, pp. 1 *et seq*.

[122] See also P. Beckmann, A. Colombi Ciacchi, et al., 'Germany', in G. Brüggemeier, A. Colombi Ciacchi, and G. Comandé (eds), *Fundamental Rights and Private Law in the EU* (Cambridge: CUP, 2010), p. 261.

[123] For the English translation of the German Basic Law, see: <http://www.gesetze-iminternet.de/englisch_gg/index.html>.

[124] For the full constitutional text in English see: <http://www.president.ee/en/republic-of-estonia/the-constitution/index.html>.

[125] More on this topic in de Schutter (n 83).

[126] See Butt, Kübert, & Schultz (n 33), pp. 25 and 29.

is clear that, in these countries, social provisions do not need to be enshrined in constitutions for the public to be assured of basic social services.

4.2. *The impact of constitutional rights and principles on contracts*

The inclusion of social state principles and other basic rights in the constitution have sometimes strengthened the position of the 'weaker party' in contract law cases in a number of Member States. While basic or human rights were generally conceived to protect the individual against the state, its application in private law cases is now becoming more frequent, exerting the so-called 'horizontal effect' of fundamental rights.[127] This implies that fundamental rights or basic rights are not applied in a 'vertical' relationship between a private person and a public body, but in the 'horizontal' relationship between two private parties, such as a company and an individual.[128]

One example of the effect of constitutional rights on contract law is the seminal German suretyship (*Bürgschaft*) case of 19 October 1993, which was based, in part, upon the principle of the social state enshrined in the German Basic Law described in subsection 4.1.[129] This case before the German Federal Constitutional Court concerned the validity of a personal guarantee for DM 100,000 given by a 21-year-old unskilled factory worker, with no assets of her own, for her father's business loan. When the father defaulted the bank claimed the repayment from the guarantor (i.e. his daughter). She contested the validity of the guarantee agreement by arguing that not only had she not been informed about the consequences of signing a personal guarantee, but the financial risks had been minimized and misrepresented by the bank. She based her defence upon the German Constitution, in particular upon 'human dignity' (Article 1(1) GG), her party autonomy (Article 2(1) GG) in conjunction with the principle of the social state (Article 20(1) and 28(1) GG), and was successful in her appeal. As a consequence, she was able to withdraw from the contract with the bank, among other things, because she had not been

[127] For a German approach see G. Krings, *Schutzansprüche: Die subjektiv-rechtliche Rekonstruktion der grundrechtlichen Schutzpflichten und ihre Auswirkung auf die verfassungsrechtliche Fundierung des Verbrauchervertragsrechts* (Berlin: Duncker & Humblot, 2003), p. 307.

[128] M. Hesselink, 'The Horizontal Effect of Social Rights in European Contract Law' in *Diritto Privato Europeo* (Milan: Giuffré Editore, 2003), p. 4; M. Hunt, 'The Horizontal Effect of the Human Rights Act', (1998) *Public Law*, p. 429

[129] BVerfGE 89, 214, (NJW 1994, 36).

duly informed of the consequences of the guarantee contract. This case will be further discussed in Chapter 5 of this book.

In Italy as well, constitutional rights have been used as arguments to strengthen the position of the weaker party in contract litigation.[130] In *Pedrazzoli v Mediolanum*, the constitutional right to freedom of association led to a first pronouncement in favour of a consumer. Back in 1988 and 1994, Marcello Pedrazzoli had subscribed two insurance contracts with the life insurer Mediolanum, committing to the payment of premiums until 2008. Some time after the signing of the contracts, the majority shareholder of Mediolanum, the future Italian Prime Minister, Silvio Berlusconi, entered into politics, and his company started to support and fund his party (Forza Italia) in a direct and systematic way. Disagreeing with the political agenda of Forza Italia, Pedrazzoli argued that being bound to the insurance for another 14 years de facto limited his freedom of political association (Articles 18 and 49 of the Italian Constitution). Pedrazzoli thus claimed the rescission of the contract, and the repayment of the previously paid premiums. A first decision was in favour of Pedrazzoli,[131] according to which the consumer could withdraw from the insurance contract, without losing his paid premiums. The 'Tribunale di Milano' held that the contract clause constituted a violation of freedom of association (Article 18 of the Italian Constitution) and was contrary to good faith. However, the final ruling was eventually decided in favour of the insurance company.

Despite its final outcome, the whole history of this case exemplifies the increasing influence that specific constitutional rights may have indirectly on consumer protection.

4.3. *The protection of health and safety*

The right to health and safety is a human right,[132] which has been recognized in the Universal Declaration of Human Rights, adopted in 1948.[133] Article 25(1) of the Declaration states that everyone has the 'right to a standard of living adequate for the health and well-being of himself and of his family', including medical care and the right to security in the event of sickness, disability, or

[130] For a more in-depth analysis, see Wilhelmsson, 'The Ethical Pluralism of Late Modern Europe and Codification of European Contract Law' (n 107), pp. 143 *et seq*.

[131] Trib. Milano, *Pedrazzoli v Mediolanum Vita*, 30 March 1994, Foro it, 1994, I, 1572.

[132] See G. Robbers, *Menschenrecht auf Sicherheit—Aspekte der Geschichte, Begründung und Wirkung einer Grundrechtsfunktion* (Baden-Baden: Nomos, 1987).

[133] See the Universal Declaration at: <http://www.un.org/en/documents/udhr/hr_law.shtml>.

old age. The right to health has been confirmed by Article 12 of the ICESCR, which enshrines 'the right of everyone to the enjoyment of the highest attainable standard of physical and mental health', including the prevention of diseases and availability of medical services.[134] Furthermore, at the EU level, Article 35 of the Charter of Fundamental Rights provides the right of access to healthcare.[135]

Besides, and as a consequence of, these general pronouncements, there is a global, ongoing tendency to give shape to health and safety rights in precise legal instruments that also have an effect on consumer protection. The UN took the lead with the adoption of its 1985 Guidelines for Consumer Protection, discussed at the beginning of this chapter, which enshrine the right to safety. A second important step has been the adoption of the EC Directive 92/59/EEC[136] on general product safety (later replaced by Directive 2001/95/EC).[137] At the national level, the right to health protection has been integrated in a number of national constitutions.

Whilst the right to health and safety has certainly been strengthened and further promoted by legal initiatives over the last decades, the tension remains as to how health and safety measures should be weighed against freedom of trade and patent rights. This is particularly evident in developing countries, where a jarring contrast emerges between fundamental rights and economic principles, and where the constitutional inclusion of the right to healthcare is having a significant impact in protecting individuals, including consumers.

For example, the Constitution of the Republic of South Africa was rewritten in the 1990s (and entered into effect in February 1997), containing numerous economic and social rights inspired by the UN International Covenant on Economic, Social and Cultural Rights. The right to health is mentioned in section 27, which states: '(1) Everyone has the right to have access to (a) healthcare services, including reproductive healthcare; (b) sufficient food and water; and (c) social security.' This right has to be respected, promoted, and fulfilled by the state.

Driven by the strategic activism of non-governmental organizations, this right has, in particular, played a significant role in cases on access to essential medicine in relation to the HIV epidemic. For instance, in 2001, the Treatment Action Campaign (TAC), in an effort to promote affordable treatment for

[134] General Assembly resolution 2200A (XXI) of 16 December 1966.

[135] T. Hervey, 'The Right to Health in EU Law' (n 72), p. 196.

[136] OJ L 228, 11.8.1992, 24.

[137] OJ L 11, 15.1.2002, 4.

people with HIV, successfully supported the South African Government against a legal challenge from pharmaceutical companies.[138] These companies challenged the validity of the amended South African 1997 Medicine Act,[139] which allowed the parallel import of generic drugs, arguing that this would violate their patent rights.[140] However, they eventually withdrew the action against the South African Government owing to considerable public pressure.[141]

In the landmark *Nevirapine* case,[142] the TAC filed a suit against the South African Government, claiming that its restriction on the availability of Nevirapine (a drug capable of reducing the transmission of HIV from mothers to infants) violated the right to health. The trial court decided that limiting Nevirapine in the public sector 'is not reasonable and is an unjustifiable barrier to the progressive realisation of the right to healthcare'.[143] In July 2002, the Constitutional Court of South Africa decided that the government's policy violated the healthcare rights of women and new-born children under the South African Constitution. It thus confirmed an obligation on the government to facilitate the use of Nevirapine at public hospitals and, moreover, it required the government to implement a publicly funded programme to ensure access to health services to pregnant women and new-born children.

The right to health is inextricably linked to consumer protection, because access to safe products and to essential services at an affordable price plays an important role in both fields of law. The cases just discussed illustrate how constitutional rights may help to shift the balance of power in favour of the weaker party and away from large corporations. Moreover, they show that

[138] Notice of Motion in the High Court of South Africa (Transvaal Provincial Division), Case No. 4183/98.

[139] Medicines and Related Substances Control Amendment Act No. 90 of 1997, South African Government Gazette No. 18,505 of 12 December 1997 amending the Medicines and Related Substances Control Act No. 101 of 1965.

[140] For more information see L. Forman, '"Rights" and Wrongs: What Utility for the Right to Health in Reforming Trade Rules on Medicines?', (2008) 10(2) *Health and Human Rights: An International Journal*.

[141] D. Barnard, 'In the High Court of South Africa, Case No. 4138/98: The Global Politics of Access to Low-Cost AIDS Drugs in Poor Countries', (2002) 12 *Kennedy Inst. of Ethics J.*, pp. 159–74; G.J. Annas, 'The Right to Health and the Nevirapine Case in South Africa', (2002) 346 *New England Journal of Medicine*, pp. 750–4.

[142] *Minister of Health and Others v Treatment Action Campaign and Others*, 2002 (5) SA 721 (CC), para. 25, 2002 (10) (BCLR 1033) (CC).

[143] High Court of South Africa, Transvaal Provincial Division, *Treatment Action Campaign v Minister of Health*, (2002) 4 BCLR 356; Annas, 'The Right to Health and the Nevirapine Case in South Africa' (n 141), pp. 750–4.

constitutional rights can have a significant practical judicial impact, obliging governments to effectively implement these rights, and are thus not merely abstract statements.

4.4. *Consumer codes*

The constitutional dimension of consumer law is well established in Southern European countries and Latin America.[144] Countries such as Brazil, Spain, and Portugal include provisions regarding access to justice in their constitutions and have adopted general consumer laws or codes, based upon their respective constitutions.

Brazil adopted its Federal Constitution in 1988, incorporating consumer protection and access to justice as fundamental provisions.[145] The Constitution mentions, in section XXXII of Article 5, that the 'state will promote consumer protection in the form of law'. Article 48 of the subsequent Interim Constitutional Provisions Act stipulates that the 'Congress shall, within 120 days of enactment of the Constitution, draft a consumer protection code'. The code was adopted in 1990 and contains detailed consumer law provisions, mentioning in particular consumer policy, access to justice, the prohibition of unfair practices, and collective consumption conventions. This code amounted to a legal revolution for Brazil, because many of the new rights created had not existed previously in Brazilian case law, nor in its legal tradition. In particular, this change affected the right to access to justice,[146] with the new constitutional provisions being applied in various court cases.[147]

5. Conclusions

This chapter has explored the intersection of consumer protection and human rights. At the international level, consumer protection has not been addressed expressly in human rights provisions. However, consumer protection considerations have been taken into account in some cases by the European

[144] A. de Moraes, *Direitos Humanos Fundamentais, Teoria Geral*, 7th edn (Saõ Paulo: Editora Atlas S.A., 2006), pp. 186–9; A. Benjamin, 'Group Action and Consumer Protection in Brazil', in T. Bourgoignie (ed.), *Group Actions and Consumer Protection* (Brussels: Bruylant, 1992), pp. 140 *et seq.*

[145] According to the 1988 Constitution, the Attorney General and associations as well as other entities, can file legal action not only to protect diffuse interests or rights but also collective interests or rights of any kind (Art. 129, II, and 129, para. 1).

[146] Benjamin, 'Group Action and Consumer Protection in Brazil' (n 144), pp. 140 *et seq.*

[147] For more information, see de Moraes (2006), *Direitos Humanos Fundamentais, Teoria Geral* (n 144), pp. 186–9.

Court of Human Rights, for example in relation to the human right to freedom of expression. Furthermore, the UN Guidelines for Consumer Protection, albeit not a human rights document, promotes universal recognition of consumer protection, including a new dimension on responsible consumption.

At the EU level, consumer protection has been recognized as a policy objective in the Charter of Fundamental Rights. The Charter contains a number of social and economic provisions, including an explicit reference to consumer protection, which goes beyond the scope of traditional human rights. Although the consumer provision in the Charter is conceived as a policy objective, it might, over time, develop into more specific rights, especially if combined with other relevant fundamental rights, such as the right to privacy or the right to a due process.

The Charter can be seen as the start of a process whereby European institutions become closer to EU citizens, by making human rights more visible and central in the integration process. As mentioned in this chapter, the Commission has become more active in promoting EU fundamental rights in the EU and the ECJ increasingly refers to the Charter in its jurisprudence.

However, besides its potential, the Charter also has important limitations. In particular, the Charter provision regarding consumer protection is short and abstract. It does not provide additional competences to the EU and consumer protection remains difficult to enforce. At the same time consumer law as a human rights topic remains controversial, especially at an international level. Against the background of a predominantly market-based concept of the consumer and of a Charter of still limited practical effect, the next chapter explores new approaches to EU consumer law.

4

A Broader Perspective on Consumer Protection and Human Rights

1. Introduction

As illustrated in Chapter 2, EU consumer law seems trapped in a market-orientated perspective. Arguably the Charter of Fundamental Rights indicates a shift in relation to the ethic of the EU by integrating consumer protection in its 'Solidarity' chapter, but this initiative has some shortcomings.[1] Therefore it remains unclear whether, beyond its symbolic nature, the Charter and the Lisbon Treaty will contribute to a paradigmatic shift and in particular have an invigorating effect on consumer protection.

This chapter looks at consumer protection and human rights from a theoretical and interdisciplinary perspective. Starting from the observation that the Union needs to move beyond market integration objectives, this chapter analyzes some theories which could help integrate ethical and social considerations into a novel consumer law approach. In particular, Sen's and Habermas' theoretical approaches may help rethink the interplay of consumer law and fundamental rights, promoting 'substantive freedoms' and participatory procedures.

Applying such a perspective, the role that fundamental rights can play in defining a broader consumer law approach transcends the traditional function of protecting individuals' freedom against state interference. Such rights can influence the relationship between private parties, and may be used as a way to promote market ethics. As we will see, the legal framework developed since Lisbon may help to strengthen particular aspects of consumer law, complementing the traditional EU consumer model in some respects.

[1] For an assessment of the scope and limitations of the EU Charter of Fundamental Rights, see ch. 3.

To develop these arguments, this chapter proceeds as follows. It starts with a description of recent changes in the market and in the European consumer landscape, which pose challenges to consumer protection. Then, it analyzes a number of theoretical approaches, which may provide new perspectives on the development of EU consumer law and human rights. The final part of the chapter examines how in practice these theoretical insights may influence the EU law framework.

2. The Transformed Role of the Consumer

The position and the role of the European consumer have changed significantly in recent decades. Markets have expanded under the influence of globalization, which has led to a marked growth in goods and services. Furthermore, regulatory reforms, leading to liberalization of key consumer sectors, have enhanced competition and consumer choice. Finally, consumers themselves have also changed, for demographic, economic, and ethical reasons.

At the same time, new challenges have emerged, ranging from health risks, to threats to privacy, and difficulties in the enforcement of cross-border rights. This has led to a weakening of the consumer position in some respects, and thus stimulated a reflection on how such trends can be counterbalanced by legal initiatives. As we saw in the previous chapter, some of these initiatives have been linked to a fundamental rights discourse, resulting in a process of convergence between the previously distant areas of consumer and fundamental rights.[2]

However, it is now apparent that the connection between the consumer and fundamental rights not only stems from a need or desire of policy-makers to restore a balance of power; it emerges directly from new trends in the markets and in society. In an effort to reclaim their powers in global markets, specific groups of consumers are gradually becoming a more active part of the market. They do so by promoting or boycotting certain products on moral grounds, by establishing associations, and by taking a political stance, as

[2] See ch. 3 of this book. See also S. Deutch, 'Are Consumer Rights Human Rights?' (1994) 32(3) *Osgoode Hall L. J.*, pp. 540–53; S. Gan, 'Essay: Consumer Rights: A Part of Human Rights', (2008) 1(1) *J. Int'l Bus. Ethics*, pp. 18 *et seq.*

for example in the movements for ethical purchasing and fair trade.[3] For these consumers, purchasing is not only regarded as a means to consumption, but also as a way of promoting moral values, ethical principles, or human rights.

The following sections illustrate these trends in a broad context, looking at some socio-legal, economic, and human rights theories which may help in considering consumer protection from different perspectives. The chapter will then close with an exploration of how a new EU consumer law approach may apply these theories to address some of the current challenges.

2.1. *Changes in markets and regulation*

The last few decades in Europe have been characterized by dramatic changes in the markets, driven by technological development and regulatory reforms. This trend has had a positive impact on consumer welfare, as it has spurred innovation, leading to lower prices and to a greater range of choice.[4] The downside has been the exacerbation of old-standing problems of free-market economies: asymmetric information, externalities, and increased risks.[5] On the other hand, the powers of Member States freely to determine matters of consumer protection have shrunk, without being replaced by an equivalent framework at EU level.[6]

Global markets have entailed a socio-political and economic change. They have become more anonymous and they are now characterized by long and complex production chains. All this has had a number of effects. First, externalities in the international context are difficult to measure and to compensate for, as they stretch across national boundaries and affect larger numbers of individuals. Secondly, products have become more complex and varied, which makes effective choices more difficult,[7] and in the case of related damage, this may render the proof of causal links between damage and product defects

[3] M. Micheletti and A. Follesdal, 'Shopping for Human Rights'—Special Issue, (2007) 30(3) *J. Consumer Policy*, pp. 167–75; N. Stehr, C. Henning, & B. Weiler (eds), *The Moralization of the Market* (New Jersey: Transaction Publishers, 2006), pp. 8 *et seq*.

[4] J. Stiglitz, *Globalization and its Discontents* (London: Penguin Books, 2002), p. 9.

[5] U. Beck, *Risk Society: Towards a New Modernity* (translated from the German *Risikogesellschaft*, published in 1986) (New Delhi: Sage, 2002), pp. 87–93.

[6] See ch. 2 of this book.

[7] For a detailed description see the OECD chapter: 'The Changing Consumer and Market Landscape', in *OECD Consumer Policy Toolkit* (Paris: OECD, 2010), pp. 16–17.

more challenging.[8] Furthermore, consumer rights enforcement is particularly challenging at the cross-border level.[9] Finally, markets have become increasingly anonymous, severing the trust relationship that used to exist in local markets. This has caused a sense of alienation and reluctance to participate in cross-border markets, reinforced by the fact that negative events such as food scandals and financial frauds have become, if not more frequent, better known to the general public owing to improved means of communication.

At the same time, multinationals have increased their influence on the lives of individuals because of a reduction in the scope of welfare states.[10] Privatization renders consumers increasingly dependent on businesses for the purchase of services of general interest, such as telecommunications or energy. As a result, in some cases companies have taken over functions that were previously a state prerogative, substituting the (at least theoretical) 'public good' objective with a private profit objective.

Moreover, the formation of large business groups has meant greater economic and lobbying power for firms to defend their interests at EU policy level.[11] Consumer organizations, in contrast, often lack the necessary financial means and are too fragmented to have the same impact on international regulators, contributing to a tilting of the balance of power in favour of large companies.[12]

At the same time, national powers are slowly diminishing in the area of consumer protection. Member States are increasingly unable to protect their citizens independently, as they are influenced by supra-national institutions such as the EU. As some scholars have pointed out, this is accompanied by a growing legitimacy deficit in the European decision-making process, which has inadvertently brought about a progressive alienation of citizens from

[8] Consumers often lack resources and access to information in order to investigate highly technical products so as to prove the defect or the causal link to the product. See also the EU Commission, *Third Report Concerning Liability for Defective Products*, COM(2006) 496 final, 14.9.2006, p. 9.

[9] See the case law description on collective redress in ch. 7.

[10] C. Harding, U. Kohl, & N. Salmon, *Human Rights in the Market Place: The Exploitation of Rights Protection by Economic Actors* (Aldershot: Ashgate Publishing, 2008).

[11] Harding, Kohl, & Salmon, *Human Rights in the Market Place* (n 10).

[12] On the difficulties of establishing political power for consumers, see F. Trentman & M. Bevir (eds), *Governance, Citizens, and Consumers: Agency and Resistance in Contemporary Politics* (Basingstoke: Palgrave Macmillan, 2007); see the explanation on interest groups and consumer protection in I. Ramsay, *Consumer Law and Policy: Text and Materials on Regulating Consumer Markets* (Oxford: Hart Publishing, 2007), p. 31.

public institutions and political participation.[13] Just as the powers of single states are weakening, so is the ability of citizens to influence important decisions that affect their lives.

In such a context, consumer law finds a new *raison d'être* and a novel role: that of protecting from risks, but also of ensuring 'substantive freedoms' for consumers, enabling them to participate actively in policy-making and in the market. Human rights could support such a process as, according to some, they may empower consumers and help create a 'level playing field' in the changing global marketplace.[14] Furthermore, a human rights perspective in law and policy may promote ethical market behaviour,[15] which will be discussed in the next section.

2.2. *Changes in consumers, vulnerable groups, and ethical trends*

European consumers also have evolved in the last decades and their behaviour and impact on markets has changed. On the one hand secular trends, dictated by demographics and long-term growth, are slowly but inexorably changing the composition and purchasing power of this side of the market. On the other hand, a clearer distinction between groups of consumers can be drawn, which vary considerably in their ability or preferences depending, amongst other things, on age, cultural background, and ethical awareness.

A 2010 OECD consumer study describes some of these changes, highlighting in particular that the percentage of the elderly population has increased and will continue to rise.[16] According to the study, this age group might have more difficulties in adjusting to fast-changing complex markets and technological development and in dealing with the digital environment. At the same time, the percentage of very young consumers (e.g. teenagers) has declined, but as a result of a general increase of income in industrial countries, this age band has become more active in the marketplace. They may, however, lack sufficient knowledge and experience to make well-reasoned decisions. Putting these two facts together one concludes that an increasing share

[13] J. Habermas, 'Making Sense of the EU: Toward a Cosmopolitan Europe', (2003) 14 *J. Democracy*, p. 89; J.H.H. Weiler, 'The Transformation of Europe', (1991) 100 *Yale L. J.*, p. 2403, at 2410.

[14] Deutch, 'Are Consumer Rights Human Rights?' (n 2), pp. 540–53; Harding, Kohl, & Salmon (n 10).

[15] Gan, 'Consumer Rights' (n 2), pp. 18 *et seq*.

[16] OECD Document, 'The Changing Consumer and Market Landscape' (n 7), pp. 24–7.

of consumers may be relatively more vulnerable in their decision-making, and face barriers to effective participation in the market.[17]

Besides such long-term trends, shorter-term cyclical changes dictated by the economic conjuncture constantly influence the expectations and behaviour of consumers. For example, as a result of the economic and financial crises which began in 2008, consumer confidence has dropped and so has the income or purchasing power of part of the population, weakening the position of these consumers, and putting some at risk of social exclusion.[18] Other groups may equally be more disadvantaged in the current environment, such as disabled consumers, who may have more difficulties in accessing information or finding adequate goods or services.[19] The development of increasingly distinct consumer groups with different abilities and knowledge will require targeted policy answers to protect and ensure inclusion of vulnerable groups.

The demographic, economic, and social changes have induced an evolution in behaviour too. An increase in information and in financial means in the global marketplace has led to more ethical awareness, which is reflected in purchasing behaviour. By their choices, a growing number of consumers express social preferences, more or less consciously promoting ethical, ecological, and human rights objectives.[20] These ethical purchasing trends have sometimes been successful in raising public awareness and in pushing companies to adopt ethical standards; by so doing, they have induced a 'moralization of the markets'[21] and contributed to the promotion of human rights.[22]

However, these movements are still relatively small and do not seem to possess sufficient organizational continuity to attain long-term effects.[23] Given that they express legitimate and pertinent concerns—in particular, considering the

[17] OECD Document, 'The Changing Consumer and Market Landscape' (n 7), pp. 24–7.

[18] See the Communication from the European Commission, A European Consumer Agenda—Boosting confidence and growth, COM(2012) 225 final, 22.5.2012.

[19] See the Communication from the European Commission, A European Consumer Agenda—Boosting confidence and growth (n 18).

[20] This consumer trend has been particularly discussed by social science and humanities scholars; see Micheletti and Follesdal, 'Shopping for Human Rights' (n 3), pp. 167–75; Stehr, Henning, & Weiler (eds), *The Moralization of the Market* (n 3), pp. 8–12; Gan (n 2), pp. 18 *et seq*.

[21] Stehr, Henning, & Weiler (n 3), pp. 8–12.

[22] See A. Fagan, 'Buying Rights: Consuming Ethically and Human Rights', in J. Dine and A. Fagan (eds), *Human Rights and Capitalism: A Multidisciplinary Perspective on Globalisation* (Cheltenham: Edward Elgar Publishing, 2006), p. 115; for a political science perspective on ethical consumption behaviours as a source of human rights mobilization, see L. Scruggs, S. Hertel, S.J. Best, & C. Jeffords, 'Information, Choice and Political Consumption: Human Rights in the Checkout Lane', (2011) 33 *Hum. Rts. Quarterly*, 1092–121.

[23] Stehr, Henning, & Weiler (n 3), pp. 8 *et seq*.

growing environmental challenges—the promotion of sustainable consumption can be regarded as an important policy objective. The European legal system is now faced with the challenge of adapting to, or at least addressing, these changes.

2.3. *Adapting consumer law to economic and social changes*

As we have just seen, the consumer landscape has undergone important changes in the last decades. How has the legal system responded?

The previous chapters have shown that the current consumer law model in the EU is still ill-equipped to respond fully to these developments. Important steps have been the adoption of the Charter, now with binding force. However, as already discussed in Chapter 3, the Charter is abstract and includes consumer protection as a policy goal, rather than as a set of enforceable rights. At the same time, the EU's full-harmonization approach is based on market efficiency rationales, which generally limit broader consumer protection initiatives unless they have a clear market integration focus.

The recent policy approach reflected in the European Commission 2012 Consumer Agenda identifies a number of new societal and consumer challenges such as unsustainable consumption, social exclusion, and vulnerable consumers, as described in previous sections. This indicates that the EU recognizes these challenges and part of this Agenda will be briefly discussed later. However, at the same time, the Agenda mainly refers to market rationales, describing the consumer as the 'engine of growth', and focusing on cross-border market participation, with the objective of increasing choice.[24] Consumer welfare is mentioned only marginally, and is referred to as something which needs to be achieved again, by ensuring broader choice (e.g. by promoting online shopping).

An efficient market, leading among other things to a more ample choice, is an important precondition to ensure consumer welfare. However the promotion of efficiency is only one dimension of consumer protection, which also touches upon social objectives and considerations of fairness and justice. The EU approach is still struggling to incorporate these broader dimensions.[25] This is all the more surprising considering, for example, the benchmark offered by the UN's international consumer model, and the protective approaches developed by some Member States.

[24] Communication from the European Commission, A European Consumer Agenda—Boosting confidence and growth (n 18).

[25] For the legal debate on the EU consumer concept see ch. 2.

The UN has issued a set of Consumer Guidelines providing directions on how to build consumer protection systems which also promote social objectives, such as sustainable consumption and access to essential services. Furthermore, the complementary UNCTAD Manual on Consumer Protection includes an extensive list of consumer protection rationales. Besides economic efficiency, a key objective is the protection of the individual consumer's right to dignity, regarded as part of a 'new range of social rights that individuals are entitled to claim in a modern society'. Other purposes of consumer law mentioned by the UNCTAD Manual are distributive justice, participatory decision-making, and communal values.[26] Although the UN Guidelines are not binding, they have been adopted as a common denominator at the international level, and have had a considerable impact on consumer protection systems in several countries across the globe.[27]

Furthermore, as we have seen previously, some European Member States have adopted higher levels of consumer protection than the one provided by EU law. These countries may have to lower their standards if full-harmonization EU measures are adopted, as described in Chapter 2.

The EU remains thus anchored to a rather restrictive model of consumer law, relying on the notion of the reasonably well-informed and observant 'average market participant'.[28] As discussed previously, this market consumer approach and full-harmonization strategy has come under increasing criticism, as a number of scholars have argued in favour of a model based on justice and other values.[29] Undermined by the new 'behavioural economics' (showing that consumers may struggle to take rational decisions and can be easily manipulated by marketing strategies), the 'informed and rational' consumer hypothesis has been challenged by the 'irrational and uneducated' consumer who, as such, is also a 'vulnerable' consumer.[30]

[26] United Nations, *UNCTAD Manual on Consumer Protection* (New York and Geneva, 2004), pp. 7–9.

[27] Secretary-General of the United Nations, Consumer Protection Report, (1993) 16(1) *J. Consumer Policy*, 1 pp. 97–121.

[28] See chs 2 and 3 of this book.

[29] M. Hesselink, 'European Contract Law: A Matter of Consumer Protection, Citizenship or Justice', (2007) 15 *Eur. Rev. Private Law*, pp. 323–48. For a good overview of the general debate and challenges in EU consumer law, see: N. Reich, 'Crises or Future of European Consumer Law', (2009) *Ybk Eur. Consumer Law*, pp. 3 *et seq.*

[30] H.-W. Micklitz, L. Reisch, & K. Hagen, 'An Introduction to the Special Issue on Behavioural Economics, Consumer Policy and Consumer Law', (2011) 34 *J. Consumer Policy*, pp. 271–6; M. Lissowska, 'Overview of Behavioural Economics Elements in the OECD Consumer Policy Toolkit', (2011) 34 *J. Consumer Policy*, pp. 393–8.

On the other hand, according to some, interference with free markets may lead to paternalistic regulation, which ultimately has a negative impact on consumers.[31] Overprotection might lead to less diligent behaviour on the part of consumers, and impose extra costs which will eventually be passed on to them.[32]

Given that both views contain some truth, the question is how to strike a compromise between apparently competing objectives. In particular, what is the role and competence of the EU in ensuring consumer autonomy and protecting vulnerable groups, without imposing a solution that restricts freedoms and interferes unnecessarily with the market and with Member States' policies? How can consumers be enabled to take decisions that benefit their welfare and are sustainable in the long term?

The next section will discuss different theories, some of which might help to answer these questions, by providing the foundations for a legal framework that reconciles efficiency, freedom, protection, and welfare.

3. Freedom, Capabilities, Human Rights, and Procedures

The previous section has placed consumer law in a broad socio-economic context, uncovering challenges which cannot be fully solved by a legal model, which is focused on economic efficiency alone. Consequently, this section will explore theoretical approaches that might provide different perspectives on consumer protection, market freedoms, and human rights. It will assess, among other things, contributions to legal theory, welfare economics, and human rights. The final section of this chapter will then provide new insights on how a theoretical underpinning may inspire a novel approach to consumer law, based on a broader set of rationales such as freedom, inclusion, participation, and sustainability.

3.1. *Economic efficiency, freedom, and justice*

Friedrich Hayek, who was awarded the Nobel Prize for economics in 1974, contributed to legal theory and has been influential in shaping the policy of

[31] T. Hartlief, 'Freedom and Protection in Contemporary Contract Law', (2004) 27(3) *J. Consumer Policy* (2004), pp. 253–67.

[32] See; e.g. H. Kötz & A. Flessner, *European Contract Law, Vol. 1: Formation, Validity, and Content of Contracts; Contract and Third Parties* (Oxford: Clarendon Press, 1998), p. 129.

several countries during the last century.[33] His approach has also recently been debated as an inspiration for the development of European private law.

One of the fundamental concepts in Hayek's system is the distinction between two types of coexisting 'orders' which mirror the distinction between 'society' and 'government': the self-generating or 'spontaneous order' and the 'made order' or 'deliberate organization'.[34] The 'spontaneous order' is the way the society and economy organize themselves, reaching the most efficient allocation of resources and at the same time realizing the liberty of the individuals, who can pursue their own interests. According to Hayek the 'universal rules of just conduct' form the foundation of this spontaneous order of the free society.[35] In such an order, an important role of law is to defend rules of 'just conduct', instead of formulating 'specific commands that deprive its members of the possibility of using their knowledge for their purposes'.[36] Conversely, in the 'deliberate organization', individuals have to follow the commands of an authority (the government), which, may conflict with the interests of the individuals.[37]

The firm belief in a spontaneous order is the basis of Hayek's liberalism and his aversion towards the concept of 'social justice'. This latter is, in his own words, an 'empty phrase without determinable content'[38] and even 'the Trojan Horse through which totalitarianism has entered' [society][39]—with clear reference to fascism and national socialism on one side, and to communism on the other, which both undermine individual liberties. Similarly, Hayek criticizes the economic and social rights recognized in the 1948 Universal Declaration of Human Rights, arguing in particular that these rights conflict with the traditional civil rights and lamenting their soft or vague nature which, according to him, may undermine the respect and legitimacy of the whole rights system.[40]

Hayek's theory has sparked debate about its potential to inspire EU private law. Several scholars have argued that such an approach could encourage

[33] Regarding the influence of Hayek's theory in the UK on the approach of the Conservative Government 1979–97, see G. Howells & S. Weatherill, *Consumer Protection Law* (Aldershot: Ashgate, 2005), pp. 80 *et seq*.

[34] F.A. von Hayek, *Law, Legislation and Liberty, Vol 1: Rules and Order* (London: Routledge and Kegan Paul, 1973), pp. 36 *et seq*.

[35] Hayek, *Law, Legislation and Liberty, Vol 1: Rules and Order* (n 34), pp. 124–5.

[36] Hayek (n 34), pp. 50–1.

[37] Hayek also referred to the distinction between rules of just conduct and rules of organization as being equivalent to the difference between private law (including criminal law) and public law; Hayek (n 34), p. 132.

[38] F.A. von Hayek, *Law, Legislation and Liberty, Vol. 2: The Mirage of Social Justice* (London: Routledge and Kegan Paul, 1976), p. 133.

[39] Hayek, *Law, Legislation and Liberty* (n 38), p. 136.

[40] Hayek, (n 38), pp. 103–4.

European private law to develop in a liberal direction as a 'spontaneous legal order' with limited interference from the EU.[41] Others instead have contested the use of Hayek's approach as a general theoretical framework for European private law, because it is too 'absolute and deterministic' and does not leave room for intermediate approaches reflecting the EU 'mixed economy'.[42]

This raises the question of how Hayek's theory would influence the particular field of European consumer law. A careful reading of Hayek's own writings reveals that he did attribute a specific role to the government and, interestingly, in the area of consumer protection. For example, in his book on *Law, Legislation and Liberty*, he recognizes a role for governments to protect consumers, albeit only briefly.[43] In particular, he recognizes the need to establish a *certification* system, managed by the state or by other organizations, on the quality of products and services, to facilitate the choice of consumers. He also highlights the importance of health and safety regulation (in particular, minimum hygiene standards for food products) and the need to restrict dangerous products. However, in line with his liberal views, Hayek argues that such protection is necessary to facilitate consumer choice and promote market functioning, and not to promote 'social justice' which he sees as rhetorical at best.

Hayek's discussion of consumer protection is only tangentially related to his main discourse, as these issues are touched upon only in order to provide examples of the role of the government. Two points are, however, particularly interesting for our analysis of consumer law. First, Hayek argues that the government functions should as far as possible be undertaken at the *regional* or *local* level. Central government should limit itself to enforcing law and order through general rules, while the 'positive services' should be provided by smaller governmental organizations.[44] In the context of EU consumer law, this can be seen as an argument in favour of minimum harmonization and in defence of national regulation—which is by definition more 'regional' than EU regulation. Secondly, Hayek is acutely wary of the limits of human

[41] J.M. Smits, 'European Private Law: A Plea for a Spontaneous Legal Order' in D.M. Curtin, J.M. Smits, A. Klip, and J. McCahery (eds), *European Integration and Law* (Antwerp and Oxford: Intersentia, 2006), pp. 55–107.

[42] See also M. Hesselink, 'A Spontaneous Order for Europe?' in H.-W. Micklitz & F. Caffaggi (eds), *European Private Law after the Common Frame of Reference* (Cheltenham: Edward Elgar, 2010), pp. 123–45.

[43] See, F.A. von Hayek, *Law, Legislation and Liberty, Vol. 3: The Political Order of a Free People* (Chicago/London: Chicago Press and Routledge & Kegan Paul, 1979), pp. 62–3.

[44] See Hayek, *Law, Legislation and Liberty, Vol. 3: The Political Order of a Free People* (n 43), pp. 62–3.

knowledge, which, he argues, make it difficult to impose centrally planned regulatory measures.[45] In the spontaneous order, law has instead developed over time, adjusting to the requirements of particular society contexts. Translated into the EU current situation, this would suggest that EU consumer law should be closely built on established national legal traditions and on the international law model—which is the result of an interaction between peers (nations) and hence, Hayek would argue, is the fruit of a 'spontaneous' order.[46]

However, Hayek's profoundly liberal approach has now been surpassed and cannot usefully be applied to fundamental rights and consumer challenges in the EU that have emerged and have been recognized in more recent times. Among these, the distortions caused by unequal bargaining power, incomplete information and externalities, and market failures which cause the 'spontaneous order' to deviate from efficiency. Furthermore, even the arguments, for example, about quality certification requirements, have very much the flavour of early views on consumer protection, lacking an analysis of the issues of potential conflicts of interest, balanced representation, and impartiality. In particular, Hayek's minimalistic view of the state would be unable to address the burning issues of market fairness, sustainability, social exclusion, and participation of vulnerable consumers.

This casts doubts on Hayek's approach as a model to interpret the present, and to suggest a way forward for a European consumer law model. If the EU law-making process were to follow it too closely it would fail to reflect current consumer challenges, and lose legitimacy.

Another approach is proposed by John Rawls, who in his seminal work *A Theory of Justice* (1971),[47] set out to reconcile *freedom* with the seemingly competing principle of *equality*. To this aim, the American philosopher devised a theory of *fairness* based on two 'principles of justice'. The first principle states that, in a fair system, 'each person is to have an equal right to the most extensive basic liberty compatible with a similar liberty for others'.[48] The second principle instead defines the conditions under which 'social and economic inequality' can be regarded as just: first, inequality should only be introduced to benefit the least advantaged; secondly, inequality can only be 'attached to offices and positions open to all under conditions of fair equality of opportunity'.[49]

[45] See also the critical appraisal by A.I. Ogus, 'Law and Spontaneous Order: Hayek's Contribution to Legal Theory', (1989) 16(4) *J. Law and Society*, pp. 393–409.

[46] See also Hesselink, 'A Spontaneous Order for Europe?' (n 42), pp. 123–45.

[47] J. Rawls, *A Theory of Justice* (Cambridge, MA: Harvard University Press, 1971).

[48] Rawls, *A Theory of Justice* (n 47), p. 60.

[49] Rawls (n 47), p. 302.

As the next subsection will discuss, Rawls' second principle has been taken further by Sen who developed the idea of opportunity into 'capability'—stressing that what matters is not the resources one is given, but the use that can be made of them.

The next subsection explores Sen's approach to human rights, welfare, and justice which, while focusing on individual freedom, recognizes that the state plays a role in ensuring effective freedom in the market.

3.2. *Substantive freedoms, capability, and ethical demands*

Amartya Sen, recipient of the Nobel Prize in Economics in 1998, is most famous for his contributions to welfare economics and for his freedom-based 'capability' approach. Developed in the context of social choice theory, the idea of capability has found application in a number of other fields, such as human development and, more recently, in the context of human rights and justice theory.[50] This section will argue that Sen's capability approach can contribute to a new perspective on consumer law, as it bridges the ideas of substantive freedom, welfare, ethics, and human rights, which, in turn, are increasingly important aspects of consumer life. The capability perspective may also be particularly relevant for the European case, because it has been suggested as an approach that can combine social justice with economic development.[51] Before discussing the applicability of the capability approach to EU consumer law and human rights, we briefly review some key concepts in Sen's theoretical approach.

'Capability'—the cornerstone of Sen's theory—is defined as 'a substantive freedom to achieve alternative functioning combinations'.[52] In turn, 'functioning' (or more simply, a function) refers to the objectives or 'things' that a person may value, or may enjoy doing or being,[53] which range from basic needs or activities such as nutrition and health, to more sophisticated ones, such as taking part in the political life of the community.[54] The capability concept

[50] A. Sen, *Commodities and Capabilities* (Oxford: OUP, New Delhi, 1985); M. Nussbaum and other scholars have further developed the capability approach: M. Nussbaum, 'Capabilities and Human Rights', (1997) 66 *Fordham L. Rev.*, p. 273.

[51] In EU law the capability approach was initially mainly tested in the field of EU employment law and fundamental rights: R. Salais & R. Villeneuve, 'Introduction: Europe and the Politics of Capabilities', in R. Salais & R. Villeneuve (eds), *Europe and the Politics of Capabilities* (Cambridge: CUP, 2004), pp. 3–5; S. Deakin & J. Browne, 'Social Rights and Market Order: Adapting the Capability Approach', in T. Hervey & J. Kenner, *Economic and Social Rights under the EU Charter of Fundamental Rights: A Legal Perspective* (Oxford: Hart Publishing, 2003), pp. 33 *et seq*.

[52] A. Sen, *Development as Freedom* (Oxford: OUP, 1999), p. 75.

[53] Sen, *Commodities and Capabilities* (n 50), p. 18.

[54] A. Sen, *The Idea of Justice* (Penguin Books, 2010), pp. 231–3; Sen, *Development as Freedom* (n 52), p. 75.

focuses in particular on the 'real opportunity' of individuals to achieve valuable outcomes, as opposed to concentrating merely on the means to achieve these outcomes.[55] In particular, this approach puts an emphasis on effective freedom and on what individuals can achieve with their resources, rather than focusing on the resources themselves and their allocation (e.g. on commodities or income). This sets Sen apart from previous economists.[56]

Sen stresses that similar material resources need not lead to equal capabilities, because people have different abilities and opportunities to convert the means at their disposal into 'functions', depending on personality traits, education, and, importantly, the environment. In particular, the legal system in which individuals live can determine the capacity to exercise certain functions, therefore having an important impact on capabilities.[57] For example, inequality may be reduced by an opportune legal design.[58] An economic, social, or legal system, Sen argues, should expand the capabilities of individuals.

Furthermore, Sen sees a close link between freedom, ethical values, and responsibility—sometimes also called 'agency'. He argues that a focus on substantive freedom, providing the opportunity to choose between options, empowers individuals, but this comes with an increase in responsibility or obligations. According to Sen: 'Since a capability is the power to do something, the accountability that emanates from that ability—that power–is a part of the capability perspective, and this can make room for demands of duty.'[59]

Sen's concepts and ideas have influenced policy-makers at the international level, and in particular in developing countries, where issues of social justice are very pressing. However, they have also received attention in developed countries. They have, for example, surfaced in European social policy; notably, in the Supiot Report[60] and have been discussed as an inspiration to develop European contract law.[61]

[55] Sen, *The Idea of Justice* (n 54), pp. 231–3 and p. 287.

[56] See also Arango, who argues that Sen's approach to social justice appears more realistic and contextualized than the approach taken by liberal scholars such as von Hayek: R. Arango, 'Basic Social Rights, Constitutional Justice, and Democracy', (2003) 16 *Ratio Juris*, p. 151.

[57] See, Deakin & Browne, 'Social Rights and Market Order' (n 51), pp 27 *et seq.*

[58] See also Deakin & Browne (n 51), pp. 27 *et seq.*

[59] Sen, *The Idea of Justice* (n 54), p. 19, and pp. 270–1.

[60] Supiot Report, *Au-delà de l'emploi: Transformations du travail et l'avenir du droit du travail en Europe, Rapport pour la Commission Européenne* (Paris: Flammarion, 1999). Salais & Villeneuve, 'Introduction: Europe and the Politics of Capabilities' (n 51).

[61] S. Deakin, '"Capacitas": Contract Law and the Institutional Precondition of a Market Economy', (2006) 3 *Eur. Rev. Contract Law*, p. 317; M. Hesselink, 'European Contract Law: A Matter of Consumer Protection, Citizenship, or Justice?' (2007) 2 *Eur. Rev. Private Law*, pp. 323–48.

Sen's approach to substantive freedom may provide new perspectives in the field of EU consumer policy too, for several reasons, which will be discussed in what follows: its focus on substantive freedom and choice, its attention to diversity, responsibility, and ethics, and because of its links to the debate on human rights.

The capability approach stresses the importance of substantive freedom and effective choice, which makes Sen's theory immediately relevant for any theoretical discourse on consumers, who constantly have to choose between goods and services in the global marketplace. While most daily purchasing choices are trivial, others are complex and can have a major impact on the life of consumers, for instance binding them financially to long-term contracts. At the same time, while the variety of products and services have increased considerably, rational and effective choices are sometimes rendered more difficult or hindered by a number of factors, such as aggressive advertising, and lack (or overflow) of information.[62] From a capability perspective, these difficulties are particularly relevant because they constrain the substantive freedom of consumers and thus provide a strong case for policy actions and development of EU consumer law towards enhancing consumer knowledge. For example, this could be achieved by requiring firms to provide simple and comparable information and by building consumer knowledge through education or independent advice, particularly in complex areas such as financial services, where choices may have important and lasting effects on consumer welfare. Interestingly, as we will see in the next chapter, a *financial capability* approach has inspired the UK consumer policy precisely in this sector.

Sen's focus on substantive freedom and real opportunity also implicitly calls for empowering and inclusive measures. Such a perspective could inspire an approach that focuses on enabling consumers to exercise their rights effectively and promote their interests, thus reducing a discrepancy that has been noted between formal recognition of rights and the ability to defend these latter. Indeed, it has been observed that although the law provides consumers with an increasing number of rights and protection provisions, individuals sometimes face barriers to solving practical problems effectively and refrain from seeking help, a challenge compounded by the limited resources of enforcement authorities.[63]

[62] See e.g. J. Davies, 'Consumer Protection in a Normative Context', in J. Devenney and M. Kenny (eds), *European Consumer Protection: Theory and Practice* (Cambridge: CUP, 2012), p. 370. Regarding the limits of consumer freedom from a philosophical perspective see Y. Silier, *Freedom: Political, Metaphysical, Negative, And Positive* (Aldershot: Ashgate, 2005), pp. 55–6.

[63] European Commission, Eurobarometer 2010 Report 342, 'Consumer empowerment' survey. This survey revealed that only 16% of consumers who experience problems seek help

Another core feature of the capability approach is that it acknowledges human diversity, highlighting that individuals have different abilities and opportunities to use resources or participate in economic activities. As discussed at the beginning of this chapter, this is relevant for EU consumer law. The OECD and EU have recently highlighted the existence of an increasing number of consumers who can be considered as 'vulnerable', for example due to their age, limited economic resources, or lack of knowledge.[64] These consumers may struggle to participate actively in complex markets and thus risk social exclusion. Sen's theoretical system, recognizing differences in individuals' capabilities, would then be a natural foundation for a consumer framework flexible enough to respond to the needs of different consumer groups, and therefore able to address these social challenges.

A final feature of Sen's theory which may inspire consumer law is its focus on ethics and responsible behaviour. In his book *On Ethics & Economics*, Sen criticizes mainstream economic theory for separating ethics from economics, and argues instead that human behaviour and choices are not only determined by self-interest, but are also driven by other goals, values, and ethical considerations.[65] To describe this dualism, Sen uses the terms 'well-being' and 'agency'. Well-being concerns the individual's personal advantage.[66] Agency, in contrast, 'takes a wider view of the person' as an actor pursuing broader objectives, commitments, or values, which may go beyond the realization of personal well-being. The separation of agency and well-being in Sen's approach introduces the possibility of moral conflict, that is to say, a discrepancy between what a person does in obedience to a moral principle, and what a person 'would like to do', in the absence of such a moral imperative. Sen argues that economics could be made more productive by paying explicit attention to the ethical motivations that influence human choice. For example, in his book on *The Idea of Justice* Sen shows how the concepts of agency,

from consumer organizations or public authorities to resolve them and seldom consider courts for dispute resolution; Communication from the European Commission, A European Consumer Agenda—Boosting confidence and growth, COM(2012) 225 final, 22.5.2012.

[64] OECD Document, 'The Changing Consumer and Market Landscape' (n 7), pp. 24–7; see the Communication from the European Commission, A European Consumer Agenda—Boosting confidence and growth (n 63).

[65] A. Sen, 'Well-being, Agency and Freedom: The Dewey Lectures 1984', (1985) 82 *J. Philosophy*, pp. 203 *et seq*.

[66] Sen, 'Well-being, Agency and Freedom (n 65), pp. 203–4; see also A. Sen, *On Ethics and Economics* (Oxford: Basil Blackwell, 1987), pp. 40–1 and 58–9.

freedom, and capability can be relevant to approach environmental challenges and further sustainable development objectives, focusing on a broad view of the quality of life.[67]

Sen's theoretical approach could thus provide the basis to develop a legal approach which takes into account market ethics and sustainable development, reflecting the broader dimension of modern consumption.[68] This would require law and policy incentives in the form of information and education to promote consumer awareness. The application of the capability perspective in consumer law may thus generate a dyad of autonomy and responsibility whereby consumers are empowered, but also have a bigger role to play in terms of sustainable behaviour.

In conclusion, Sen's theory may help to reconcile conflicting dimensions of EU consumer law: freedom and market goals on the one hand, and social and ethical values on the other, showing that these are all promoting substantive freedoms. This is further confirmed by looking at these issues from a human rights angle, which is prominent in Sen's work, as discussed next.

3.3. *Human rights*

As discussed in the previous subsections, Hayek's and Sen's theories can provide different perspectives on the consumer law discourse. This section argues that another dimension is added by theories on human rights.

A consideration of human rights is present in the works of both Hayek and Sen. While the topic is rather marginal in the theory of the former, described in section 3.1,[69] human rights play an important role in Sen's framework. Sen identifies a link between these rights and positive freedoms, arguing that human rights, seen as articulation of 'social ethics' or 'ethical demands',[70] are *entitlements* to substantive freedoms.[71] Sen stresses that these rights are not confined to 'coercive legal rules' and 'judicial enforcement' (which are still important to make human rights effective), but they can also be expressed and

[67] Sen, *The Idea of Justice* (n 54), p. 248.

[68] Sen, *Development as Freedom* (n 52), pp. 18–19.

[69] As seen previously, Hayek rejects the recognition of economic and social rights as human rights.

[70] A. Sen, 'Human Rights and the Limits of Law', (2006) 27(6) *Cardozo L. Rev.*, p. 2916.

[71] A. Sen, 'Human Rights and Capabilities', (2005) 6(2) *J. Human Development*, p. 152.

promoted in alternative ways, such as through social monitoring and support by NGOs.[72]

Furthermore, Sen is a strong proponent of including economic and social rights among human rights, even if these are not practically enforceable in a given economic and political situation.[73] To explain this position, which contrasts with the approach of some human rights scholars (e.g. Cranston) discussed in Chapter 3,[74] Sen argues that the potential difficulty of implementing a right does not eliminate the utility of declaring such a right. On the contrary, the formal recognition of these rights contributes to their feasibility and realization in the future. After all, Sen argues, civil and political rights may also be difficult to realize in practice, but this does not mean they should not be acknowledged as human rights.[75] Sen's arguments thus provide a justification to integrate and recognize the value of economic and social rights, and may serve as a lens to interpret existing fundamental rights. For example, the express provision in the Charter to protect consumers as a 'solidarity' objective may receive a new *raison d'être*: although drafted as a policy goal and not as a subjective right, this provision may be regarded as an intermediate step towards a social-focused consumer law and policy model.

A different view is expressed by Joseph Raz. This legal philosopher distinguishes between *moral* and *human* rights, arguing that human rights are such only when an authority declares and actively protects them.[76] It then follows that human rights which lack an explicit promotion and enforceability do not fully qualify as human rights. Raz laments a proliferation of rights which are erroneously called 'human', while being (only) 'moral', for lack of implementation by impartial and effective institutions.[77]

These conclusions contrast with Sen, who instead sees a value in declaring human rights even just as a matter of principle, in order to promote their

[72] Sen, 'Human Rights and the Limits of Law' (n 70), pp. 2916–19; A. Sen, 'Elements of a Theory of Human Rights', (2004) 32(4) *Phil. & Pub. Affairs*, pp. 319–28: see also Sen, *The Idea of Justice* (n 54), p. 364.

[73] Sen, 'Human Rights and the Limits of Law' (n 70) p. 2924.

[74] Cranston contests the usefulness of economic social rights in poor countries which do not have sufficient financial means to guarantee them. See M. Cranston, *Are There Any Human Rights?* (1983) 1 12 *Daedalus*, p. 1; see also the broader academic debate on social human rights and international consumer rights described in the previous chapter.

[75] Sen, 'Human Rights and the Limits of Law' (n 70), p. 2924.

[76] J. Raz, 'Human Rights in the Emerging World Order', (2010) *Transnational Legal Theory*, pp. 31–47. J. Raz, 'Human Rights Without Foundation', in S. Besson & J. Tasioulas (eds), *The Philosophy of International Law* (Oxford: OUP, 2010), pp. 321 *et seq*.

[77] Raz, 'Human Rights in the Emerging World Order' (n 76), pp. 31–47.

future realization. Another point of disagreement between Sen and Raz stems from the fact that, for Raz, certain human rights (e.g. the right to privacy) cannot be regarded as freedoms, while for Sen, human rights are inextricably connected, and even to a certain extent emanate from the right to substantive freedoms.

Despite these differences, Raz's emphasis on the importance of active realization of human rights brings him close to Sen's idea of empowerment. Raz argues that human rights play an important role not only as they bring to the fore the issue of human life; but, just as importantly, because, in a globalized world, they empower individuals in the face of powerful governments, international organizations, and large corporations.[78] Raz is acutely aware of the international dimension of human rights; perhaps as a reflection of this, he stresses that human rights are not absolute (in the sense of abstractly identical across states), but need to be adapted to different cultural contexts, and be balanced with other objectives.

Yet another perspective on human rights is that of Sandra Fredman, who argues that human rights are not limited to individual freedom and opportunities, but also embed wider societal objectives such as care, dignity, and the promotion of responsible behaviour.[79] As we have seen, the idea that human rights may include obligations (e.g. to promote responsible actions) is also present in Sen's agency concept, and it neatly dovetails with recent trends in modern consumption, while of course addressing the ever-pressing issue of sustainable consumption. In conclusion, from a theoretical point of view, there seems to be disagreement on whether economic and social rights, relevant in a consumer law context, can be fully seen as human rights. However, because social considerations are becoming increasingly relevant in consumer policy and law, it seems likely that human rights and consumer law will become progressively more intertwined.

In practice, the entry of human rights in the field of consumer law will provide a strong defence or tool of empowerment of the 'weak party', in particular in an international context. Moreover, the trend of framing consumer protection as a matter of fundamental rights could be regarded as an ethical or moral complement to the market integration focus in the EU. However, the issue of enforcement and actual implementation of these rights may remain an open question and could, in the extreme, undermine the credibility of

[78] Raz, (n 76), pp. 31–47.

[79] S. Fredman, *Human Rights Transformed: Positive Duties and Positive Rights* (Oxford: OUP, 2008), pp. 15–16.

a legal system. In turn, a discourse on the enforcement and realization of human and consumer rights leads to the topic of procedures, which are discussed in the next section.

3.4. *Procedural rights and participation*

Procedural rights are a necessary complement to substantive rights, as they significantly influence the realization and the development of the latter.[80]

Procedural rights in general have been a key topic in theoretical debates. For example, in constitutional theory, Robert Alexy described the increasing prominence of procedural rights for the effective protection of constitutional rights.[81] Denis Galligan stressed the importance of procedural fairness and participation mechanisms, focusing in particular on administrative processes, which are seen as a precondition for the effectiveness of fair treatment standards.[82]

In what follows, we will consider procedural rights of two types: those that enable the effective protection of existing rights, and those that help to shape and define rights. These latter are also called participatory procedures, which allow individuals (in our case, consumers) to participate in the policy- and law-making processes.

Procedural rights of the first type are clearly essential to ensure effective protection of consumer rights.[83] For human rights, which are often abstract, they serve an even more important role: they help to shape and define the content of these rights by facilitating their application. Chapter 7 will further discuss procedural consumer rights, focusing in particular on the right to access to justice and on collective redress.

Sen's framework is essentially silent on the first type of procedural rights but includes a treatment as to the second type of participatory procedures when discussing 'political freedoms'. A key theoretical reference in this respect is Jürgen Habermas, who developed a 'discourse theory'.[84] This theory is particularly

[80] See e.g. F. Francioni (ed.), 'The Rights of Access to Justice under Customary International Law', in *Access to Justice as a Human Right* (Oxford: OUP, 2007), pp. 1 *et seq*.

[81] R. Alexy, *A Theory of Constitutional Rights* (Oxford: OUP, 2002), pp. 314 *et seq*.

[82] D. Galligan, *Due Process and Fair Procedures: A Study of Administrative Procedures* (Oxford: Clarendon Press, 1996), p. 100.

[83] See ch. 7; see also M. Cappelletti & B. Garth (eds), *Access to Justice: a World Survey* (Milan: A. Giuffre, 1978).

[84] See J. Habermas, 'Remarks on Legitimation through Human Rights', in *The Postnational Constellation, Political Essays* (Cambridge: The MIT Press, 2001), pp. 113 *et seq*; J. Habermas, *Between Facts and Norms* (Cambridge: Polity Press, 1996).

interesting for our context, as it also places an important focus on the problem of legitimacy of legal systems which is, as we saw, strongly felt in the EU. Habermas highlights the core role of democratic rights for legitimate law-making, thus shifting the attention away from freedom rights, which are the main objective of the liberal approach.[85]

In his theoretical construct Habermas distinguishes five fundamental categories of basic rights.[86] The first three comprise civil rights, whose role is to guarantee the greatest possible subjective freedom of action for all individuals. A fourth category pertains to political rights, through which citizens enact legitimate law and participate in the democratic process. Finally, a fifth category of rights comprises social and ecological rights which, in turn, are necessary to exert the rights in the first four categories, and are, therefore, assigned a derivative status.[87]

All of these five categories form the basis for the institutionalization of 'action norms', and ensure that individuals can participate in a rational discourse about law. In turn, if such a discourse is absent or impaired, public action turns into technocratic policy-making not supported by the consent of the governed.[88]

While Habermas' discourse theory remains rather abstract, his approach could be particularly relevant for the European context for several reasons. First, as already stated, it addresses the question of legitimacy, which is particularly pertinent for the EU. Secondly, being centred on an argumentative notion, it is well adapted to the European legal system, based on a relatively non-hierarchical network of institutions, which are therefore natural dialectic actors.[89] Finally, the discourse approach is clearly well suited to culturally diverse societies like the European one. Particularly in these cases, the discourse approach may facilitate a legitimate law-making process, as it allows better exploration of all the alternatives and of their effects on the parties involved.

[85] J. Habermas, 'Reconciliation through the Public Use of Reason, Remarks on John Rawls' Political Liberalism' and J. Rawls, 'Reply to Habermas', (1995) 92 *J. Phil.*, p. 3; Habermas, *Between Facts and Norms* (n 84).

[86] This system of rights is universal, but needs to be adapted to the particular national context, see Habermas, (n 84), pp. 122 *et seq*.

[87] Habermas, (n 84), pp. 123 *et seq*; see also the comments by J. Tweedy & A. Hunt, 'The Future of the Welfare State and Social Rights: Reflections on Habermas', (1994) 21 *J. Law and Society*, p. 307.

[88] Habermas, (n 84).

[89] The state still has a corrective function, but it can no longer be conceived as a hierarchical control mechanism; see Ch. Joerges, 'The Impact of European Integration on Private Law: Reductionist Perceptions, True Conflicts and a New Constitutional Perspective', (1997) 3 *Eur. L. J.*, p. 389.

Constitutional scholars have made a case for adopting a discursive approach in the EU constitutional process through an assembly, which would merge national Parliaments and the European Parliament into a real discourse.[90] This approach was effectively adopted in the creation of the EU Charter of Fundamental Rights, which indeed was the result of an articulated dialogue incorporating opinions from a large variety of sources.[91]

In the specific context of consumer law, a stronger focus on participatory rights would imply that: (1) relevant information relating to European public action should be available to consumers; (2) citizens should be educated, so they can form their own judgement on consumer-related issues; and (3) citizens should be given institutional means to express their judgement, either indirectly (through their vote) or directly (through unions, associations, media, etc.).[92] For point (3), in particular, adequate mechanisms have to be established, so that consumers can affirm their identity as consumers, through participation at every level of the European system.[93]

The next section discusses in more detail how these theoretical considerations surface in various existing legal provisions, at the EU and at a global level too. Moreover, it will show how these theoretical insights point to a way to extend and to interpret existing legislation, moving towards a new framework for consumer law.

4. Reassessing EU Consumer Law and Fundamental Rights

As demonstrated in the previous chapters, EU consumer law has focused mostly on market integration objectives and is now struggling to resolve several pressing economic and societal challenges that cannot be fully addressed

[90] R. Bieber, 'Steigerungsform der Europäischen Union: Eine Europäische Verfassung', in J. Ipsen, H.W. Rengeling, J.M. Mössner, & A. Weber, *Verfassungsrecht im Wandel* (Cologne: Festschrift zum 180 jährigen Bestehen des Carl-Heymanns-Verlags, 1995), pp. 291 *et seq.*

[91] J. Elster, 'Forces and Mechanisms in the Constitution-Making Process', (1995) 45 *Duke University L. J.*, pp. 364 *et seq.*

[92] See also F. Kandil, 'Economic Efficiency and Social Justice: A Prudential Approach for Public Actions', in Ch. Joerges, B. Stråth, & P. Wagner (eds), *The Economy as a Polity: The Political Constitution of Contemporary Capitalism* (London: UCL Press, 2005), pp. 207–9.

[93] A large number of actors participate in the European multi-level system, which requires a legal order that facilitates deliberative actions; see Ch. Joerges, 'On the Legitimacy of Europeanizing Europe's Private law', EUI WP 2003/3, pp. 36 *et seq.*

by the traditional approach. A number of modern theories discussed above may inspire a broader conceptual framework, able to integrate social principles, economic objectives, and fundamental rights, and may thus address some of these challenges.

While the Charter's specific provision on consumer protection (Article 38) is rather short and, as some have argued, limited, a number of other Charter Articles, in conjunction with the Lisbon Treaty, provide a fertile ground to rethink and shape EU consumer law and policy. This section describes how the theories presented in this chapter, in conjunction with these provisions, could inspire a more comprehensive framework that strengthens the protection and empowerment of consumers.

4.1. *Economic and social dimensions of consumer law*

As discussed in Chapter 2, the EU consumer law framework presents some limitations. The capability theory discussed in subsection 3.2 has in particular two elements which may help policy- and law-makers to overcome some of these limitations: first, the idea of maintaining and strengthening 'substantive freedoms'; secondly, the idea of promoting social and economic objectives along with human rights.[94]

Sen's focus on freedom and opportunities and their meaning for consumer law have been discussed in section 3. Here we recall that they may underpin a legal model with the desirable quality of being protective but at the same time non-intrusive. Hence, Sen's theory may inspire a system able to solve the dilemma of choosing between a paternalistic, over-protective state, which stifles growth and competition, and an under-protective system, narrowly focused on economic growth.[95]

The other important element in Sen's discourse is the recognition of the importance of economic and social rights. Interestingly, the legal framework developed after Lisbon has placed an increasing weight on such social objectives, as can be inferred from new provisions. The most important legal novelties in this sense appear in the Lisbon Treaty and in the Charter of Fundamental Rights.

The Lisbon Treaty enumerates several social goals in a catalogue of EU objectives (Article 3 TEU).[96] Article 3(3) TEU, for example, states that the

[94] Sen, 'Elements of a Theory of Human Rights' (n 72), p. 315.

[95] See also Deakin & Browne (n 51), pp. 37 *et seq.*

[96] Arguably, the Treaty also seems to downplay traditional market-oriented goals. For example, the objective of protecting competition, which figured prominently in Art. 3(1)(g) of the pre-Lisbon EC Treaty, has been omitted from the current list, and has been relegated to a Protocol on 'Internal

Union 'shall work for (...) a competitive social market economy'. First proposed as an intermediate solution between laissez-faire and planned economy, the concept of 'competitive social market' has been very influential in the policy of the Federal Republic of Germany, thus proving its practical applicability in a national context.[97] The question remains as to whether such a concept can also influence the policy of the Union. For example, Joerges and Rödl argue that it may have little impact at the supra-national level, as the EU lacks the competences required to implement it.[98] Despite this, the reference to a social market economy is a clear recognition of the need for an equilibrium between freedom objectives and social goals.

Besides such a social market concept, Article 3 TEU contains other 'solidarity' objectives ranging from the goal to 'combat social exclusion and discrimination', to the aim to 'promote social justice and protection'. The inclusion of these objectives is an innovative transformation of the pre-Lisbon Article 2 TEU, and may well directly influence EU policy and the interpretation of Treaty provisions by the ECJ. Moreover, such provisions may inspire institutions, which can influence new legislative proposals, particularly if considered in conjunction with the rights recognized in the Charter.[99]

As mentioned, important steps towards a stronger recognition of social values also appear in the Charter of Fundamental Rights.[100] This has several provisions not strictly referring to consumers, but which can be relevant nonetheless—for example, Article 26 on access to services of economic interest, discussed in Chapters 5 and 6 of this book.

As we have seen in previous chapters, a specific Charter provision regarding consumer protection figures in Article 38, which states that 'Union policies shall ensure a high level of consumer protection'. This norm does not establish a subjective right but, evidently, has been designed to give guidance to

Market Competition'. The Protocols have the same legal value as the rest of the Treaty, so this change is mostly formal. And yet it may reveal a change in the legislator's attitude.

[97] The 'social market economy' concept was first formulated by economist Müller-Armack in 1946. See also A. Müller-Armack, *Wirtschaftslenkung und Marktwirtschaft* (Munich, Kastell Verlag, special edition, 1990).

[98] C. Joerges and F. Rödl, '"Social Market Economy" as Europe's Social Model?', in L. Magnusson & B. Stråth (eds), *A European Social Citizenship?: Preconditions for Future Policies from a Historical Perspective* (Brussels, Peter Lang, 2004), pp. 125 *et seq.*

[99] See e.g. the House of Lords, European Union Committee, *The Treaty of Lisbon: an Impact Assessment*, 10th Report of Session 2007–08, p. 22.

[100] See regarding the influence of the Charter: A.J. Menendez, 'Some Elements of a Theory of European Fundamental Rights', in A.J. Menendez & E.O. Eriksen (eds), *Arguing Fundamental Rights, Law and Philosophy*, Vol. 77 (Dordrecht: Springer, 2006), pp. 155 *et seq.*

EU policy and future legal initiatives. Moreover, this provision can also become a reference point for the ECJ. As we will see in Chapter 7, the ECJ already referred to this provision when it had to decide on issues of consumer protection.

The Charter and the post-Lisbon legal framework may thus indicate a rebalancing of priorities in favour of social objectives.[101] However, in the light of some important ECJ cases, the long-term implications of these provisions remain unclear, in particular in those cases when fundamental rights clash with economic (free movement) rights.[102] For example, in *Schmidberger* the Court had to balance economic rights against fundamental rights.[103] It decided that the blocking, by environmental protestors, of a motorway, posing an obstacle to cross-border trade, was justified because of the importance of the freedom of expression of the protestors. In contrast, in the more recent *Viking* and *Laval* cases the ECJ had to balance economic freedoms with collective labour rights, and gave precedence to the former.[104] While the Court acknowledged collective action as a fundamental right, it held that in the specific cases the collective actions carried out had not been proportionate to the aim pursued and were thus unlawful.

These cases dealt with fundamental rights in *environmental* and *labour* law. Nevertheless, they are interesting examples, as similar conflicts could occur in consumer law. More specific examples will be considered later, analyzing recent cases where the Court had to balance different conflicting fundamental rights, such as the rights to information and privacy as opposed to the right to property.[105]

4.2. *Social responsibility and sustainable behaviour*

As discussed earlier in this chapter, human rights contain an ethical component. They can be regarded as moral or ethical demands, which may also generate obligations to support such rights.

[101] See S. Weatherill, 'From Economic Rights to Fundamental Rights', in S. de Vries, U. Bernitz, & S. Weatherill, *The Protection of Fundamental Rights in the EU After Lisbon* (Oxford: Hart Publishing, 2013), pp. 32–4; N. Nic Shuibhne, 'Margins of Appreciation: National Values, Fundamental Rights and EC Free Movement Law' (2009) 34(2) *Eur. L. Rev.*, pp. 230–56.

[102] For a discussion on recent fundamental rights case law see S. Douglas-Scott, 'The European Union and Human Rights after the Treaty of Lisbon', (2011) 11(4), *Hum. Rts. L. Rev.*, pp. 645–82.

[103] Case C-112/00, *Eugen Schmidberger v Republik Österreich* [2003] ECR I-5659.

[104] Case C-438/05, *Viking Line* [2007] ECR I-10779; and Case C-341/05, *Laval un Partneri* [2007] ECR I-11767.

[105] The impact of fundamental rights and of the Lisbon Treaty on particular areas of consumer law will be discussed in detail in later chapters (5–7).

This finds a parallel in the consumer space, where purchasing patterns but also the lifestyle of consumers can have an important impact on environmental protection or ethical goals.[106] As we have already mentioned, the EU and other affluent economies are witnessing a still limited but visible trend towards a 'moralization' of markets, with consumers promoting environmentally friendly consumption while at the same time boycotting immoral production methods.[107]

The current consumer law framework in the EU deals neither with ethical nor sustainable consumption.[108] However, a close analysis of the Charter and of the Lisbon Treaty reveals several new provisions that may influence consumer policy in this sense.

The Charter stipulates in its preamble that 'Enjoyment of these rights entails responsibilities and duties with regard to other persons, to the human community and to future generations', reflecting, to a certain extent, the responsibility dimension mentioned earlier. Furthermore, Article 37 of the 'Solidarity' chapter of the Charter of Fundamental Rights concerns environmental protection, and expressly stipulates that: 'A high level of environmental protection and the improvement of the quality of the environment *must be integrated into the policies of the Union* and ensured in accordance with the *principle of sustainable development*' (emphasis added). Thus, this includes an obligation for EU policies to integrate environmental protection and to respect the principle of sustainable development.[109] Given that EU consumer policy can play a key role in promoting sustainable consumption, Article 37 may be regarded as a legal basis to establish such a policy.

Similarly, sustainable development and environmental protection are given an important place in the Lisbon Treaty. For example, Article 191 TFEU enshrines for the first time the objective of 'combating climate change' and reinforces the 'polluter pays' principle. Furthermore, Title XXI on Energy aims, among other areas, to promote renewable and efficient energy. Finally,

[106] See beginning of this chapter regarding ethical market behaviour; see also M. Lori, 'Fighting for Human Rights: Consumption Behaviour as Political Praxis', in *Rethinking Consumer Behaviour for the Benefit of All* (Council of Europe, 2009), pp. 94 *et seq*.

[107] Stehr, Henning, & Weiler (n 3), pp. 8–12.

[108] OECD, *Promoting Sustainable Consumption: Good Practices in OECD Countries* (Paris: OECD, 2008). However, DGs Environment, and Enterprise and Industry of the European Commission have become increasingly active in the field of sustainable consumption, see: <http://ec.europa.eu/environment/eussd/escp_en.htm> and <http://ec.europa.eu/enterprise/policies/sustainable-business/environment-action-plan/>.

[109] See also N. de Sadeleer, 'Droits fondamentaux et protection de l'environnement dans l'ordre juridique de l'UE et dans la CEDH', in C. Vedure, 'Environmental Law and Consumer Protection', (2011) 1 *Eur. J. Consumer Law*, pp. 25–6.

Article 11 TFEU states that environmental protection requirements must be integrated into the Union's policies, with a view to promoting sustainable development, thus echoing Article 37 of the Charter of Fundamental Rights.

While these provisions do not explicitly relate environment protection to consumer law (for this latter the key reference is Article 169 of the TFEU, discussed in Chapter 2), they may have an important effect on consumer policy too, as environmental protection and consumer law are related. This link is explicitly recognized by the UN Guidelines for Consumer Protection,[110] which define sustainable consumption as 'meeting the needs of present and future generations for goods and services in ways that are economically, socially and *environmentally sustainable*' (emphasis added).[111] In addition, the Guidelines cover provisions on recycling and sustainable government practices, encouraging life-cycle thinking and eco-products.

The UN Guidelines therefore make an explicit link between the 'right' and the 'duty' dimensions of consumer policies, and by so doing they establish a principle which is likely to influence future regulation.[112] While in the EU sustainable consumption has played a minor role in the Consumer Policy Strategy 2007–2013,[113] it seems to be gaining momentum with the new EU Consumer Policy Agenda issued in 2012.[114] According to this Agenda the EU would have the task of rendering consumers more conscientious on the topic of sustainable consumption and promote such an approach through coherent policy actions.

This new 'responsibility' trend is in line with Fredman's and Sen's general theoretical considerations mentioned in section 3 of this chapter. Moreover, the increasing moral awareness of consumers suggests that responsible behaviour is not totally extraneous to the current attitude of a growing group of European citizens.

[110] This new version of the UN Guidelines including sustainable consumption was incorporated by the Economic and Social Council in July 1999 and adopted by the General Assembly in its Decision 54/449.

[111] At the international level, sustainable consumption was first established in the UN declaration adopted at the Rio summit in 1992. UN Guidelines, cl. 42.

[112] Even though, it should be remembered, the UN Guidelines do not have a binding status.

[113] See the European Commission's website: <http://ec.europa.eu/consumers/strategy/index_en.htm>.

[114] Communication from the European Commission, A European Consumer Agenda—Boosting confidence and growth, COM(2012) 225 final, 22.5.2012; sustainable consumption is also promoted by the EU 'Resource Efficiency Roadmap', COM(2011) 571.

4.3. *Procedural rights—a catalogue for consumer law?*

Procedural rights have been recognized as an essential part of human rights and have been codified in several fundamental documents. The 1948 Universal Declaration of Human Rights, for example, includes several procedural rights. Article 8 enshrines the right to an effective remedy for acts violating fundamental rights, while Article 10 guarantees fair procedures. Article 20 ensures freedom of association and Article 21 concerns the right to take part in government.

These rights have taken a specific and prominent role in the field of environmental protection which, just like consumer law, deals with the issue of protecting diffuse interests.[115] The 1998 UNECE Convention on Access to Information, Public Participation in Decision-making and Access to Justice (the Aarhus Convention)[116] recognizes in its preamble that procedural rights are a significant prerequisite for an adequate protection of the environment, underlying their importance for the enjoyment of human rights.[117] Accordingly, the Convention contains procedural rights to increase public involvement in decision-making and to facilitate access to justice. The procedural rights of the Aarhus Convention may provide inspiration for consumer protection, which has been equally recognized as a fundamental policy objective in the Charter of Fundamental Rights. In such a context, procedural rights may encompass, for example, the right to: information (as a precondition of participation), fair administrative actions, public participation, and access to justice.

Procedural guarantees, and in particular the concept of access to justice, have also played an important role in the European human rights discourse and EU case law.[118] Key provisions in the Charter of Fundamental Rights are the right to good administration (Article 4) and the right to an effective remedy (Article 47).[119] Furthermore, the European Convention on

[115] D. Anton & D. Shelton, 'Procedural Human Rights and the Environment', in *Environmental Protection and Human Rights* (Cambridge: CUP, 2011), pp. 356 *et seq.*

[116] Text of the Convention can be found at: <http://www.unece.org/env/pp/documents/cep43e.pdf>. The Convention entered into force in 2001.

[117] M. Pallemaerts, 'Proceduralizing Environmental Rights: The Aarhus Convention on Access to Information, Public Participation in Decision Making and Access to Justice in Environmental Matters in a Human Rights Context' (UNEP for the Geneva Environment Network, 2004), pp. 17–19; see also in the same publication, F.X. Perrez, 'Key Questions concerning the Human Rights and Environment Debate. An Introduction', p. 6.

[118] E. Storskrubb & J. Ziller, 'Access to Justice in European Comparative Law', in F. Francioni (ed.), *Access to Justice as a Human Right* (Oxford: OUP, 2007); A. Ward, 'Access to Justice', in S. Peers & A. Ward (eds), *The EU Charter of Fundamental Rights* (Oxford: Hart Publishing, 2004), pp. 123–40.

[119] For the impact of procedural human rights on competition law see W. Wils, 'EU Antitrust Enforcement Powers and Procedural Rights and Guarantees: The Interplay Between EU Law,

Human Rights (ECHR) contains core procedural human rights guarantees in Article 6 on the right to a fair trial and in Article 13 on the right to an effective remedy.

Despite these broad provisions at the human rights level, procedural rights are not fully developed in EU consumer law. While recent legal innovation has strengthened alternative dispute resolution procedures,[120] consumers still face barriers to access justice, in particular in cases of collective actions. As we will see in Chapter 7, effective consumer protection could be improved by stronger procedural rights, facilitating amongst other things cross-border collective actions.

Another class of procedural rights that could be strengthened in the EU system is that of participatory procedures, whose theoretical underpinning has been considered when discussing Habermas' discourse approach. Participatory procedures provide citizens and interest groups with the possibility to be involved in the law-making process, giving them a chance to see their aspirations reflected in the legal system. Moreover, they strengthen the legitimacy of the law. At present, consumers often lack the means and the understanding to make their voice heard at the regulatory level,[121] requiring strong and permanent organizations to play a systematic role in representing their interest.

This discussion suggests that a catalogue of procedural rights for EU consumer law might be an appropriate complement to the protective provisions which are already being developed.[122] Such a catalogue would both promote and legitimate a system built around the figure of an active consumer. It could include three key procedural rights for consumers: (1) the right to information; (2) the right to participation in the policy debate; and (3) the right to access to justice.

The right to information and advice or education is an essential starting point: adequate information and advice enhance the capabilities of consumers

National Law, the Charter of Fundamental Rights of the EU and the European Convention on Human Rights', (2011) 34(2) *World Competition: Law and Economics Rev*, pp. 189–213.

[120] See Regulation (EU) No 524/2013 of 21 May 2013 on online dispute resolution for consumer disputes (Regulation on consumer ODR), Directive 2013/11/EU of 21 May 2013 on alternative dispute resolution for consumer disputes (Directive on consumer ADR).

[121] See e.g. H.-W. Micklitz, 'European Consumer Law', in E. Jones, A. Menon, & S. Weatherill (eds), *The Oxford Handbook of the European Union*, online version, 2013, p. 16.

[122] A similar recommendation has been put forward by the European Economic and Social Committee, which underlined the importance of participatory measures for consumers and the focus on collective redress. See the opinion of the European Economic and Social Committee on the Legal Framework for Consumer Policy, INT/263, Brussels, 20 April 2006.

to participate effectively in market transactions and policy-making.[123] The right to information of consumers is already included in Article 169(1) TFEU and was implemented in a number of directives, which will be explained in the following chapters.

Participation in the policy debate ensures that consumer interests are taken into account in law-making procedures.[124] Participatory democracy is recognized in Article 11 TEU, which stipulates, inter alia, that: 'The institutions shall, by appropriate means, give citizens and representative associations the opportunity to make known and publicly exchange their views in all areas of Union action'. This can be regarded as an important means for non-institutional actors, such as consumer organizations, to take part in EU decision-making.[125] This is also in accordance with a concept of democracy emerging from the discourse and capability approach, whereby a system should ensure material conditions for the effective exercise of rights.[126] Chapter 6 will explore this issue further.

Finally, the right to access to justice and due process assists consumers in enforcing their rights. Access to justice can be facilitated by rules supporting the effective protection of consumer interests by collective actions, alternative dispute resolution, and litigation funding schemes. Chapter 7 discusses this topic in more detail, exploring how effective judicial protection of consumers may be strengthened as a fundamental right.

4.4. *Feasibility and policy implications*

The previous sections have proposed potential developments for EU consumer law: a shift towards social and sustainability objectives, and a strengthening of procedural rights. Would the EU have sufficient competences to promote such a broader consumer approach?

The EU has developed consumer law, mainly on the basis of Article 114 TFEU (ex Article 95 EC). As the *Tobacco Advertising* case has shown, there are competence limitations for the EU to legislate by invoking Article 114 without a clear market-making objective.[127] However, the ensuing case law

[123] See also Harding, Kohl, & Salmon (n 10).

[124] The link between social objectives and market choices has to be openly debated to increase political legitimacy, see S. Weatherill, *Consumer Law and Policy* (Cheltenham: Edward Elgar Publishing, 2005).

[125] For the definition of participation see J. Mendes, 'Participation and the Role of Law after Lisbon: A Legal View on Article 11 TEU', (2011) 48 *CML Rev.*, p. 1849.

[126] Sen, *Development as Freedom* (n 52), p. 84; Habermas, *Between Facts and Norms* (n 84), p. 82.

[127] Case C-376/98, *Germany v Parliament and Council* [2000] ECR I-08419.

has been more permissive with regard to new directives,[128] so that broader measures may be adopted in consumer law on the basis of this Article, if they also promote market integration.

However, for the adoption of provisions that have no economic integration goals, Article 169(2)(b) TFEU (ex 153(3)(b) EC) can serve as an appropriate basis, which states that the EU shall contribute to the realization of consumer protection objectives 'through measures which support, supplement and monitor the policy pursued by the Member States'.

It may be argued that this norm does not confer an outright power on the EU to legislate, as its competence is made conditional on the existence of Member State policies, which the EU can support, supplement and monitor. However, given that each Member State does have policies and legal provisions which protect consumers, it would appear that the EU de facto has some competence to legislate in this area. In particular, the reference to measures to 'support, [and] supplement' perfectly supports the creation of empowering procedures and protective measures.

Given that the Commission possesses the legal means to propose a broader model of consumer law, the question is then whether there is the political will within the EU to change its approach. At the moment there does not seem to be a strong political willingness to initiate a regulatory reform in primary law. However, the EU would already have some competence to adopt a broader approach like the one proposed in this chapter. The first signs of a trend towards strengthened procedural and social objectives have appeared in specific areas of secondary consumer law. The next chapters will examine these first steps by looking at a number of consumer areas.

5. Conclusions

This chapter started by illustrating the new challenges posed by global markets and by a changing consumer landscape, arguing that the current EU approach, influenced by a market-making consumer concept, is unable to meet these challenges.

[128] See ch. 2 of this book.

Drawing on different theories, including those of Sen and Habermas, this chapter has proposed a complementary framework, based, inter alia, on fundamental rights values and effective procedural rights.

The chapter explored how these approaches can be adapted to consumer law, and discussed to what extent fundamental rights and the new legal framework since Lisbon could support an evolution of the EU consumer model in this direction. The Charter provision explicitly mentioning consumer protection is limited. However, the legal framework provided by the Lisbon Treaty, in conjunction with specific provisions of the newly binding EU fundamental rights, may nonetheless develop into a tool to reshape some aspects of consumer protection. Furthermore, the 'Solidarity' chapter of the Charter may foster an approach towards social protection and sustainable consumption, responding to important trends in the market and establishing new perspectives in EU law. Finally, Article 169(2) of the Treaty offers some grounds for the EU to legislate in defending the health, safety, and economic interests of consumers, with the potential of transcending the narrow market-making perspective adopted so far. Recent initiatives at the European level discussed in this chapter show a growing propensity to follow this path, although the process is likely to be long, and will require strong political will.

The following three chapters show how the analytical framework presented in this chapter can be made operational and supported by fundamental rights.[129] Enlarged markets require the development of new capabilities and procedural rights for consumers, such as through collective actions, democratic participation in regulation and education. Chapter 5 thus examines the impact of fundamental rights on consumer law in financial contracts, demonstrating the importance of clear information, advice, and access to essential services to promote consumer knowledge and inclusion. Chapter 6 analyzes the fundamental rights dimension of access to services of general interest and regulatory involvement of consumers, using electronic communication as an example. Finally, Chapter 7 explores the availability of procedural consumer rights, in particular assessing the issue of access to justice, analyzing collective redress mechanisms and litigation funding.

[129] For reasons of space, the intersection of ethical consumption, human rights, and environmental protection will not be further discussed in this book.

5

Consumer Protection and Financial Contracts

1. Introduction

This chapter explores the potential impact of fundamental rights on financial consumer contracts, with a special focus on credit agreements. As we have seen in previous chapters, constitutional and fundamental rights play an increasing role in private law in several Member States.[1]

With the legally binding Charter, the influence of fundamental rights in contractual relationships can be expected to increase. This raises questions on how fundamental rights may affect consumer law, in particular in the area of financial agreements, where the complexity of the market renders informed choice more difficult, and where contracts may have important long-term effects on an individual's welfare.[2]

In Chapter 2, we have seen that EU consumer protection is informed by a market-making perspective, and is focused on full harmonization. This tendency has become particularly visible in contract law and also surfaces in the new directive on credit agreements for consumers from 2008. Although this directive improves the information provided to consumers, there are still doubts on whether this is sufficiently effective in addressing interrelated

[1] See comparative studies on this topic: G. Brüggemeier, A. Colombi Ciacchi, & G. Comandé (eds), *Fundamental Rights and Private Law in the European Union* (Cambridge: CUP, 2010); C. Busch and H. Schulte-Nölke (eds), *EU Compendium—Fundamental Rights and Private Law: A Practical Tool for Judges* (Munich: Sellier, 2010); C. Mak, *Fundamental Rights in European Contract Law: A Comparison of the Impact of Fundamental Rights on Contractual Relationships in Germany, the Netherlands, Italy and England, vol. 12* (Alphen aan den Rijn: Kluwer Law, 2008).

[2] O. Cherednychenko, *Fundamental Rights, Contract Law and the Protection of the Weaker Party: A Comparative Analysis of the Constitutionalisation of Contract Law, with Emphasis on Risky Financial Transactions* (Munich: Sellier, European Law Publisher, 2007).

challenges such as rising over-indebtedness[3] as well as financial exclusion.[4] Market studies have demonstrated that consumers often lack financial understanding and adequate assessment of future risks,[5] which in turn raises a number of questions regarding the prevention of unsustainable lending practices, and on how to improve consumers' financial capability.[6]

It is argued here that the EU should focus on a coherent approach in relation to consumer credit inspired by a capability approach, promoting information, responsible lending, and inclusive instruments, which are prerequisites for a long-term sustainable market.

The section below starts by exploring consumer protection in financial services, focusing on consumer credit regulation, tracing its evolution and illustrating its emphasis on information and responsible credit. The following section then examines the potential role of fundamental rights in protecting weaker parties in contractual relationships and in promoting specific principles in financial agreements. Finally, the last section explores mechanisms that enhance the consumers' understanding of financial issues and assesses approaches that may help to address over-indebtedness, such as social lending schemes and special bankruptcy rules.

2. Financial Consumer Protection and Credit Regulation

The EU established rules for financial services operators in order to enhance consumer protection in the key areas of financial services, including banking,[7] insurance,[8] and securities.[9]

[3] M. Westphal, 'The EU Financial Service Policy and its Effect on Consumer Law', in M. Kelly-Louw, J. Nehf, & P. Rott (eds), *The Future of Consumer Credit Regulation, Creative Approaches to Emerging Problems (Markets and the Law)* (Aldershot: Ashgate Publishing, 2008), pp. 69–90.

[4] Opinion of the European Economic and Social Committee on the Proposal for a Directive concerning credit for consumers, COM(2002) 443 final—2002/0222 (COD), INT/159, 17 July 2003.

[5] See J. Leskinen & A. Raijas, 'Consumer Financial Capability—a Life Cycle Approach', in European Credit Research Institute, *Consumer Financial Capability: Empowering European Consumers* (Brussels: ECRI, 2006), pp. 8–9.

[6] See for example: OECD/INFE, High-level Principles on National Strategies for Financial Education (Paris 2012).

[7] E.g. Directive 2008/48/EC of 23 April 2008 on credit agreements for consumers, OJ L 133/66-92, 22.5.2008.

[8] E.g. Directive 2002/92/EC of 9 December 2002 on insurance mediation, OJ L 009, 15/01/2003.

[9] E.g. Directive 2004/39/EC of 21 April 2004 on markets in financial instruments, OJ L 145, 30.4.2004.

Moreover, the recent financial crisis placed a renewed focus on stronger supervision of the financial markets and on consumer protection.[10] In 2010 the European Commission presented several reforms in the financial sector, focusing on four core principles, one of which consisted of strengthened responsibility and consumer protection to restore confidence in the financial markets. The other principles were: transparency in the financial market; effective supervision through new independent authorities and enforcement;[11] and finally enhanced resilience and financial stability.[12]

As a result of the EU reforms, three supervisory authorities and a European System Risk Board were established at the beginning of 2011.[13] The three supervisory authorities are responsible for supervising different financial areas at the micro-financial level, covering banking, insurance, and occupational pensions and securities. They were also given specific powers and tasks to protect consumers. Their regulations expressly state that they 'shall take a leading role in promoting transparency, simplicity and fairness in the market for consumer financial products or services across the internal market'.[14] They can do this by different means, including collecting, analyzing, and reporting on consumer trends, reviewing and coordinating financial literacy and education initiatives, and by developing training standards for the industry.[15] The European Banking Authority (EBA) is responsible for banking supervision, dealing also with issues of consumer credit and over-indebtedness.

The regulation of consumer credit, a key area of EU consumer protection, has already existed for some time. However, retail financial services have

[10] At the international level the World Bank issued a document on 'Good Practices for Financial Consumer Protection', June 2012.

[11] See <http://ec.europa.eu/internal_market/finances/committees/index_en.htm>.

[12] Communication from the Commission of 2 June 2010—Regulating financial services for sustainable growth [COM(2010) 301—Not published in the Official Journal].

[13] Regulation 1093/2010 establishing a European Banking Authority; Regulation 1094/2010 establishing a European Insurance and Occupational Pensions Authority, Regulation 1095/2010 establishing a European Securities and Markets Authority (adopted on 24 November 2010).

[14] See Art. 9 of Regulation 1093/2010 establishing a European Banking Authority; Regulation 1094/2010 establishing a European Insurance and Occupational Pensions Authority, Regulation 1095/2010 establishing a European Securities and Markets Authority (adopted on 24 November 2010).

[15] Furthermore, they have to monitor financial activities and 'may adopt guidelines and recommendations with a view to promoting the safety and soundness of markets and convergence of regulatory practice' and can temporarily prohibit or restrict certain financial activities in the Union.

evolved rapidly over the last decade. On the one hand, credit products available to consumers have become more varied and widespread; on the other, financial innovation has allowed lenders to more easily sell on their loans, making the credit intermediation chain longer and more articulated. While creating benefits, this process has also introduced new risks, and thus new challenges for regulation.

The diffusion of credit and the creation of new credit products have increased consumers' choice and purchasing power, benefitting buyers and sellers alike. At the same time, the abundance of credit and the proliferation of complex credit products have made financial exposures higher and more difficult to understand and manage. This has increased the risk of consumer over-indebtedness, which may crystallize following a fall in income (due to e.g. redundancy or illness)[16] or following a change in general economic conditions which may negatively affect financial commitments.

Similarly, the possibility for lenders to sell on their loan portfolios has increased credit supply, but has also weakened the incentives for lenders to assess the ability of consumers to sustain their financial commitments. As shown by the recent crisis, this has resulted in reckless lending and over-indebtedness, imposing considerable costs on the economy and ultimately on consumers—in particular on weak consumers. The Council of Europe highlighted in a Memorandum on 'legal solutions to debt problems' the serious negative effects that over-indebtedness can have on the welfare of individuals, which may impinge on the human right to dignity.[17]

This issue raises difficult questions on how the access to credit in the market can be regulated in a coherent way, in order to facilitate financial participation, but at the same time prevent over-indebtedness. EU consumer law seems to have provided only a partial answer to this dilemma, focusing in particular on the issue of information in credit regulation. The following section will analyze the evolution of consumer credit regulation in the EU and assess the current Consumer Credit Directive.

[16] G. Howells, 'Whose Responsibility to Plan for Future Changes in Circumstances—Debtor, Creditor or the State?', in T. Wilhelmsson & S. Hurri (eds), *From Dissonance to Sense: Welfare State Expectations, Privatization and Private Law* (Aldershot: Ashgate Publishing, 1999), p. 438.

[17] See the Council of Europe, Explanatory Memorandum to Recommendation on Legal Solutions to Debt Problems, June 2007; see also G.M. Duhl, 'International Developments in Consumer Financial Services Law 2007–2008', (2009) 64 *Business Lawyer*, pp. 683–4.

2.1. *The rise of consumer credit and EU regulation*

The past two decades have seen a marked increase in consumer credit, which has become a common feature in the European Union.[18] Lending first appeared in the form of payment by instalments provided directly by the seller, and was eventually supplemented by the involvement of the financier, as a third party. Accordingly, banks or financial intermediaries have today become the usual lender. The expansion of the credit sector has occurred for two main reasons. First, the reduction of the welfare state has transformed credit into a necessity for many of the poor in order to balance their budget. Secondly, the liberalization of financial services has led to easier access to credit, which is now increasingly available to all groups in society. This development has been described as the 'democratization' of credit.[19]

For many years, consumer credit has developed freely in the European Member States, without any specific regulation. However, the apparent ease of access to borrowing led to over-indebtedness on the part of consumers.[20] Thus, there were different reasons that called for a particularly high level of protection for the consumer. First, in many cases, there was a considerable amount of money involved and long-term commitments in agreements had the potential to seriously affect consumer well-being and autonomy. Secondly, consumers lacked the experience to judge the impact of complex credit contracts, something which only became apparent after some time.[21]

In order to prevent any abuse by financial institutions and consumer over-indebtedness, the European Community and Member States gradually adopted legislative measures.[22] The Community regulated consumer credit for the first time through the Consumer Credit Directive 87/102, in 1987.[23] The 1987 directive aimed at promoting competition and greater transparency in contractual clauses and at providing detailed information on the costs and conditions of consumer credit. The information requirement consisted

[18] J. Niemi-Kiesiläinen, I. Ramsay, & W. Whitford (eds), *Consumer Bankruptcy in Global Perspective* (Oxford: Hart Publishing, 2003), p. 2.

[19] Niemi-Kiesiläinen, Ramsay, & Whitford (eds), *Consumer Bankruptcy in Global Perspective* (n 18), p. 2.

[20] Howells, 'Whose Responsibility to Plan for Furture Changes in Circumstances' (n 16), p. 438.

[21] See P. Rott, 'Consumer Credit', in H.-W. Micklitz, N. Reich, & P. Rott, *Understanding EU Consumer Law* (Antwerp: Intersentia, 2009), pp. 177–212.

[22] See e.g. the French Act no. 78-22, 10 January 1978, concerning the information and protection of consumers in certain credit operations.

[23] Council Directive 87/102/EEC concerning consumer credit OJ [1987] L042, p. 48. This was later complemented by other Acts and culminated in the adoption of a new Directive 2008/48/EC of 23 April 2008 on credit agreements for consumers repealing Council Directive 87/102/EEC.

of establishing strict rules to ensure that the signing of the contractual agreement would be treated with due seriousness, drawing the consumer's attention to the economic and legal contents of the operation. These information conditions have influenced the contract law of the Member States, standardizing the rules on the rights of withdrawal and the remedies available for private individuals.

While the directive harmonized national measures in the field of consumer credit, it also contained a 'minimum-harmonization formula'. As we saw in Chapter 2, this meant that Member States were still allowed to provide a higher level of consumer protection, if they decided that this was necessary.[24] As a result, most Member States had gone far beyond the minimum EU standards.[25]

Owing to the fast development of the credit sector, the EU developed a new consumer credit proposal in 2002.[26] The reason was that markets had, by then, changed considerably, requiring an extension of the legal scope to cover new types of payments. Furthermore, Member States had included new types of credit agreements in their legislation, with provisions often more detailed and stringent than those contained in the directive itself. These different provisions, for example in terms of the periods of time for a withdrawal or for the cancellation of a contract, had led to a fragmentation of the market,[27] imposing legal challenges on firms that wanted to offer products in different Member States.[28]

Aimed at reducing market fragmentation, the first proposal of the new directive in 2002 moved away from the initial minimum-harmonization trend and opted for a maximum harmonization of consumer credit provisions.[29]

[24] N. Reich and H.-W. Micklitz, *Europäisches Verbraucherrecht*, 4th edn (Baden-Baden: Nomos, 2003), p. 45; G. Howells & T. Wilhelmsson, *EC Consumer Law* (Aldershot: Dartmouth Publishing, 1997), pp. 315–20; N. Reich.

[25] S. Weatherill, *EU Consumer Law and Policy* (Cheltenham: Edward Elgar Publishing, 2005), p. 88.

[26] COM/2002/443 Proposal for a Directive of the European Parliament and the Council on the harmonisation of the laws, regulations and administrative provisions of the Member States concerning credit for consumers, Brussels, 11.9.2002.

[27] More on the credit proposal in K. Nemeth & H. Ortner, 'The Proposal for a New Directive concerning Credit for Consumers', (2003) 4 *German L. J.*, pp. 801–13.

[28] COM/2002/443 Proposal for a Directive of the European Parliament and the Council on the harmonisation of the laws, regulations and administrative provisions of the Member States concerning credit for consumers, Brussels, 11.9.2002. See also the EESC Opinion of 07/17/2003, OJ, C/2003/234.

[29] COM/2002/443 Proposal for a Directive of the European Parliament and the Council on the harmonisation of the laws, regulations and administrative provisions of the Member States concerning credit for consumers, presented by the Commission Brussels, 11.9.2002.

In practice, this meant that Member States would have been prohibited from maintaining stricter rules in the area covered by the directive.

An important shortcoming of this full-harmonization strategy was its failure to capture the variety of financial needs and resources of consumers in different Member States. As mentioned earlier, a large number of scholars have, criticized the full-harmonization trend.[30] This would leave Member States without sufficient autonomy to determine their own consumer policy and learn from each other through a cooperative process.[31] Full harmonization might also be too inflexible, hindering Member States from introducing new legislation promptly to address developments in national consumer credit markets.[32] These problems were soon recognized by the Commission and so the draft directive was modified and made more flexible, allowing Member States, in some cases, to provide higher protection. In particular, the scope of the draft directive was reduced, with the result that most of the harmonized rules related to the provisions of contractual and pre-contractual information.

The draft directive also intended to extend the scope of its 1987 predecessor (which applied only to credit agreements) to include guarantors, stating that they should be provided with a minimum amount of information and protection, similar to that enjoyed by the consumer. Moreover, the proposal focused on enhanced market stability by putting in place a set of provisions on responsible lending, obligatory consultation of databases, and providing information and protection both when the credit agreement is concluded and during its performance. After six years of debate, the new directive on credit agreements for consumers was finally adopted on 7 April 2008 and became effective on 21 June 2008.[33] In the final version, several protective provisions

[30] See chapter 2 of this book. See also T. Wilhelmsson, 'The Legal, the Cultural and the Political—Conclusions from Different Perspectives on Harmonisation of European Contract Law', (2002) *Eur Bus. L. Rev.*, p. 541; U. Reifner, *Ausgewählte Auszüge aus Normen und Begründung aus der Sicht des Verbraucherschutzes des Geänderten Vorschlags für eine Richtlinie über Verbraucherkreditverträge und zur Änderung der Richtlinie 93/13/EWG des Rates, 7.10.2005 COM (2005) 483* (Hamburg: Institut für Finanzdienstleistung e.V., 2005), p. 1 *et seq*; for a different view, see Nemeth & Ortner, 'The Proposal for a New Directive concerning Credit for Consumers' (n 27), pp. 809–12.

[31] See more on this debate in chapter 2 of this book.

[32] House of Lords, European Union Committee, 13th Report of Session 2005–06, Proposed EU Consumer Credit Harmonisation Directive, Paper 37, p. 8.

[33] Directive 2008/48/EC of 23 April 2008 on Credit Agreements for Consumers, OJ L 133/66-92, 22.5.2008.

were reduced or dropped (among them, that on guarantors' protection and some aspects on responsible lending).[34] However, the complex drafting process of the directive at least demonstrates that new concerns and objectives are now present in the policy debate, and that EU consumer law may be evolving from the narrow market-building approach of its beginnings.

2.2. *The 2008 Credit Agreements Directive and its focus on information*

A main objective of the new directive is to promote a single credit market through legal harmonization, on the basis of Article 114 TFEU (ex Article 95 EC). The directive aims to increase cross-border services and to provide a high level of consumer protection, focusing on transparency and consumer rights.[35] The biggest innovations are the harmonized rules concerning the early repayment of credit, the standardized information provided to consumers, and the consumer's right to withdraw within 14 days, as well as responsible lending to prevent over-indebtedness.

The scope of the directive is set out in Article 2. The directive applies generally to all credit agreements ranging from 200 Euros to 75,000 Euros, with the exception of the exclusions under Article 2(2). Credit agreements that are exempted include, for instance, (a) mortgages; (d) most of the leasing agreements; (e) credit agreements in the form of an overdraft facility, and where the credit has to be repaid within one month; (f) credit agreements where the credit is granted free of interest or charges; and (g) credit granted by employers to the employees.

Article 3(c) of the directive offers a definition of credit agreement as 'an agreement whereby a creditor grants or promises to grant to a consumer credit in the form of deferred payment, loan or other similar financial accommodation'. The consumer is described as 'a natural person who, in transactions covered by this Directive, is acting for purposes which are outside his trade, business or profession' (Article 3(a)). In turn, Article 3(b) defines creditors as a natural or legal person who grants or promises to grant credit in the course of his profession.

The 2008 directive features three types of instruments that aim to protect consumers and to increase market transparency: (1) information requirements; (2) a standard method of cost calculation; and (3) specific rights. They

[34] Rott, 'Consumer Credit' (n 21).

[35] See preliminary notes of the new Credit Agreements Directive, notes 4–9 and Art. 1 of this directive.

are meant to balance the asymmetrical contractual position of the consumer in relation to the professional in the market. In particular, the disequilibrium in knowledge and bargaining power is compensated through increased information and additional reflection time for consumers after a contract has been agreed.[36]

First, the directive is based on the main regulatory technique of 'information disclosure' for consumers. This means that detailed information has to be provided to the consumer at different stages of the pre-contractual and contractual process. Already at the early stage of the credit advertising of a particular interest rate, standard information must be included on credit conditions, such as maximum amount, fees, and annual percentage rate of charges (Article 4). Later, at the pre-contractual stage, Articles 5 and 6 oblige the creditor to provide detailed information on the conditions of the loan before the transaction of the final credit agreement.[37] This information should be provided to consumers well in advance, so that they have time to compare the different options available (Article 5(1)). Furthermore, it has to be made available on a 'durable medium' and by means of a 'Standard European Consumer Credit Information' form (included in Annex II of the directive). The information required includes inter alia (a) the type of credit; (b) the identity and address of the creditor; (c–d) the total amount and duration of the credit; (g) the annual percentage rate of charge and the total amount payable; and (h) the amount, number, and frequency of payments to be made by the consumer (Article 5(1)).[38] Finally, at the contractual stage, key information must be included in the actual credit agreement, which is mentioned in Article 10. The objective is to render the consumer aware of the total cost, risks, and conditions, which is facilitated by the use of standard agreements, as well as to eliminate hidden costs or unfair business practices.

Secondly, this objective is also promoted by the use of a harmonized Annual Percentage Rate of Charge (APR), which should facilitate comparison and better evaluation of credit costs. Article 19 of the directive defines the APR as a unified calculation method of charges, which provides the consumer with a simple cost indicator, allowing quick and simple comparison of different

[36] A cooling-off period gives consumers the possibility to reflect on their decision and to withdraw from the contract within 14 days; Weatherill, *EU Consumer Law and Policy* (n 25), p. 84.

[37] Directive 2008/48/EC of 23 April 2008 on credit agreements for consumers, OJ L 133/66, 22.5.2008.

[38] Other important information requirements concern (m) a warning on the consequences of payments; (o) the right of early repayment; and (r) the right to be supplied with a copy of the draft credit agreement (Art. 5(1)).

credit offers. This facilitates comparison of credit conditions, which is clearly beneficial for consumers, and can promote market integration by improving competition.[39]

Thirdly, the directive provides consumers with two key instruments so that they can release themselves from the contract: the right of withdrawal from a credit agreement (Article 14) and the possibility of early repayment, limiting penalty impositions by the provider (Article 16). According to Article 14, the consumer can withdraw from the credit agreement within 14 days of the conclusion of the contract without need of justification. In turn, Article 16 provides the consumer with the option of terminating the agreement through early repayment, conditional on adequate compensation being paid to the creditor. Finally, the directive newly includes a provision to facilitate dispute resolution. Article 24 mentions that Member States should ensure that adequate and effective out-of-court dispute resolution procedures for the settlement of consumer disputes concerning credit agreements are put in place.

Over all, the new directive shows a strong tendency to increase consumer information as a regulatory tool. This will augment consumer financial capability, by helping them to understand and compare different financial services. However, information alone is not sufficient to ensure an adequate level of financial understanding. Various studies have demonstrated that only a small proportion of European consumers possess sufficient financial knowledge.[40] Even when information is provided, lack of financial experience and complex contractual terms often impede an adequate assessment of the credit agreement and of the financial transaction. Thus, it is essential to improve the financial literacy of consumers[41] through education and adequate advice. The importance of raising financial education and awareness has been highlighted by a number of public and international institutions, including the OECD, which will be discussed later in this chapter.[42]

[39] G. Nicolini, 'A Regulatory Perspective on Consumer Financial Capability', in European Credit Research Institute (ECRI) (ed.), *Consumer Financial Capability, Empowering European Consumers* (Brussels: ECRI, 2006), pp. 78–9.

[40] See also the report of European Credit Research Institute, *Consumer Financial Capability: Empowering European Consumers* (n 39), pp. 1 and 78–90; see OECD study: *Improving Financial Literacy: Analysis of Issues and Policies* (Paris: OECD, 2005).

[41] See G. Pearson, 'Financial Literacy and the Creation of the Financial Citizen', in M. Kelly-Louw, J. Nehf, & P. Rott (eds), *The Future of Consumer Credit Regulation, Creative Approaches to Emerging Problems (Markets and the Law)* (Aldershot: Ashgate Publishing, 2008), pp. 3–29.

[42] See section 4.2 of this chapter.

Interestingly, the new EU directive introduces, to some degree, a shift of responsibility, imposing on the lender an obligation to provide 'responsible credit'. This includes the duty to advise the consumer adequately not withstanding the potential conflict of interest between the consumer and the lender, and can be considered one way to enhance financial literacy.

2.3. *Responsible lending*

As seen above, an important complement to consumer financial capability is responsible lending by the banking sector. The 2008–09 financial crisis has demonstrated that aggressive and risky lending behaviour causes damage to markets, companies, and to society as a whole. Thus, for the good of the market, not only should the financial capability of consumers be improved, but firms should also be given the responsibility of evaluating the borrower's creditworthiness, in order to prevent over-indebtedness. Concrete legislative action in this sense was missing from EU provisions until 2002, when the Commission proposed the aforementioned draft directive,[43] where the concept of 'responsible credit' was introduced.[44] 'Responsible credit' imposed on banks (and other credit providers) an obligation to assess the applicant not only on his or her ability to repay a specific loan, but from a broader financial soundness perspective.[45] This would, for example, involve lenders checking a central database of late payments before agreeing to supply further credit.[46]

Owing to pressure from financial institutions, the 2004 draft that followed was, however, less ambitious. The principle of responsible lending only became applicable to pre-contractual disclosure of information.[47] Lenders were still obliged to evaluate the creditworthiness of consumers by asking them certain information, and by consulting databases on the credit history

[43] Proposal for a Directive of the European Parliament and the Council on the harmonisation of the laws, regulations and administrative provisions of the Member States concerning credit for consumers, COM/2002/443, Brussels, 11.9.2002.

[44] N. Didier, 'Evaluation of the Consumer's Financial Capacity', in European Credit Research Institute (ECRI) (ed.), *Consumer Financial Capability: Empowering European Consumers* (Brussels: ECRI, 2006).

[45] In this context, the consumer had to provide reliable information to the creditor. Article 31, preamble note 29, and the explanatory memorandum of the draft directive; more in Didier, 'Evaluation of the Consumer's Financial Capacity' (n 44), p. 93.

[46] Article 9 and the explanatory memorandum of the draft Consumer Credit directive of 2002, COM/2002/443, presented by the Commission.

[47] Amended proposal for a Directive on the harmonisation of the laws, regulations and administrative provisions of the Member States concerning credit for consumers, COM(2004) 747 final, 2002/0222 (COD), Brussels, 28.10.2004.

of the consumer in question. However, no particular sanctions were determined in the case of non-compliance by the creditor.[48]

This approach to responsible lending, which remained largely unchanged in the final 2008 Consumer Agreements Directive,[49] is based upon two pillars: (1) the obligation to provide pre-contractual information and advice on the advantages and disadvantages of a product; and (2) the assessment of the creditworthiness of the consumer.

As for (1), the 2008 directive's preliminary remark, note 24 states that 'the consumer needs to be given comprehensive information before he concludes the credit agreement', placing on the creditor the burden of providing such information and, except in some cases,[50] on the intermediary too. Preliminary remark 26 then affirms 'that creditors should not engage in irresponsible lending and give out credits without prior assessment of creditworthiness, and the Member States should enact the necessary supervision to avoid such behaviour and should determine the necessary means to sanction creditors in the event of their doing so'.

Pillar (2), is established by Article 8 of the directive, entitled 'Obligation to assess the creditworthiness of the consumer'. According to this provision, Member States are to ensure that 'before the conclusion of the credit agreement, the creditor assesses the consumer's creditworthiness on the basis of sufficient information, where appropriate obtained from the consumer and, where necessary, on the basis of a consultation of the relevant database'.

Furthermore, in the case of a change in the amount of credit, the creditor has to update the financial information on the consumer and re-evaluate his or her creditworthiness (Article 8(2)). Finally, the directive stipulates that creditors should receive non-discriminatory access to databases concerning consumers in a Member State in which they are not established (Article 9(1)).

These measures are an important initial step in the direction of responsible lending, placing greater responsibility on credit providers for checking the creditworthiness of consumers and for informing them adequately. However, according to some scholars, these legal innovations might be of limited use for two main reasons. On the one hand, the directive does not provide specific

[48] Amended proposal for a Directive concerning credit for consumers, COM (2004) 747 final, 2002/0222 (COD), Brussels, 28.10.2004.

[49] Directive 2008/48/EC on credit agreements for consumers, OJ L 133/66, 22.5.2008.

[50] These cases are those where 'suppliers of goods and services act as credit intermediaries in an ancillary capacity', i.e. when 'their activity as credit intermediaries is not the main purpose of their trade, business or profession'.

sanctions in the event of non-compliance. On the other, the compulsory check on creditworthiness could have a counterproductive effect by paradoxically excluding from credit the poorest individuals, who are those most in need of it.[51]

2.4. *Social justice debates*

This subsection places consumer credit within the wider social justice debate in contract law, which highlights the limitations of information as the sole tool to achieve consumer protection. Consumer credit forms part of contract law, which is based upon the basic, and in a sense conflicting, principles of autonomy and solidarity. While liberalism is often associated with contractual freedom, information, and the binding force of the contract, solidarity is linked with the idea of fairness, the duty of good faith, as well as compulsory provisions to protect the weaker party.[52]

The new 2008 directive on credit agreements is a clear advance in protecting consumers by increasing the amount of information that the lender has to provide in credit agreements. In this regard, the directive seems inspired by the liberal proponents who, in general, prefer information provisions to substantive mandatory law, as a lighter form of intervention.[53] In particular, some scholars argue that an under-estimation of the consumer's own abilities to make an adequate judgement leads to overprotective regulation and might encourage careless behaviour.[54] According to them, social protection of consumers creates an unnecessary financial burden for society, which is ultimately paid by the consumer.[55]

However, behavioural economics has shown that consumers are not always able to take rational decisions, and are often manipulated by advertising.[56]

[51] See e.g. U. Reifner, 'Verantwortungsvolle Kreditvergabe im europäischen Recht', in L. Thévenoz & N. Reich (eds), *Liber amicorum Bernd Stauder, Droit de la Consommation/Konsumentenrecht/Consumer Law* (Baden-Baden/Zurich: Nomos/Schulthess, 2006), pp. 383–403.

[52] F. Nicola & U. Mattei, 'A Social Dimension in European Private Law? The Call for Setting a Progressive Agenda', (2006) 41 *New England L. Rev.*, pp. 1–66; Study Group on Social Justice in European Private Law, 'Social Justice in European Contract Law: A Manifesto', (2004) 10 *Eur. L. J.*, p. 653.

[53] See S. Grundmann, 'Information, Party Autonomy and Economic Agents in European Contract Law', (2002) 39 *CML Rev.*, p. 269.

[54] See e.g. H. Kötz & A. Flessner, *European Contract Law, Vol. 1: Formation, Validity, and Content of Contracts; Contract and Third Parties* (Oxford: Clarendon Press, 1998), p. 129; and T. Hartlief, 'Freedom and Protection in Contemporary Contract Law', (2004) 27 *J. Consumer Policy*, pp. 258 *et seq.*

[55] Kötz & Flessner, *European Contract Law, Vol. 1: Formation, Validity, and Content of Contracts; Contract and Third Parties* (n 54), p. 129.

[56] See C. Sunstein (ed.), *Behavioural Law and Economics* (Cambridge: CUP, 2000). On producer manipulation of irrationalities in consumer information processing, see J.D. Hanson & D.A.

Furthermore, information per se may not help consumers as too much information may lead to 'information overload', decreasing the ability of consumers to make rational choices. Hence, special attention should be given to the way information is presented and received, not just to the amount of it,[57] requiring, for example, that contractual terms are drafted in plain and understandable language.

This argument has been extended further by some scholars who have noted that information disclosure does not provide a coherent standard of fairness.[58] It also does not take account of a social dimension in contract law.[59] If consumers fail to behave in an alert and rational manner, regulatory intervention based upon information disclosure may not yield the intended benefits.[60] Particularly vulnerable groups in society, such as elderly people or uneducated consumers, do not meet the regulator's model of an attentive consumer.

However, the right to information and the right to fair contractual conditions are complementary rather than alternative. Adequate information and fairness could constitute two pillars of a consumer credit regulation,[61] able to re-establish an equitable equilibrium between contractual parties,[62] and thus promoting consumer participation in financial markets.[63]

The concept of capability is ideally placed to realize this synthesis. Deakin arrives at similar conclusions for labour law, where he proposes the idea of

Kuysar, 'Taking Behavioralism Seriously: Some Evidence of Market Manipulation', (1999) 112 *Harv. L. Rev.*, p. 1420.

[57] Consumers lack knowledge of their rights and often do not read or understand the small print in contracts; see the study of E. Kempson, S. Collard, & N. Moore, 'Measuring Financial Capability: An Exploratory Study for the Financial Services Authority', in ECRI, *Consumer Financial Capability: Empowering European Consumers* (Brussels: ECRI, 2006), pp. 56–67.

[58] Howells & Wilhelmsson, *EC Consumer Law* (n 24); Howells & Wilhelmsson, 'Private Law in the EU: Harmonized or Fragmented Europeanization?', (2002) 10 *Eur. Rev. Private Law*, p. 77; Weatherill (n 25), p. 84.

[59] U. Mattei & F.G. Nicola, 'A "Social Dimension" in European Private Law? The Call for Setting a Progressive Agenda', (2007) 7 *Global Jurist* (Frontiers); G. Alpa, 'New Perspectives in the Protection of Consumers: A General Overview and some Criticism on Financial Services', (2005) 16 *Eur. Bus. L. Rev.*, p. 722.

[60] See e.g. G. Howells, 'The Potential and Limits of Consumer Empowerment by Information', (2005) 32 *J. Law and Society*, pp. 349–70.

[61] Reich and Micklitz, *Europäisches Verbraucherrecht* (n 24), p. 45.

[62] S. Deakin, '"Capacitas": Contract Law and the Institutional Pre-conditions of a Market Economy', (2006) 3 *Eur Rev. Contract Law*, pp. 319–28; M. Hesselink, 'Capacity and Capability in European Contract Law', AMCLE WP No. 2005-09.

[63] See ECRI, *Consumer Financial Capability: Empowering European Consumers* (Brussels: ECRI, 2006).

contract 'capacity', defined as 'a status conferred by law for the purpose of empowering the holder to participate in the operations of the market economy'.[64] Strengthening capabilities would not only enhance consumer information, an objective already considered by the 2008 directive, but could also address the issues of unfair contractual terms and over-indebtedness from a broader perspective: that is, by seeing them as social justice issues—something which is instead beyond the scope of the directive. The next sections will explore whether fundamental rights and alternative measures might help to move in this direction.

3. Fundamental Rights, Social Principles, and Non-Discrimination

The Credit Agreements Directive represents an improvement in information requirements and is concerned with aspects of responsible lending. However, it does not address related social issues and is limited in scope. For example, it does not provide protection to vulnerable contractual parties, such as non-professional guarantors for consumer credit.

Given these limitations, it is important to establish whether the progressive influence of constitutional and fundamental rights in Europe may lead to more extensive protection. In particular, will these provisions help protect weaker contractual parties, by promoting fair business practices or specific fundamental rights values, thus going beyond an information-focused approach?[65]

Signs that this is starting to happen are emerging in the national case law.[66] For example, as we have seen previously, a jurisprudential trend has developed in Germany whereby constitutional principles are applied in credit guarantee disputes in order to protect weaker contractual parties. Similarly, there are reasons to believe that such a trend may be developing at the EU level.

[64] S. Deakin, "Capacitas" (n 62), p. 319.

[65] T. Wilhelmsson, 'The Ethical Pluralism of Late Modern Europe and Codification of European Contract Law' in J. Smits, *The Need for a European Contract Law: Empirical and Legal Perspectives* (Groningen: Europa Law Publishing, 2005), p. 145; Hesselink, 'European Contract Law' (n 6), pp. 323 *et seq*.

[66] Cherednychenko, *Fundamental Rights, Contract Law and the Protection of the Weaker Party, A Comparative Analysis of the Constitutionalisation of Contract Law, with Emphasis on Risky Financial Transactions* (n 2).

Certain provisions of the Charter of Fundamental Rights can be seen as steps in this direction; moreover, as exemplified by a recent case before the ECJ that we will examine later on, fundamental rights may strengthen general values such as that of non-discrimination.

3.1. *The role of the Charter*

The Charter of Fundamental Rights may influence financial consumer protection in a number of ways, some of which are not specific to consumer law but highlighted here as relevant examples. First, an increasing number of financial services directives which deal with consumer issues now expressly refer to fundamental rights. Second, the Charter contains several provisions that may directly affect EU policy or the reasoning of the Court in matters of financial services. Third and closely related to the previous points, the Charter may function as a yardstick to assess the validity of legislative acts, directly influencing financial regulation.

The first role is exemplified by the aforementioned 2008 directive on credit agreements, whose preamble explicitly refers to the Charter, by stating that the directive respects fundamental rights and observes the principles recognized by the Charter. Paragraph 45 of the preamble is more specific as it stipulates that 'the Directive seeks to ensure full respect for the rules on protection of personal data, the right to property, non-discrimination, protection of family and professional life, and consumer protection *pursuant to the Charter*' (emphasis added).[67] This shows that the Charter has influenced EU financial legislation, at least formally, requiring compliance with its standards, and being expressly and increasingly referred to. As for the second role, the Charter itself includes a number of provisions that may be relevant for financial consumer protection. We analyze some of these provisions, which are scattered around the Charter.

Article 38 of the Charter, which has already been mentioned in Chapter 3, is a key provision regarding consumer law, because it stipulates that 'Union policies shall ensure a high level of consumer protection'. This may influence EU policies in financial matters to take account of consumer interests.[68] The recent Consumer Agenda of 2012 expressly mentions the objective to develop 'a systematic approach to integrating consumer interests into all

[67] OJ L 133/66-92, 22.5.2008.

[68] See also Institute for Financial Services, Fundamental Rights and Consumer Credit, *Are these Rights still Taken Seriously in the European Credit Society?* (2006).

relevant policies' focusing in particular on financial consumer protection.[69] The Agenda contains a number of concrete actions for the Union. Some that are particularly noteworthy include: a recommendation to combat unfair practices in the financial services sector, and a commitment to evaluate the implementation of the Consumer Credit Directive, to assess whether this needs a revision, in particular regarding what concerns the protection of vulnerable consumers. Furthermore, it mentions the provision of basic bank accounts as a measure to prevent financial and social exclusion. This has been followed up by a recent legislative initiative which proposed, among other things, to promote this type of financial service.[70] Interestingly, the Agenda refers precisely to Article 38 of the Charter, and to Article 12 TFEU, thus clarifying the source of its inspiration.[71]

Another important provision of the Charter is Article 33, which states that 'The family shall enjoy legal, economic and social protection'. This provision may, for example, be applied, together with other relevant binding provisions, to protect family members who act as consumer credit guarantors for a relative, if they have received misleading information by a financial institution. As will be seen in the next subsections, a growing number of such cases have emerged in Member States where individuals have acted as financial guarantors for their relatives, sometimes without having received proper information from the bank regarding the related risks.

The last article of the Charter to be considered here is Article 36 concerning access to services of general economic interest. This provision states that 'The Union recognises and respects access to services of general economic interest as provided for in national laws and practices, in accordance with the Treaty establishing the European Community, in order to promote the social and territorial cohesion of the Union'. The reason why this is relevant in our context is that basic financial services are increasingly acknowledged in Member States as services of general interest, so such a provision may promote a stronger focus on financial inclusion. This is in line with the aforementioned Consumer Agenda, which also expressly recognizes financial

[69] Communication from the Commission, A European Consumer Agenda—Boosting confidence and growth, COM(2012) 225 final, 22.5.2012, Brussels.

[70] Proposal for a Directive on the comparability of fees related to payment accounts, payment account switching and access to payment accounts with basic features, COM(2013)0266 final - 2013/0139 (COD).

[71] Communication from the Commission, A European Consumer Agenda - Boosting confidence and growth, COM(2012) 225 final, 22.5.2012, Brussels.

services as essential services for consumers. As we saw before and as we will discuss in more depth later, the Union is starting to enquire into how the financial inclusion of consumers may be improved.[72]

A third role that the Charter may play in financial consumer protection is that of a yardstick to examine the legality of specific measures. This is best illustrated by the recent *Test-Achats* case, discussed at more length later on, where the ECJ referred inter alia to Article 21 of the Charter, which forbids discrimination. This provision was used by the Court as part of the assessment of the validity of secondary law in the insurance sector, and eventually led to an interpretation which was favourable to the consumer organization that brought the claim.

The following subsections describe the influence that constitutional rights can have on financial services agreements in specific Member States, to assess whether the Charter might have a similar effect.

3.2. *Constitutional principles in financial guarantor cases*

Constitutional principles are increasingly used in contract cases to protect 'weaker parties' from unfair agreements. This has been particularly visible in the so-called 'guarantor (or suretyships) cases', a recent series of judgments across several EU countries, where, in particular, the principles of solidarity, autonomy, good faith, or morality have been invoked to free individuals from burdensome guarantee contracts.[73] In these cases, the fact that, for example, a relative had exerted undue influence over a person to sign a contract, or the guarantor had not been duly informed about the consequences of the guarantee contract played an important role in allowing the guarantor to withdraw from her (or his) contractual obligations.[74] The judge plays an important role to determine a balanced approach, between the creditor's contractual autonomy and the guarantor's rights of protection and autonomy.

A seminal case in this context is the German suretyship (*Bürgschaft*) case[75] already partially discussed in Chapter 3, which revolved around the validity of a personal guarantee given by a 21-year-old daughter in favour of her father's

[72] See the report financed by and prepared for the European Commission and drafted by Réseau Financement Alternatif, *Financial Services Provision and Prevention of Financial Exclusion* (2008).

[73] See M. Hesselink, 'The Horizontal Effect of Social Rights in European Contract Law', in *Europa e diritto privato* (Milan: Giuffré Editore, 2003), p. 4.

[74] Howells (n 16), pp. 450 *et seq.*

[75] BVerfG 19 October 1993, BVerfGE 89, 214.

business debt.[76] As we saw, the daughter was allowed to withdraw from her contractual obligations as a guarantor, because she had, inter alia, not been properly informed by the bank. In this case, the constitutional principles of private autonomy and of the social state played an important role. Indeed, while the German Constitutional Court recognized that contracts must usually be upheld according to the constitutional right of private autonomy guaranteed by Article 2(1) German Grundgesetz (GG),[77] in particular circumstances the civil courts have an obligation to intervene in favour of the weaker party based upon the constitutional right of private autonomy (Article 2(1) GG) and the principle of the social state (Articles 20(1) and 28(1) GG).[78] Such an intervention is required if a contract presents a substantial structural imbalance of bargaining power and turns out to be exceptionally onerous for the weaker party.[79] In the present case, the contractual imbalance existed because the financial risk in relation to the guarantee was exceptionally high and did not provide any economic benefit to the daughter. In addition, this risk was very difficult to estimate, in particular for the 21-year-old daughter, who did not benefit from a professional education and because the contract lacked clear information on significant additional costs related to the guarantee, such as information on credit interests. In this context, exact information by the bank on the financial implications of the contract would have been of particular importance. However, the bank had failed to provide information about the risk relating to the surety and in contrast downplayed the obligation resulting from the contract.

As mentioned, the German *Bürgschaft* case was only one of several cases resolved in favour of guarantors in Member States including France, the UK, and the Netherlands. Despite reaching similar conclusions, the courts of the different countries followed different models.[80] Comparative legal studies[81] show that UK and Dutch courts based their judgments mostly on private law principles, such as on the duty to inform and the principle of good faith, to

[76] BVerfG 19 October 1993, BVerfGE 89, 214; see also Howells (n 16), p. 450.

[77] BVerfG 19 October 1993, BVerfGE 89, 214.

[78] Also important were general clauses of good morals (§ 138(1)) and good faith (§ 242) of the German Civil Code.

[79] BVerfG 19 October1993, BVerfGE 89, 214.

[80] See further Cherednychenko (n 2), p. 231; see A. Colombi Ciacchi, 'Protection from Unfair Suretyships', in S. Vogenauer & S. Weatherill, *The Harmonisation of European Contract Law* (Oxford: Hart Publishing, 2006), p. 205.

[81] See further Cherednychenko (n 2), p. 231; see Colombi Ciacchi, 'Protection from Unfair Suretyships' (n 80), p. 205.

protect the weaker party in contract law.[82] German and French courts instead based their decisions mainly on constitutional principles or specific legislative provisions respectively, recognizing the invalidity of significant disproportionate contractual obligations, thus granting to the weaker party a higher level of protection.[83]

The constitutional case law is particularly interesting as an inspiration in the EU context. As we have seen before, the EU Charter grants special legal, economic, and social protection to the family (Article 33) and mentions consumer protection (Article 38), which may also serve as a basis for such a higher-level protection of weaker parties in contractual disputes. This might, however, take some time, considering also that some contrasting signs have emerged from former judgments of the ECJ (which were, however, delivered before the adoption of the Charter), as we will discuss in the next subsection.

3.3. *Protection of guarantors by the ECJ*

The new 2008 directive on credit agreements discussed above does not mention the protection of consumer guarantors and the literature has extensively debated whether this directive (and its predecessor) might be applicable to consumer guarantors.[84] Two related cases suggest that the answer is likely to be negative.

In *Dietzinger* (1998), a case similar to the German guarantee case discussed in subsection 3.2, the ECJ showed judicial self-restraint and decided that a consumer directive which potentially could have protected a guarantor was not applicable.[85] Mr Dietzinger, who was without a regular income, had provided a guarantee for his parents' business debts. He tried to free himself of the contractual obligation by arguing that the guarantee had been signed away from business premises, and that he had not acted rationally. Moreover, he maintained that he had not been informed of his right of withdrawal, basing his claim on the Doorstep Selling Directive 85/577, implemented by the German law. The ECJ, however, ruled that the directive was not applicable in

[82] O. Cherednychenko, 'The Constitutionalization of Contract Law: Something New under the Sun?', (2004) 8 *Electronic J. of Comparative Law*, pp. 10 *et seq*.

[83] See more in A. Colombi Ciacchi, 'The Constitutionalisation of European Contract Law: Judicial Convergence and Social Justice', (2006) 2 *Eur. Rev. Contract Law*, pp. 167–80; Cherednychenko, 'Constitutionalization of Contract Law' (n 82), pp. 4 *et seq*.

[84] See e.g. Colombi Ciacchi (n 80), p. 205.

[85] Case C-45/96, *Bayerische Hypotheken- und Wechselbank AG v Edgar Dietzinger* [1998] ECR I-1199.

this case. Indeed, it stated that, even if a guarantee contract has been concluded by a person who is not acting in the course of his or her profession, it still does not fall within the scope of the directive if the guaranteed debt itself has been contracted by another person who is acting in the course of his or her profession.

Thus, the ECJ expressed a formal opinion on the applicability of the directive, without entering into the merits of the contract itself. This attitude of the Court, which is plainly different from that of the German court mentioned in the previous subsection, was criticized by a number of scholars.[86] On the other hand it could be argued that the ECJ lacked a precise legal reference on which it could have reached a different conclusion, such as the basis which exists for courts in Germany under its national law.

An even stronger suggestion that the 2008 directive on credit agreements will *not* protect guarantors comes from the *Berliner Kindl Brauerei AG v Siegert* case (2000). Here, the ECJ explicitly negated the applicability of the predecessor of the 2008 directive (the Consumer Credit Directive 87/102) to a contract of guarantee for the repayment of a credit.[87] A German brewery (the Berliner Kindl Brauerei—BKB) had granted a loan to a principal debtor for the opening of a restaurant. In turn Mr Siegert, a private citizen, acted as a surety to BKB for the repayment of the loan, acting outside his trade or profession. When he tried to withdraw from the contract, Mr Siegert argued that he had validly cancelled the contract pursuant to the German Consumer Credit Law (*Verbraucherkreditgesetz* 1990), which had implemented the former Consumer Credit Directive 87/102. The case was referred by the Potsdam Court to the ECJ for a preliminary ruling and the ECJ ruled that the directive does not cover a contract of guarantee for repayment of credit.[88] In particular, the ECJ argued that the exclusion of the guarantor from the directive could be inferred, because it aims to provide information to the debtor on the conditions and effects of the agreement, but barely mentions the guarantors and does not concern itself with their protection.

These cases show that the non-professional guarantor did not benefit from specific protection in a number of consumer laws.[89] However, these judgments took place before the adoption of the Charter in 2000 and were limited

[86] For criticism, see O. Gerstenberg, 'Private Law and the New European Constitutional Settlement', (2004) 10 *Eur. L. J.*, p. 766, at 785; however, another view is defended by Joerges, who welcomes this development, as it enables diverse legal approaches; see Ch. Joerges, 'Interactive Adjudication in the Europeanization Process? A Demanding Perspective and a Modest Example', (2000) 8 *Eur. Rev. Private Law*, pp. 1–16.

[87] Case C-208/98, *Berliner Kindl Brauerei* [2000] ECR I-1741.

[88] Case C-208/98, *Berliner Kindl Brauerei* [2000] ECR I-1741, paras 22 and 26–7.

[89] Reich & Micklitz (n 24), p. 740.

because of the restrictive scope of the relevant directive. More recent ECJ jurisprudence on consumer credit and doorstep selling already puts more emphasis on the protection of the consumer as the weaker party, albeit without referring to the Charter.[90] It seems likely that, as time goes by, the Charter will play a growing role in consumer protection. As we have seen in previous chapters, fundamental rights have increasingly been recognized in the EU, reaching binding status, and have been referred to by the ECJ more regularly since the adoption of the Lisbon Treaty.

In addition to this, fundamental rights may play an important role in strengthening specific principles or values in the financial services field. This can occur in a different context and way than in the cases we have just seen, as will be shown in the next section.

3.4. *The fundamental right of non-discrimination*

In the *Test-Achats* case the ECJ had to determine whether it is compatible with fundamental rights to use gender as a factor to assess insurance risks.[91] This high-profile case raised strong reactions by scholars and by representatives of the insurance sector, and had a significant impact on EU regulation regarding non-discrimination.[92]

The case concerned Directive 2004/113/EC, which forbids discrimination based on gender in the access to and supply of goods and services. In particular, the directive prohibits the use of gender as a factor in calculating an insurance premium and benefits in insurance contracts. However, one exception was included in Article 5(2), permitting the taking into account of gender differences, if this was a determinant risk factor, whose influence could be substantiated by relevant and accurate data.

This case was initiated in 2008 by a Belgian consumer organization (*Association Belge des Consommateurs Test-Achats*) and two individuals who lodged an action for the annulment of a Belgian law[93] transposing the aforementioned directive,

[90] See e.g. Case C-509/07, *Luigi Scarpelli v NEOS Banca SpA* [2009] ECR I-3311; Case C-481/99, *Heiniger* [2001] ECR I-9945 fn. 28; P. Rott, 'Heininger und die Folgen für das Widerrufsrecht', (2002) *Verbraucher und Recht*, pp. 49–55.

[91] Case C-236/09 *Association Belge des Consommateurs Test-Achats ASBL and Others v Conseil des ministres* 1 March 2011.

[92] See C. Tobler, 'Case C-236/09 *Association Belge des Consommateurs Test-Achats ASBL and Others v Conseil des ministres*' (2011) 48 *CML Rev.*, pp. 2041–60, at 2051.

[93] Law of 21 December 2007 amending Law of 10 May 2007 combating discrimination between men and women with respect to gender in insurance matters (*Moniteur belge* No. 373 of 31 December 2007, p. 66175).

and in particular the exception of Article 5(2). The applicants claimed that the Belgian Law, allowing for such exception, did not comply with the principle of equal treatment for men and women, and infringed in particular Articles 20, 21, and 23 of the Charter of Fundamental Rights, Article 14 ECHR, and Article 26 of the International Covenant on Civil and Political Rights. As a result of the action, the Belgian Constitutional Court submitted a reference for a preliminary ruling to the ECJ asking whether Article 5(2) of the directive was compatible with Article 6(2) EU, and with the principle of equality and non-discrimination guaranteed by that provision.

Advocate General Juliane Kokott applied a fundamental rights analysis to assess the matter. She started by underlining that 'a condition of the lawfulness of all European acts is respect for fundamental and human rights'. The basis for this lies in Article 6 TEU, which states that the Union is founded on the respect for fundamental rights included in the Charter.[94] In particular, equal treatment and non-discrimination between men and women are fundamental rights included in Article 21(1) and Article 23(1) of the Charter. As a consequence, difference in treatment between genders may only be allowed in exceptional cases, when it is clearly demonstrable that gender differences have a material impact on the matter in hand.

Kokott was of the opinion that the exception in the directive was not supported by clear evidence that gender differences have a determinant impact on risks. In fact, many other factors equally influence the evaluation of insurance risks. For instance, life expectancy also depends on the economic and social condition and lifestyle of each insured person.[95] Therefore, Kokott concluded against the validity of Article 5(2). In her view, it was incompatible with EU fundamental rights and the principle of equal treatment for men and women to take the gender of an insured person into account as a risk factor in insurance contracts.[96]

The ECJ followed Kokott's recommendation (albeit applying a slightly different reasoning) as it ruled on 1 May 2011 that the exemption in Article 5(2) of the 2004 directive is invalid.[97] The ECJ started by stressing the core importance

[94] Opinion of Advocate General Kokott on 30 September 2010 in Case C-236/09, *Association Belge des Consommateurs Test-Achats ASBL and Others*, paras 27–8.

[95] See also EU Court of Justice Press Release no. 93/10, 30 September 2010, Advocate General's Opinion in Case C-236/0, *Association Belge des Consommateurs Test-Achats ASBL and Others*.

[96] Opinion of Advocate General Kokott on 30 September 2010 in Case C-236/09, *Association Belge des Consommateurs Test-Achats ASBL and Others v Conseil des ministres* 1 March 2011, paras 69–87.

[97] Case C-236/09, *Association Belge des Consommateurs Test-Achats ASBL and Others v Conseil des ministres* 1 March 2011, not yet reported.

of fundamental rights, referring to Article 6 TEU, which provides that the EU is to respect fundamental rights as guaranteed by the ECHR and as they result from the constitutional traditions common to the Member States. Those fundamental rights are included in the Charter, which has the same legal status as the Treaties.[98] Then the ECJ stated that since Articles 21 and 23 of the Charter are expressly mentioned in Directive 2004/113, the validity of Article 5(2) of that directive must be assessed in the light of these fundamental rights.[99]

The Court then examined a number of Treaty provisions concerning the right to equal treatment for men and women, such as Article 157(1) TFEU on the principle of equal pay for men and women and Article 19(1) TFEU, which confers a competence on the Council to combat discrimination. For the substantive assessment of Article 5(2) of the directive the Court referred to the principle of equal treatment applied in its former jurisprudence requiring 'that comparable situations must not be treated differently, and different situations must not be treated in the same way, unless such treatment is objectively justified'.[100] The comparability of situations must be examined in the light of the concrete subject-matter and bearing in mind the aim of the EU measure under consideration. Thus, in the present case, the Court relied on Directive 2004/113 to assess the comparability of situations in the present case[101] and concluded that in accordance with Articles 21 and 23 of the Charter the directive is based on the premise that 'the respective situations of men and women with regard to insurance premiums and benefits contracted by them are comparable'. Accordingly, the Court found that the exception included in Article 5(2) of the directive, allowing Member States to maintain without temporal limitation an exemption from the rule of unisex premiums and benefits, works against the achievement of the objective of equal treatment. According to the Court this meant that the derogation might continue indefinitely, which would be incompatible with the purpose of Directive 2004/113 and with Articles 21 and 23 of the Charter.[102]

[98] Case C-236/09, *Association Belge des Consommateurs Test-Achats ASBL and Others v Conseil des ministres* 1 March 2011, para. 16, not yet reported.

[99] Case C-236/09, *Association Belge des Consommateurs Test-Achats ASBL and Others v Conseil des ministres* 1 March 2011, para. 17, not yet reported.

[100] Case C-236/09 *Association Belge des Consommateurs Test-Achats ASBL and Others v Conseil des ministres* 1 March 2011, para. 28, not yet reported; see Case C-127/07, *Arcelor Atlantique et Lorraine and Others* [2008] ECR I-9895, para. 23.

[101] See the critical analysis by Tobler, 'Case C-236/09 *Association Belge des Consommateurs Test-Achats ASBL and Others v Conseil des ministres*' (n 92), p. 2051.

[102] See also ECJ Press Release No 12/11, 1 March 2011; Case C-236/09, *Association Belge des Consommateurs Test-Achats ASBL and Others v Conseil des ministres* 1 March 2011, not yet reported.

Therefore, the Court concluded that Article 5(2) of Directive 2004/113 was invalid with effect from 21 December 2012.

This case shows that the Charter plays an increasingly important role in the Court's decision-making. The ECJ affirmed the central function of fundamental rights as a benchmark to assess the validity of secondary law.[103]

As a practical result of the case, insurers had to change their policies, determining policy terms on a gender-neutral basis.[104] Furthermore, the *Test-Achats* case may open the door for a wider fundamental rights and equality debate in financial services contracts. For example, legislative acts and financial services contracts may also be assessed in terms of non-discrimination on the basis of age, disability,[105] or even of social origin (explicitly mentioned in Article 21 of the Charter).

Also of special interest is the background of this judgment. The fact that a consumer organization brought this case, in order to defend broader fundamental rights and general principles such as equality between men and women, may indicate a new trend of consumer activism, based on strategic litigation, to promote specific principles or fundamental values in the EU.[106]

In conclusion, there are clear signs that fundamental rights are increasingly influencing consumer protection in financial services.[107] As argued, the Charter is playing a role in this evolution and may fill, to a certain extent, the gap left by the current financial services legislation, by promoting new policies and new principles which find application in consumer law. However, it is still too early to make clear predictions in this field. The future will largely depend on how active the EU policy-makers will be, and how far the ECJ will go with its interpretation.

4. Financial Capability and Over-Indebtedness

With the reduction of the welfare state, access to financial services has gained new significance as a service of general interest for consumers. For example, access to

[103] Case C-236/09, *Association Belge des Consommateurs Test-Achats ASBL and Others v Conseil des ministres* 1 March 2011, not yet reported.

[104] Insurers had to change their pricing policies by 21 December 2012.

[105] See e.g. the European Insurance and Occupational Pension, Authority (the EIOPA), which has started to assess the potential implications of this case for the insurance sector.

[106] Another case brought by Test-Achats was recently decided by the General Court regarding consumer protection, also dealing partially with fundamental rights, which will be discussed in ch. 7 in this book.

[107] O. Cherednychenko, 'Fundamental Rights and Contract Law', (2006) 4 *Eur. Rev. Contract Law*, p. 503. The Study Group on Social Justice, 'European Private Law, A Manifesto' (n 52), p. 653, at 667.

a basic payment account is nowadays a precondition to obtaining a number of essential goods and services. The importance of this is also demonstrated by a current legislative initiative, at EU level, on access to banking accounts as a measure of financial inclusion for consumers.[108] Similarly, consumer credit is now used, to a growing extent, as a means of funding basic services, such as education and healthcare.[109] Paradoxically, it is in affluent societies in particular that financially disfavoured consumers can suffer from exclusion, as they struggle to afford services and goods that are commonly viewed as essential requirements in society. At the same time, the wider use of credit and financial instruments has also created new challenges for the consumer, for example by increasing the risk of over-indebtedness.

In the legal literature, calls to tackle financial exclusion have intensified in the last decade.[110] Consequently, the question arises concerning which legal mechanisms would encourage the access of consumers in the credit market and also fight over-indebtedness? This section examines how current EU financial services regulation could be complemented. Specific legal models will be explored, such as social lending and consumer bankruptcy, which exemplify how the capability approach could be applied to extend market participation to otherwise disadvantaged groups.

4.1. *Corporate responsibility and social banking*

Corporate social responsibility (CSR) is a good example of a 'soft law' mechanism which can complement the 2008 directive on credit agreements for consumers. Mentioned as part of the European 2020 strategy for sustainable and inclusive growth, CSR is defined by the European Commission as a concept whereby companies integrate social and environmental concerns in their business operations and in their interaction with their stakeholders on a voluntary basis.

[108] Proposal for a Directive on the comparability of fees related to payment accounts, payment account switching and access to payment accounts with basic features, COM(2013)0266 final - 2013/0139 (COD); see also the Commission Recommendation on access to a basic payment account, C(2011) 4977/4.

[109] C. Williams & J. Windebank, 'The "Excluded Consumer": A Neglected Aspect of Social Exclusion', (2002) 30 *Policy and Politics*, p. 501; I. Ramsay, 'Consumer Law, Regulatory Capitalism and the "New Learning" in Regulation', (2006) 28 *Sydney L. Rev.*, p. 30.

[110] P. Cartwright, *Banks, Consumers and Regulation* (Oxford: Hart Publishing, 2004), p. 214; T. Wilhelmsson, 'Services of General Interest and European Private Law', in C. Rickett & T. Telfer (eds), *International Perspectives on Consumers' Access to Justice* (Cambridge: CUP, 2003), pp. 149–66; Ramsay, 'Consumer Law, Regulatory Capitalism and the "New Learning" in Regulation' (n 109), p. 29.

Such a concept was introduced in 2001, when the European Commission adopted the Green Paper 'Promoting a European Framework for Corporate Social Responsibility'.[111] This paper encourages companies to go beyond compliance with existing regulatory standards, highlighting the economic advantage of such an approach for the companies themselves. Indeed, CSR can be considered as an investment in order to improve the corporate reputation and attract the interest of consumers and investors.[112] Paragraph 51 of the Green Paper explicitly mentions consumers, and states that companies should aim at making services usable by as many people as possible, including disabled consumers.[113] This is particularly relevant in consumer credit, given that financial institutions usually do not lend to low-income consumers.[114] Thus, facilitating access to financial services at an affordable rate could be considered as an important example of corporate social responsibility.[115]

A concept related to social responsibility, but specifically centred on finance is 'social (or ethical) banking'. While there is no universally accepted definition, it can be said that 'Social Banking describes the provision of banking and financial services that consequently pursue (...) a positive contribution to the potential of all human beings to develop (...)'.[116] Social banking usually functions as a best practice approach and as a social assessment tool for mainstream banking and is an institution that helps to tackle exclusion. The roots of this idea go back to at least the 1977 US Community Reinvestment Act (CRA), which introduced a social rating system on banks.[117]

[111] See: <http://eur-lex.europa.eu/LexUriServ/LexUriServ.do?uri=COM:2001:0366:FIN:EN:PDF>, COM(2001) 366.

[112] For an example of corporate social responsibility and the capability approach, see J. Browne, S. Deakin & F. Wilkinson, 'Capabilities, Social Rights and Market Integration', in R. Salais & R. Villeneuve, *Europe and the Politics of Capabilities* (Cambridge: CUP, 2005), pp. 212–13.

[113] Low-income consumers are particularly common among the disabled, see e.g. the Joseph Rowntree Foundation Report, *Enduring Economic Exclusion: Disabled People, Income And Work* (2000).

[114] T. Wilson, 'Responsible Lending or Restrictive Lending Practices? Balancing Concerns regarding Over-indebtedness with Addressing Financial Exclusion', in M. Kelly-Louw, J. Nehf, & P. Rott (eds), *The Future of Consumer Credit Regulation, Creative Approaches to Emerging Problems, (Markets and the Law)* (Aldershot: Ashgate Publishing, 2008), pp. 91–106.

[115] U. Reifner, 'The Lost Penny, Social Contract Law and Market Economy', in T. Wilhelmsson & S. Hurri (eds), *From Dissonance to Sense: Welfare State Expectations, Privatization and Private Law* (Aldershot: Ashgate Publishing, 1999), p. 119.

[116] Institute for Social Banking: <http://www.social-banking.org/the-institute/what-is-social-banking>.

[117] U. Reifner, 'Social Banking, Ansätze und Erfahrungen über die Integration sozialer Zielsetzungen in Privatwirtschaft und Finanzdienstleistungen', in L. Schuster (ed.), *Die gesellschaftliche Verantwortung von Banken* (Berlin: Erich Schmidt Verlag, 1997), p. 205.

This Act aims to encourage deposit institutions to help meet the credit needs of the communities in which they operate, including low- and moderate-income neighbourhoods. However, this does not mean that institutions should make high-risks loans, as the operations have to be consistent with safe and sound operations of a bank.[118] The CRA requires that the performance of these financial institutions in helping meet the credit needs of their communities needs to be assessed periodically.[119] This assessment is conducted by federal agencies, which are responsible for supervising depository institutions and whose ratings are made public. The CRA does not provide specific criteria for rating the record of depository institutions; but the assessment should suit the institution's circumstances.[120] Beside their 'naming and shaming effect', these ratings are important because they are taken into account by public authorities in considering an institution's application for deposit facilities. Certain government institutions are obliged, by statute, to only deal with banks that have achieved a good rating. However, besides this, there is no direct penalty on the financial institution, in case of non-compliance, which weakens the effectiveness and control of the Act.

The CRA has been successful in motivating financial institutions to establish more inclusive and sustainable lending patterns which do not imply unprofitable credit.[121] This scheme has also led to enhanced financial education and understanding.[122] Thus, a similar legal scheme may also be an interesting inspiration in the EU context to stimulate an equitable consumer credit system.

In EU Member States, social banking is often embodied by alternative lending institutions that lend to consumers at preferential rates. Examples of these include collective bank accounts and self-help organizations, such as credit unions in the UK, which aim to facilitate access to low-income consumers.[123] In these financial cooperatives individuals lend money to one another at

[118] This Act was enacted by Congress in 1977 (12 U.S.C. 2901) and implemented by Regulation 12 CFR 228, substantially revised in May 1995, and updated again in August 2005.

[119] See the information at: <http://www.federalreserve.gov/communitydev/cra_about.htm>.

[120] See the information at: <http://www.federalreserve.gov/communitydev/cra_about.htm>.

[121] M. Barr, 'Credit Where it Counts: the Community Reinvestment Act', (2005) 80 *New York University L. Rev.* 513.

[122] According to Ramsay, this scheme can also encourage a more democratic approach as community groups have standing to participate in public hearings on a bank's performance; Ramsay (n 109), p. 31.

[123] See W.C.H. Ervine, 'Regulating Socially Harmful Lending: Reform in the United Kingdom', in L. Thévenoz & N. Reich (eds), *Liber amicorum Bernd Stauder: Droit de la Consommation/Konsumentenrecht/Consumer Law* (Baden-Baden/Zurich: Nomos/Schulthess, 2006), pp. 77–93.

comparatively low rates.[124] While this represents a good solution for certain consumers, credit unions still have to assess risks which may exclude individuals. Moreover, the organization and the consumers must present a saving pattern in order to obtain credit, which poses practical challenges for the credit union. Thus, the role of the government remains important in order to promote social lending and to provide lending to individuals who remain too risky for credit unions.[125]

4.2. *Financial literacy and education*

Improving financial capability through literacy and education is essential to help consumers make sustainable decisions in financial matters, especially because the credit market is becoming increasingly complex, requiring an advanced level of knowledge. In turn, enhancing financial capability means facilitating consumer decisions to choose financial services that are suitable for their needs and providing information that helps consumers to manage economic resources in a sustainable way.[126] This cannot be taken for granted, as the frequent episodes of consumer over-indebtedness demonstrate a significant lack of financial understanding and rational behaviour on the part of consumers. How, therefore, can financial capability of market participants be enhanced through information and education? What tools may help consumers to evaluate risks and to manage their financial means adequately?

The OECD has been leading in this regard, developing specific guidelines on financial education in the credit sector, as a tool to prevent over-indebtedness. In 2009 the OECD issued a 'Recommendation on Good Practices on Financial Education and Awareness Relating to Credit', including suggestions on how public actions, credit market players, specific platforms, and NGOs may enhance financial literacy of consumers, especially after the recent financial crisis.[127] Furthermore, the OECD proposes a wide range of tools and

Concerning the UK consumer credit movement, see N. Ryder, 'Out with the Old and in with the New? A Critical Analysis of Contemporary Policy towards the Development of Credit Unions in Great Britain', (2005) *J. Business Law*, pp. 617 *et seq*.

[124] For more on the consumer credit movement in the UK see Ryder, 'Out with the Old and in with the New?' (n 123), pp. 617 *et seq*.

[125] Reifner, 'The Lost Penny, Social Contract Law and Market Economy' (n 115), pp. 158–9.

[126] See the FSA publications at: <http://www.fsa.gov.uk/Pages/Library/Other_publications/FCP/index.shtml>. See also the consumer financial capability approach in Leskinen & Raijas (n 5), pp. 10 *et seq*; for a 'financial capability index' as a financial self-evaluation tool for the consumer, see Nicolini, 'A Regulatory Perspective on Consumer Financial Capability' (n 39), pp. 84–90.

[127] OECD, *Financial Literacy and Consumer Protection: Overlooked Aspects of the Crisis, OECD Recommendation on Good Practices on Financial Education and Awareness Relating to Credit* (Paris: OECD, June 2009).

objectives to enhance financial literacy, whose suitability may depend on specific national contexts:

- ensuring media coverage;
- the development of free and objective sources of consumer information, such as consumer information centres;
- the development of alternative information and communication channels, including Internet sites, guides, and leaflets, to help consumers compare different credit products and assess the protection and risks involved;
- the use of social networks, targeting the most vulnerable consumers; and
- ensuring the provision of clear and plain information for consumers.[128]

The concept of financial capability has been used as a model in national policy to promote financial literacy of consumers. For example in the UK, in the early 2000s, the FSA (now FCA)[129] formulated a 'National Strategy for Financial Capability', as part of its statutory duty to promote public understanding of the financial system.[130] Financial capability for the FSA meant: being able to manage money; keeping track of finances; planning ahead; choosing financial products; and staying informed about financial matters. The FSA's Financial Capability division was subsequently spun off and renamed, in April 2011, the 'Money Advice Service', an independent organization charged by the Financial Services Act 2010 with two statutory objectives: (1) enhancing the understanding of members of the public of financial matters; and (2) enhancing the ability of members of the public to manage their own financial affairs.[131]

Meanwhile, at the EU level, the Consumer Credit Directive discussed earlier in the chapter does not make any reference to financial education. However, there have been several EU-wide initiatives in this domain. An EU conference was held in 2007 on financial capability, where tools to enhance financial education were discussed.[132]

[128] OECD, *Financial Literacy and Consumer Protection* (n 127), pp. 19–20.

[129] The FSA has now become two separate regulatory authorities: the Financial Conduct Authority (FCA) (<http://www.fca.org.uk>) and the Prudential Regulation Authority (PRA) (<http://www.bankofengland.co.uk>).

[130] See e.g. the publication of the FSA: 'Towards a National Strategy for Financial Capability', (2003), at the FSA webpage: <http://www.fsa.gov.uk/Pages/Library/Other_publications/FCP/index. shtml>.

[131] <https://www.moneyadviceservice.org.uk/>.

[132] EU conference: 'Increasing Financial Capability': <http://ec.europa.eu/internal_market/finservices-retail/capability/>.

Moreover, in a 'Communication on Financial Education' (2007), the European Commission suggested eight basic principles which could help public authorities, financial services providers, or consumer organizations to establish financial education programmes.[133] These broad principles range from the recommendation that financial services providers should provide financial education in a fair, unbiased, and transparent manner, to the suggestion that national authorities should try to financially educate consumers as early as possible, beginning at school.[134]

In addition, the Commission has established 'Dolceta', a web-based consumer education tool, which covers, among other things, consumer rights and financial services.[135] This project was launched in 2003 and aims to raise the level of awareness and understanding of European consumer rights in the Member States through online consumer information and education.

Interestingly, the recently established European Insurance and Occupational Pensions Authority (EIOPA) was given a core role 'in promoting transparency, simplicity and fairness' in the market for consumer financial services. Moreover, according to Article 9 of Regulation 1094/2010, it was given a specific task to review and coordinate financial literacy and education initiatives by competent authorities.[136] Pursuing these objectives, EIOPA recently issued a report on the state of financial literacy in EU Member States and its effect on consumers.[137] This report showed that the level of financial education varies greatly between Member States, and that national strategies are rare and patchy, indicating a need to establish a coherent strategy at the European level to promote financial consumer education.

For the time being, the EU has mainly adopted a stock-taking function on this issue, which is certainly a useful step to understand the status quo. However, considering the existing gaps at national level, it might be beneficial if the EU takes a leading role assisting in the elaboration of a consistent programme promoting consumer financial understanding.

[133] See the Communication from the European Commission on Financial Education, Brussels, COM(2007) 808 final, 18.12.2007.

[134] See the Communication from the European Commission on Financial Education, Brussels, COM(2007) 808 final, 18.12.2007.

[135] <http://www.dolceta.eu/>; see also: <http://ec.europa.eu/consumers/rights/fin_serv_en.htm#other>.

[136] EIOPA's webpage: <https://eiopa.europa.eu/activities/consumer-protection-and-financial-innovation/index.html>.

[137] EIOPA, *Report on Financial Literacy and Education* (Frankfurt am Main: EIOPA, 16 December 2011).

4.3. *The 'fresh start' in consumer bankruptcy*

Over-indebtedness is only marginally mentioned in the provisions of the Consumer Credit Directive. However, in Member States, new legal mechanisms are being explored to free over-indebted consumers from high debt obligations. While this can be a socially desirable objective, it is clear that the interests of creditors have to be taken into account. Consumer bankruptcy has become a topical issue in the wake of the financial crisis, which has led to a marked increase in bankruptcy filings.[138]

The consumer bankruptcy discharge approach is historically part of US bankruptcy law, established by the American Federal Bankruptcy Act (1898).[139] This bankruptcy model aims to provide the debtor with the possibility of a 'fresh start' by terminating most of the debts existing at the time of filing in a relatively short period and to ensure that creditors are repaid to the extent that the debtor has the financial means available.[140]

The US bankruptcy law has been modified several times, most recently by the 'Bankruptcy Abuse Prevention and Consumer Protection Act' (BAPCPA) of 2005. This Act had been influenced by lenders lobbying for a less debtor-friendly bankruptcy law, in reaction to a significant growth of bankruptcy filings. Accordingly, the Act increased the costs of filing and introduced, in general, less favourable conditions for debtors, which are likely to reduce the requests for bankruptcy procedures.[141] Previous to BAPCPA, individuals could decide between two key bankruptcy procedures (Chapter 7 or 13 of the US Bankruptcy Code). The option of Chapter 7 offered a quick discharge and the debtors only had to repay from their assets above an exemption level, whereas the income received after the bankruptcy remained untouched. This type of procedure was chosen for a majority of consumer bankruptcies.[142] On the other hand, the option under Chapter 13 required debtors to repay part of their debt using their income, over a longer duration (three to five years), but exempted their

[138] M. Gerhardt, 'Consumer Bankruptcy Regimes in the US and Europe', CEPS Working Document No. 318/July 2009.

[139] C. Tabb, 'The Historical Evolution of the Bankruptcy Discharge', (1991) 65 *American Bankruptcy L. J.*, p. 325.

[140] See U. Reifner, 'Personal Bankruptcy Law and Inclusive Contract Law', in Niemi-Kiesiläinen, Ramsay, & Whitford (eds), *Consumer Bankruptcy in Global Perspective* (n 18), p. 145; Gerhardt, 'Consumer Bankruptcy Regimes in the US and Europe' (n 138), p. 2.

[141] See the report by A.B. Ashcraft, A.A. Dick, & D.P. Morgan, *The Bankruptcy Abuse Prevention and Consumer Protection Act: Means-Testing or Mean Spirited?* (Federal Reserve Bank of New York, Report no. 279, March 2007); M.J. White, 'Abuse or Protection? Consumer Bankruptcy Reform under «BAPCPA»', (2006) 18/19 *Revue de l'Institut d'Économie Publique* 1/2.

[142] Gerhardt (n 138).

assets. Debtors who wished to choose this type of procedure needed to have a regular income and their debt should remain within a specific limit.[143]

After the adoption of BAPCPA, both types of procedure remain applicable. However, debtors can no longer choose between the two options offered under Chapters 7 and 13. Instead, in order to qualify for the procedure under Chapter 7, debtors have to show that their incomes are below a specific threshold. Otherwise, they fall under the procedure in Chapter 13.[144] Moreover, under Chapter 13 debtors can no longer propose their own repayment plans, but a new 'means test' establishes the amount to pay from their income.[145] Finally, among other changes, the bankruptcy costs have been increased and the minimum time between bankruptcy filing lengthened, so that the new legal regime has generally become more burdensome for the debtor.[146] Despite these changes, according to some experts, the US bankruptcy system remains still debtor-favourable in comparison to the regimes offered by a majority of EU countries in this field.[147]

Recent comparative research on bankruptcy regimes in a number of European countries shows a large variety of models.[148] For example, the UK contains a regime that is, in certain aspects, similar to the US bankruptcy model. The 1986 Insolvency Act in the UK deals with bankruptcy procedures and has subsequently been amended by the Enterprise Act 2002 to modernize insolvency law. A major modification introduced by Part 10 of this Act reduced the required duration before debt discharge from three years to one year.[149] The courts in England and Wales can start the procedure by making a bankruptcy order after a petition by the debtor or creditor has been submitted. As a result, the assets of the bankrupt are managed by a trustee who is responsible for the sale of the assets to pay the creditors and a number of restrictions are placed on the bankrupt debtor. After a period of 12 months debtors are generally discharged from bankruptcy, relieving them from their debts.

[143] I. Livshits, J. MacGee, & M. Tertilt, 'Consumer Bankruptcy: A Fresh Start', (2007) 97(1) *Am. Econ. Rev.*, pp. 402–18.

[144] White, 'Abuse or Protection? Consumer Bankruptcy Reform under «BAPCPA»' (n 141), p. 10.

[145] White (n 141), p. 10.

[146] White (n 141), p. 10.

[147] See the report by Ashcraft, Dick, & Morgan, *The Bankruptcy Abuse Prevention and Consumer Protection Act: Means-Testing or Mean Spirited?* (n 141).

[148] See R. Anderson, H. Dubois, A. Koark, G. Lechner, I. Ramsay, T. Roethe, & H. Micklitz (eds), 'Consumer Bankruptcy in Europe: Different Paths for Debtors and Creditors', EUI WP Law 2011/09; see also Gerhardt (n 138).

[149] For more information, see Gerhardt (n 138), p. 6.

In Germany, the *Insolvenzordnung* Act of 1999 deals with insolvency of both companies and consumers. This Act also provides the possibility of debt relief, however, after a significantly longer period of 'good conduct' than in the UK. A debtor can request such a procedure, which starts with an obligatory negotiation period between creditor and debtor and then continues with a settlement before the court.[150] If these phases remain inconclusive the debtor is allowed to request the court for a discharge of residual debt, which may be granted after six years of good conduct and the regular transfer of a determined part of the income to the creditor.[151]

Other EU countries in turn have only very restrictive bankruptcy systems, such as those of Spain and Ireland.[152] However, in Europe as a whole there is a gradual trend towards adopting new bankruptcy provisions facilitating debt discharge of the debtor after a period of good conduct.[153] This is often regarded as an important social and economic policy objective to foster entrepreneurship and allow a fresh start for individuals. As we have described previously, long durations of over-indebtedness can significantly lower welfare of households, which may, in certain circumstances, impinge on the human right to dignity. On the other hand, procedures that discharge debtors too easily from their debts may be incompatible with the human right to property of the creditor.

A 2004 judgment of the European Court of Human Rights dealt with exactly this issue.[154] In *Bäck v Finland* a Finnish creditor argued that a Finnish 1993 Act on the Adjustment of Debts violated his right of property under Article 1 of Protocol 1 of the ECHR without serving a legitimate aim in the general interest. However, the Court decided that there had been no violation of property according to Article 1 of the Protocol, namely because the interference with the applicant's property rights was justified by a general public interest, given that the Finnish debt adjustment legislation served legitimate social and economic policies. Thus, this judgment recognized the important nature of the bankruptcy procedure to promote legitimate social and economic objectives from a human rights perspective. This can justify limitations to property rights, as long as the burden imposed is not excessive.

[150] See Gerhardt (n 138), p. 8.

[151] See Gerhardt (n 138), p. 8.

[152] For more information see Gerhardt (n 138).

[153] S. Viimsalu, 'The Over-Indebtedness Regulatory System in the Light of the Changing Economic Landscape', (2010) 17 *Juridica International*.

[154] ECtHR, *Bäck v Finland*, App. no. 37598/97, 20 July 2004.

The 'fresh start' philosophy inherent in the consumer bankruptcy model explained in this section in a sense reflects a capability perspective: it can quickly re-integrate consumers into the market, allowing them to regain their full capabilities, and to participate once again in the economy. Moreover, it also has a positive impact on inclusion, thus responding to a principle of solidarity.[155] Finally, by de facto imposing negative effects for improvident credit extensions, the bankruptcy discharge can also have a preventive effect on reckless lending, which has, in turn, been identified as a contributing factor to over-indebtedness.[156]

5. Conclusions

This chapter analyzed how fundamental rights, along with the application of a 'capability approach' to consumer law, may affect financial consumer contracts, focusing in particular on credit agreements.

The current framework is characterized by opposing tendencies. On the one hand, liberal views led to measures aimed at improving market functioning through harmonization, and at protecting the consumer on the basis of the 'autonomous, informed consumer concept' of the 2008 directive on credit agreements. According to this view, the main role of consumer protection is to allow well-informed choices, especially when these have long-lasting effects, as in the area of consumer credit.

On the other hand, there is an emergence of new 'social' concepts like responsible lending, which introduce a novel perspective to consumer law. This tendency is accompanied and strengthened by a progressive influence of constitutional and fundamental rights in financial contracts. As shown, constitutional social principles have been invoked in favour of weak parties in some Member States, which can lead to fairer business practices in specific contractual relations.

Furthermore, as illustrated in the controversial *Test-Achats* case, the Charter of Fundamental Rights can have significant implications for the content of existing secondary law and may influence the meaning of general principles

[155] Reifner, 'Personal Bankruptcy Law and Inclusive Contract Law' (n 140), p. 156; J. Niemi-Kiesiläinen, 'Collective or Individual? Construction of Debtors and Creditors in Consumer Bankruptcy', in Niemi-Kiesiläinen, Ramsay, & Whitford (eds), *Consumer Bankruptcy in Global Perspective* (n 18), pp. 46–7.

[156] Niemi-Kiesiläinen, Ramsay, & Whitford (n 18), p. 7.

of EU law, such as equal treatment. This indicates an increasing importance of primary EU law for consumer law and could promote a more value-based approach, strengthening a broader consumer concept.

Finally, the last part illustrated the importance of complementary legal approaches to the 2008 directive, which enhance contractual capacity for consumers to participate equally in markets in a substantive way. This inclusive role can be reached through instruments such as corporate responsibility and social lending, as well as new norms in consumer bankruptcy. Interestingly, these innovations have a strong flavour of a capability approach, which was outlined in Chapter 4. In this 'empowerment' perspective, which is a typical trait of the capability approach, this chapter has discussed four important issues that may be promoted by fundamental rights, policy objectives, or secondary law: (1) financial literacy, obtained via information and education; (2) fundamental rights protecting weaker parties; (3) the principle of non-discrimination; and (4) financial inclusion, which ensures participation in society and in the market, and the prevention of over-indebtedness.

While the current legal framework (in particular, the 2008 directive on credit agreements) is fully mindful of the information principle, protection of weaker parties and financial inclusion are only partially addressed at present.

6

Electronic Communication, Fundamental Rights Conflicts, and Consumer Participation

1. Introduction

Services of general interest usually comprise telecommunication services, postal services, and the supply of utilities, such as electricity, water, and gas. Of these, telecommunication services have been expanding most quickly in recent decades, becoming increasingly important in the daily lives of consumers, as they constitute an essential means for individuals to participate fully in society.[1] This chapter deals with consumer access to such basic services as telephone and the Internet, and examines the fundamental right to data protection and the freedom to receive or impart information.

Like other services of general interest, telecommunications were traditionally part of a state monopoly. From the 1980s onwards, an increasing trend towards privatization has spread across the whole of Europe, with the welfare state retreating to a minor role and leaving more room for private companies in a move which, coupled with deregulation, was supposed to improve efficiency and therefore consumer welfare.[2]

However, following privatization, new challenges for consumers have appeared. This is manifested by an increase in consumer actions due to, for example, mobile phone overcharging and mis-selling, unfair contract terms,

[1] T. Wilhelmsson, S. Tuominen, & H. Tuomola (eds), *Consumer Law in the Information Society* (The Hague-London-Boston: Aspen Publishers-Kluwer-Law and Business, 2000).

[2] J. Keßler & H.-W. Micklitz (eds), *Kundenschutz auf liberalisierten Märkten–Telekommunikation—Vergleich der Konzepte, Maßnahmen und Wirkungen in Europa* (Baden-Baden: Nomos, 2008), p. 7.

and misleading advertising in electronic communication.[3] At the same time, the development of new forms of communication has opened the door to 'scams' and risks of identity theft, posing threats to consumer privacy and requiring additional protective measures.[4]

As will be seen, fundamental rights play a growing role in the area of electronic communication. In a fast-changing information society, communications services, and in particular, access to the Internet, have become essential for consumers to connect with the community and to access information and key educational resources. Hence, the right of access to such services has been increasingly seen as 'fundamental'—both in itself, and because it is a precondition for the exercise of other recognized fundamental rights.

However, a number of cases recently brought to the ECJ saw these new fundamental rights clashing with established, equally important, fundamental rights. For example, some cases related to the use of the Internet show a conflict between the right to protection of personal data and the freedom to receive or impart information, on the one hand, and the right to intellectual property, on the other.

What is the role of the Charter of Fundamental Rights in this evolution? To answer this question, it is useful to describe the evolution that led to the current situation. Historically, electronic communications law has taken a competition-centred approach. However, given the growing links with fundamental rights described above, it appears crucial to consider it now in a broader consumer-citizens perspective. To do this, one has to explicitly consider issues such as social inclusion, which for example may require that services have to be provided to isolated regions, or to the disabled and the elderly. Steps in this direction have been taken in Europe in the first decade of the 2000s. For instance, the Citizens' Rights Directive 2009/136/EC[5] aims to ensure universal access to these services, paying special attention to disabled or socially disfavoured consumers. Moreover, this directive encourages consultations of consumer groups, promoting their regulatory involvement. Besides these changes, the Charter contains a number of rights that are relevant in the field of electronic communications, such as the rights to privacy and data protection. These developments suggest that a fundamental rights

[3] I. Ramsey (2003), 'Consumer Redress and Access to Justice', in C.E.F. Rickett & T.G.W. Telfer (eds), *International Perspectives on Consumers' Access to Justice* (Cambridge: CUP, 2003), pp. 17–45.

[4] Keßler & Micklitz (eds), *Kundenschutz auf liberalisierten Märkten* (n 2), p. 7.

[5] Directive 2009/136/EC, OJ L 337/11, 18.12.2009.

and broader consumer perspective is gaining momentum, and may improve market participation and regulatory involvement.

Set against this background, this chapter is organized in three sections. The first outlines the European legal framework for electronic communications and universal services. The second section describes relevant consumer rights and examines how the ECJ has tried to balance conflicting fundamental rights. The third and final section analyzes new measures that might increase regulatory involvement of consumers, such as the European Citizens' Initiative and regulatory consultation mechanisms.

2. Liberalization and Universal Services

Since the 1980s the telecommunications sector, originally in the hands of national monopolies, has been gradually liberalized leading to worldwide competition and lower prices. This privatization process caused a change in the welfare state paradigm in the European Union giving the private sector an important role in providing consumers with essential services.[6] As a consequence, the citizen's right to public services turned into a 'consumer-citizen' right.[7]

The regulation of electronic communications in the EU has, to a large extent, dealt with the supply side of the market, concentrating on market entry, licensing, and the use of the network. Now, with consumer-focused regulation, the emphasis has turned to the demand side, where two key problems are access to services, and prevention of unfair business practices.[8] How is the EU addressing these issues? Can the universal services obligations in the EU

[6] On the link between European social citizenship and services of general economic interest, see H.-W. Micklitz, 'Universal Services: Nucleus for a Social European Private Law', EUI WP Law 2009/12, pp. 12 *et seq.*

[7] Access to essential services such as telecommunications has become a novel subject of consumer law; see P. Rott, 'Consumer and Services of General Interest: Is EC Consumer Law the Future?', (2007) 30 *J. Consumer Policy*, p. 53; T. Prosser, *The Limits of Competition Law: Markets and Public Services* (Oxford: OUP, 2005), pp. 162–3; see also the EU study on consumer law and the information society, SANCO, 2006.

[8] See the OECD Report, *Enhancing Competition in Telecommunications: Protecting and Empowering Consumers* (Paris: OECD, 2008), pp. 9–32; T. Wilhelmsson, 'Services of General Economic Interest and European Private Law', in E.F. Ricket & T. Telfer (eds), *International Perspectives on Consumers' Access to Justice* (Oxford: OUP, 2008), pp. 149 *et seq.*

telecommunication framework be interpreted as a sign of a new emphasis on the citizen-consumer, and to what extent do they contribute to establishing a social model in the EU?

The next subsections intend to answer these questions, by giving an overview of the EU legal framework, and of its historic development.

2.1. *Evolution of the current legal framework*

When the telecommunications sector was controlled by public service monopolies, specific national undertakings were granted exclusive rights to install networks and services at a national level.[9] However, this changed with a marked growth in the application of information technologies and following the European Commission's promotion of competition and progressive liberalization, starting in the late 1980s.[10] Several directives were adopted to promote such liberalization, which eliminated the exclusive rights of public undertakings to provide telecommunications services or equipment. As a consequence, the Member States, albeit reluctantly, had to withdraw the exclusive rights granted to the national undertaking, so that the telecommunication market could be opened to new operators.[11] This process resulted in a liberalization of telecommunications services in the majority of the Member States by January 1998.[12] Under the new liberalized order, the provision of formerly public welfare services was now primarily determined in competitive markets, by private companies.[13]

In addition, the above liberalization was accompanied by harmonization measures. A key comprehensive regulatory framework was adopted on 24 April 2002[14] to simplify the relevant legislation. The objective of this framework was to encourage competition in electronic communications markets,

[9] See P. Nihoul & P. Rodford, *EU Electronic Communications Law: Competition and Regulation in the European Telecommunications Market* (Oxford: OUP, 2004), fn. 1.97.

[10] This change was also supported by an activist stance of the ECJ in favour of a pro-competitive reading of Art. 106(2) TFEU (ex Art. 86(2) EC, ex Art. 90(2) EEC).

[11] P. Larouche, *Competition Law and Regulation in European Telecommunications* (Oxford-Portland: Hart Publishing, 2000), pp. 35–60.

[12] See also the European Commission's website for information on Europe's information society: <http://ec.europa.eu/information_society/policy/ecomm/doc/history/index_en.htm>.

[13] For an overview, see Damjanovic & de Witte, *Welfare Integration through EU Law: The Overall Picture in the Light of the Lisbon Treaty* (Florence: EUI Law, 2008), EUI LAW WP, 2008/34, pp. 10–11.

[14] Directives 2002/21/EC on a common regulatory framework for electronic communications networks and services, OJ L 108/33, 24.4.2002, 2002/19/EC on access to, and interconnection of, electronic communications networks and associated facilities, OJ L 108/7, 24.4.2002, and 2002/20/EC on the authorisation of electronic communications networks and services, OJ L 108, 24.4.2002.

improve the function of the internal market, and guarantee basic consumer interests. Moreover, it aimed to protect users and to facilitate access to particular services for disabled persons. Article 2(c) of the Framework Directive, defines 'electronic communication service' as 'a service normally provided for remuneration which consists wholly or mainly in the conveyance of signals on electronic communications networks, including telecommunications services and transmission services in networks used for broadcasting, (...)".[15]

Consumer rights were mainly based on two directives: Directive 2002/22/EC on universal service and users' rights (USD), and Directive 2002/58/EC on the protection of privacy and of personal data.[16] These were then supported by some additional legislative acts, such as the Roaming Regulation which entered into force in June 2007.[17]

The two directives were amended on 25 November 2009 by a single 'Citizens' Rights' Directive 2009/136/EC[18] with the adoption of the 'telecom reforms package'. These new telecom reforms in 2009 were necessary to improve consistency of regulation across Europe, and to adapt to the latest technological developments, improving consumer protection on the basis of Article 114 TFEU (ex Article 95 EC). The broader legislative framework introduced by these reforms consists of two main directives, one on 'Better Regulation'[19] and another one on 'Citizens' Rights' mentioned before,[20] as well as a regulation establishing a new EU oversight authority, the 'Body of European Regulators for Electronic Communications' (BEREC).[21]

[15] Directives 2002/21/EC on a common regulatory framework for electronic communications networks and services, OJ L 108/33, 24.4.2002. This Directive was amended by Directive 2009/140/EC, as explained below.

[16] Directive 2002/22/EC on universal service and users' rights relating to electronic communications networks and services, OJ L 108/51, 24.2.2002 and Directive 2002/58/EC concerning the processing of personal data and the protection of privacy in the electronic communications sector, OJ L 201/37, 31.7.2002.

[17] Regulation (EC) No 717/2007 (amended by Regulation (EC) No 544/2009) on roaming on public mobile communications networks; now Regulation (EU) No 531/2012 of 13 June 2012 on roaming on public mobile communications networks within the Union.

[18] Directive 2009/136/EC of 25 November 2009 amending Directive 2002/22/EC and Directive 2002/58/EC and Regulation (EC) No 2006/2004, OJ L 337/11, 18.12.2009.

[19] Directive 2009/140/EC amending Directives 2002/21/EC on a common regulatory framework for electronic communications networks and services, 2002/19/EC on access to, and interconnection of, electronic communications networks and associated facilities, and 2002/20/EC on the authorisation of electronic communications networks and services, OJ L 337/37, 18.12.2009.

[20] Directive 2009/136/EC,OJ L 337/11, 18.12.2009.

[21] Regulation (EC) No 1211/2009 establishing the Body of European Regulators for Electronic Communications (BEREC) and the Office, OJ L 337/1, 18.12.2009.

The 'Citizens' Rights' Directive is particularly relevant for consumer protection, as it introduces important changes protecting and empowering users of electronic communications services.[22] It deals with access to services, contractual rights, privacy, and policy participation. This chapter will assess key provisions of this directive and examine the relevant case law, starting with the right to access electronic services.

2.2. *The concept and justification of universal services*

The 'Citizens' Rights' Directive aims to ensure the availability throughout the Union of good-quality electronic communications services. Before analyzing the relevant provisions in detail, it is important to understand the origin and rationale of universal service obligations.

During the liberalization of the EU telecommunications sector in 1998, policy-makers agreed to ensure a set of basic telecommunication services, called 'universal services', which were to be available to all, even if the market did not provide for this. The concept of universal (or general interest) services has evolved over time, following technological changes and demographic trends. In 2000, the European Commission defined universal services 'as the minimum set of services of specified quality to which all users and consumers, have access in the light of specific national conditions, at an affordable price'.[23] For consumers universal services provide 'a guarantee of universal access, high quality and affordability' of these services.[24]

In turn, the 'universality' of certain services is typically justified by economic and by social rationales. The first kind of justification is of an economic nature and is often based on the existence of strong *positive* externalities, whereby the convenience to use a service increases with the total number of users. For example, communication services become more attractive the more people are using them. Companies benefit from the ability to contact an enlarged pool of potential customers and interact with them, thereby increasing their sales opportunities; consumers, on the other hand, benefit from the ability to communicate with each other to compare products across several firms. Such benefits make a strong case for supporting the

[22] Directive 2009/136/EC, OJ L 337/11, 18.12.2009.

[23] See the Communication from the European Commission on Services of General Interest in Europe, COM(2000) 580 final, 20.9.2000, p. 16.

[24] See the Communication from the European Commission on Services of General Interest in Europe, COM(2000) 580 final, 20.9.2000, p. 7.

diffusion of such services, because this generates increasing returns for all users.

The second justification is a social one, and is founded on equity considerations. Universal services are, for example, seen as a means to combat social exclusion, and to ensure access to essential services for disadvantaged individuals.[25] Groups that are commonly cited as benefiting from universal services include disabled people, the elderly, low-income consumers, and those who live in rural areas.

2.3. *Services of general economic interest in primary law*

In primary EU law, a number of provisions refer to services of general economic interest, without, however, providing a definition of this concept.

Article 106(2) TFEU (ex Article 86(2) EC) stipulates that: 'Undertakings entrusted with the operation of services of general economic interest or having the character of a revenue-producing monopoly shall be subject to the rules contained in the Treaties, in particular to the rules on competition, in so far as the application of such rules does not obstruct the performance, in law or in fact, of the particular tasks assigned to them.' This provision was particularly important in the liberalization process promoted by the Commission explained before. In several rulings the Court established that Article 106(2) does not per se allow exclusive rights to be granted to national undertakings,[26] but under strict conditions,[27] it can allow an exception to competition law, where this is indispensable and necessary for the application of services of general interest.[28]

Article 14 TFEU (ex Article 16 EC) concerns services of general economic interest in the European Union. It states that 'given the place occupied by services of general economic interest in the shared values of the Union as well as their role in promoting social and territorial cohesion, the Union

[25] On the general universal rights, see D. Charles-Le Bihan, 'Services d'intérêt économique général et valeurs communes', (2008) 519 *Revue du Marché commun et de l'Union européenne*, pp. 356–60.

[26] Many Member States were against this liberalization trend; see e.g. Case C-202/88, *French Republic v Commission of the European Communities* [1991] ECR I-01223; and see J. Baquero Cruz, 'Beyond Competition: Services of General Interest and European Community Law', in G. de Búrca (ed), *EU Law and the Welfare State: In Search of Solidarity* (Oxford: OUP, 2005), pp. 169 *et seq.*

[27] E.g. derogations from competition have to be made available to all undertakings without discrimination and limited to specific universal service obligations.

[28] See more in J. Maillo, 'Article 86 EC, Services of General Interest and EC Competition Law', in G. Amato & C.-D. Ehlermann (eds), *EC Competition Law: A Critical Assessment* (Oxford: Hart Publishing, 2007), p. 591.

and the Member States, each within their respective powers and within the scope of application of the Treaties, shall take care that such services operate on the basis of principles and conditions (…), which enable them to fulfil their missions'. Article 14 therefore underlines the importance of services of general economic interest as representing common values in society and for enhanced cohesion in the EU.[29] However, this provision foresees no power shift between Member States and the EU.[30]

In addition, Protocol No 26 to the TFEU deals with the wider concept of 'services of general interest', which covers both 'economic' and 'non-economic' services. This Protocol provides interpretative provisions emphasizing the importance of services of general interest to ensure 'a high level of quality, safety and affordability, equal treatment and the promotion of universal access and of user rights'. While the concept of services of general interest is not defined in the Protocol, the European Commission has provided some guidance in a later document, describing them broadly as 'services, whether "economic" or not, that the Member States regard as being of general interest, and which they therefore subject to specific public service obligations'.[31]

A third relevant provision can be found in the 'Solidarity' chapter of the EU Charter of Fundamental Rights. Article 36 of the Charter explicitly stipulates that '(t)he Union recognises and respects access to services of general economic interest as provided for in national laws and practices, in accordance with the Treaty establishing the European Community (…)'. The aim of this provision is to promote the social and territorial cohesion of the EU.[32] The specific reference to 'national laws and practices' highlights that national rules and measures regarding access to services of general economic interest are to be respected by the Union.

Divergent views exist with regard to the potential effect of the Charter on services of general interest.[33] On the one hand, a number of scholars argue that

[29] W. Sauter, 'Services of General Economic Interest and Universal Service in EU Law', (2008) 33 *Eur. L. Rev.*, pp. 167–93; P. Craig & G. de Búrca, *EU Law: Text, Cases and Materials*, 4th edn (Oxford: OUP, 2008), p. 1072.

[30] M. Ross, 'Promoting Solidarity: From Public Services to a European Model of Competition?', (2007) 44 *CML Rev.*, pp. 1057–80.

[31] Commission Staff Working Document Guide to the application of the European Union rules on state aid, public procurement and the internal market to services of general economic interest, and in particular to social services of general interest, Brussels, 7.12.2010 SEC(2010) 1545 final, p. 15.

[32] Nihoul & Rodford (n 9), fn. 5.12.

[33] E. Picard, 'Citizenship, Fundamental Rights, and Public Services', in M. Freedland & S. Sciarra (eds), *Public Services and Citizenship in the European Union* (Oxford: OUP, 1998), pp. 83 *et seq.*

it may lead to more flexibility in the use of competition rules when services of general economic interest are necessary. This means that exceptional rights and state aid can be more readily granted to the operators of these services. On the other hand, some scholars argue that the Charter mainly has a political value and does not grant particular rights or obligations that can be claimed before the ECJ.[34]

At a policy level, the European Commission has proclaimed its commitment, both in a Green and a White Paper on Services of General Interest, to actively improve universal services.[35] In particular, the White Paper emphasized that universal services aim at guaranteeing access for everyone, whatever their economic, social, or geographical situation, to a service of a specified quality at an affordable price.[36]

When it comes to the specific interest of these services for the consumer, they are of importance in two ways: first, they promote affordable and easy access to basic consumer products or services; and secondly, they empower consumers in the market and provide a balanced relationship with the operators. In the 2007–2013 EU Consumer Policy Strategy the European Commission stressed its goal to promote and protect consumer rights with regard to services of general interest and specific related sectors.[37]

The evolution in electronic communications law between liberalization and increased competition on the one hand, and universal service on the other, raises questions regarding the balance of these two opposing interests. The EU legislation traditionally followed a trend towards maximum competition, and minimal guarantee of services of general interest.[38] However, the case law does show that the ECJ has taken a more favourable stance towards social values.[39] Such a trend is also visible in the recent 'Citizens' Rights' Directive which promotes an inclusive-oriented framework.

[34] See Nihoul & Rodford (n 9), fn. 5.15.

[35] See Green Paper on Services of General Interest, COM(2003) 270; the White Paper of 12 May 2004, COM(2004) 374.

[36] White Paper on Services of General Interest, COM(2004) 374 final.

[37] Communication from the Commission, Consumer Policy strategy 2007–2013, Empowering consumers, enhancing their welfare, effectively protecting them, COM(2007) 99 final, 13.3.2007.

[38] See Baquero Cruz, 'Beyond Competition' (n 26), pp. 169 et seq. Rott, 'Consumer and Services of General Interest' (n 7), p. 53; however, for a different opinion, see Prosser, *The Limits of Competition Law* (n 7).

[39] See in general e.g., Case C-67/96, Albany International BV v Stichting Bedrijfspensioenfonds Textielindustrie [1999] ECR I-5751; see also Baquero Cruz (n 26), pp. 169 *et seq*.

2.4. *Universal services in secondary law*

The new 'Citizens' Rights' Directive gives a more precise indication of the basic principles and application of universal services.[40] As stated in Article 1, the objective of the directive is to ensure the availability of good quality, publicly available services and to deal with cases where the needs of the consumers are not satisfactorily met by the market. Key provisions concern access to telephony services from all locations (Articles 4 and 26) and equal access to basic services for disabled and financially disfavoured consumers (Article 7(1)).

Article 4, on the provision of telephone services, requires Member States to ensure that all 'reasonable requests' for connections at fixed locations to a public telephone network have to be provided by at least one undertaking. This is particularly important for consumers who live in rural or isolated areas, where the connection costs would be too high for providers to spontaneously offer the service. Article 4(2) states that the connection provided must allow consumers to receive local and international telephone calls, and that it should also permit functional Internet access. Following a similar logic, Article 26 requires that emergency calls have to be made available for free, under the single number '112' to be reachable from any phone in the entire EU. An equivalent access to emergency services has to be provided for disabled users (Article 26(4)). Furthermore, Article 27(a) requires that Member States promote 'harmonised numbers for harmonised services of social values'.

Article 7 includes particular social provisions, granting to disabled users equal access to electronic communication. In particular, Article 7(1) states that 'Member States shall take specific measures to ensure that access to, and affordability of, the services identified in Article 4(3) and Article 5 for disabled end-users is equivalent to the level enjoyed by other end-users'. In turn, the services identified in Articles 4(3) and 5, which are designed especially for disabled consumers, comprise public text telephones for the deaf or speech-impaired, directory assistance for the blind, as well as special emergency services. Furthermore, depending on the national context, Member States may take specific measures, which allow disabled end-users to have

[40] Directive 2009/136/EC of 25 November 2009, amending Directive 2002/22/EC of 7 March 2002 on universal service and users' rights relating to electronic communications networks and services, OJ L 337/11, 18.12.2009.

a wider choice of service providers available to the majority of end-users (Article 7(2)).

Besides the aforementioned Articles, a set of provisions ensures the affordability of electronic communications and cost control mechanisms for consumers (Articles 9 and 10). According to Article 9, Member States may 'require that designated undertakings provide to consumers, tariff options or packages which depart from those provided under normal commercial conditions, in particular to ensure that those on low incomes or with special social needs are not prevented from accessing the network'.[41] This is important because, as a 2007 'Eurobarometer survey' on services of general interest has shown, a large number of consumers have been excluded from services of general interest owing to a lack of resources.[42]

Furthermore, Annex I of the directive describes some 'facilities and services' which, as per Article 10, should be provided to help individuals control their expenditure. These include itemized billing by the provider (which should be detailed enough to facilitate verification), the option to selectively block certain numbers, and the possibility of pre-payment in order to better control expenditures.

The national governments are bound by the directive, which defines the extent to which Member States can impose obligations within a universal service context. Furthermore, the directive determines that the costs of the universal service provisions are to be reimbursed to the provider, but only when it is shown that the service had to be provided at a loss, and that it has been provided outside normal commercial standards.[43]

The electronic communications market is evolving rapidly with technological innovations which can change the concept and scope of universal services in this field. One way of measuring the essential nature of a basic service is to determine whether the majority of consumers use a certain item of technology as a basic part of their life.[44] The directive thus set a periodical review of its scope, and the European Commission conducted a first review in 2005.[45] In September 2008, the Commission published a Communication

[41] The price of the service is determined by national regulators.

[42] Special Eurobarometer 2007 Report 260, 'Services of General Interest'.

[43] The universal provider has to be chosen by the national regulators through objective criteria.

[44] The directive is conscious of the evolving nature of universal services; the preamble to its predecessor 2002/22/EC states that 'The concept of universal service should evolve to reflect advances in technology, market developments and changes in user demand'.

[45] See the Communication from the Commission on the first review of the scope of universal service in 2005–2006: COM(2005) 203 and COM(2006) 163.

on the future scope of universal service obligation (USO).[46] One key finding was that, from 2003 to 2007, broadband use in the EU had increased significantly in households but with striking gaps between different EU countries. As the objective of the Commission was for all EU citizens to be eventually connected to high-speed Internet broadband, the report raised the question of whether the Commission should broaden the scope of universal services to broadband. The conclusion was that there was no need to extend the definition of universal services in this regard, as broadband was not yet used by the majority of people.

Access to electronic communication services can be considered a capability instrument, as it enables individuals to participate more easily in several aspects of social life, work, and economic interactions. In terms of inclusion, this is particularly important for elderly, disabled, or financially disadvantaged consumers from a capability perspective. As already discussed, increasing consumers' capability is not only socially desirable, but is also market-promoting. For instance, access to the Internet helps consumers to compare and discuss products but, above all, allows them to reach markets which would otherwise be beyond their reach. This promotes competition, consumer welfare, and ultimately market integration.

To conclude, the new 'Citizens' Rights' Directive, with its emphasis on inclusion and empowerment, is a sign that the EU consumer framework is evolving in a socially oriented direction.

3. Information, Unfair Terms, and Fundamental Rights Conflicts

Two important issues in electronic communications are the protection of privacy, and the prevention of unfair contractual terms.[47] By the nature of the service provided, telecommunication operators have access to personal information on their clients. Furthermore, telecommunication services are

[46] COM(2008) 572, Communication from the European Commission on the second periodic review of the scope of universal service in electronic communications networks and services in accordance with Article 15 of Directive 2002/22/EC, Brussels, 25.9.2008. More recently another review was undertaken by the Commission, see: COM(2011) 795 Communication from the Commission, Universal service in e-communications, Brussels, 23.11.2011.

[47] See the research of behaviour economics in the OECD Report from the Directorate for Science, Technology and Industry Committee for Information, Computer and Communications Policy, *Enhancing Competition in Telecommunications: Protecting and Empowering Consumers, Ministerial Background Report* (Paris: OECD, 2008), p. 9.

typically provided 'remotely', that is with little or no direct contact between client and provider. Considering that these services are rapidly changing owing to technological progress and thus difficult for the consumer to evaluate, it is easy to understand why in this area consumers are particularly exposed to unfair contractual terms.[48] How is the EU managing these challenges?

This section will highlight a recent trend in EU law, reflecting a new protective approach, which is also increasingly founded on fundamental rights. The first subsection will explore consumer empowerment via information, for which relevant provisions in Directive 2009/136/EC will be analyzed. The next subsection will then move on to discussing protection from unfair contractual terms, assessing an important ECJ ruling which clarified the role of national courts in consumer protection. The following subsection will then deal with the protection of personal data in electronic communication services, which is recognized as a fundamental right. However, recent case law has shown that this fundamental right may conflict with other fundamental rights, generating the need to strike a delicate balance. This is the topic of subsections 3.4 and 3.5, which comment on recent ECJ rulings on this issue in the light of the Charter.

3.1. *Consumer empowerment through information*

In the technologically complex and rapidly changing sector of telecommunications, consumers often suffer from an information asymmetry in relation to providers. This places the consumer in a vulnerable position in dealing with entities which sometimes engage in practices ranging from aggressive marketing to outright scam. Examples here are misleading pricing, non-transparent terms, and even non-consensual subscription to certain services.[49] This not only harms some consumers, but can also damage the market. Indeed, when consumers do not have sufficient information or are given inconsistent advertising, they may just refuse to participate in the market, discouraged by limited knowledge caused by lack of transparency or by information overload—which equally results in confusion.[50]

[48] For example, collective consumer actions have proliferated in this sector:<http://ec.europa.eu/information_society/newsroom/cf/itemlongdetail.cfm?item_id=3701>.

[49] Telephone slamming is an illegal telecommunications practice of changing subscribers' telephone service without their consent which has increased after liberalization; e.g., for the UK see: <http://consumers.ofcom.org.uk/2009/03/slamming-crackdown/>.

[50] 34% of consumers have difficulties in comparing offers of different providers and do not take advantage of beneficial offers; OECD Report, *Enhancing Competition in Telecommunications: Protecting and Empowering Consumers, Ministerial Background Report* (n 47), p. 9.

How, then, can reliable comparative indicators on quality and price of services empower consumers? More importantly, what information and mechanisms help to prevent abuses in the sector? There are different ways to empower consumers and thus overcome this information gap: first, improving the availability of comparative information on quality and prices; secondly, increasing the awareness of alternative suppliers and enabling consumers to switch providers easily and at an acceptable cost; finally, promoting education.[51]

Directive 2009/136/EC aims to address the first of these, promoting transparency and comparative information in the electronic communications sector. In particular, Article 21(1) provides that the national regulatory authorities can require providers to publish clear and up-to-date information on applicable prices and standard terms. In addition, according to Article 21(2) 'national regulatory authorities shall encourage the provision of comparable information to enable end-users and consumers to make an independent evaluation of the cost of alternative usage patterns, for instance by means of interactive guides or similar techniques'. These norms place an evident focus on the comparability of conditions of access and use of services. This should empower consumers, making it simpler for them to make informed choices before purchasing products.

The directive also facilitates the change of providers. Article 30 states that Member States must ensure that all subscribers 'who so request can retain their number(s) independently of the undertaking providing the service', thus giving consumers the possibility to keep their telephone number (number portability). Moreover, it allows them to switch providers within a faster period than under previous regulations, thereby enhancing mobility across providers and increasing competition in the market.

Easier access to electronic communications services already represents an improvement in the information available to consumers. This is particularly true for the Internet, which opens up a wide range of product comparisons and new participation methods for consumers. Through it, consumers can exchange information about products or services, letting others know when a company is treating its customers badly or particularly well.[52]

[51] See the OECD Report, *Enhancing Competition in Telecommunications: Protecting and Empowering Consumers, Ministerial Background Report* (n 47), pp. 9 and 43.

[52] Digital technologies have empowered consumers to become active participants by evaluating products; see N. Helberger, 'Making Place for the eConsumer in Consumer Law', (2008) 31 *J Consumer Policy*, pp. 385–91; T. Zarsky, 'Law and Online Social Networks: Mapping the Challenges and Promises of User-generated Information Flows', (2008) 18 *Fordham Intellectual Property, Media and Entertainment L. J.*, pp. 741–83.

Consumer education tools are also important to prevent abuse, and to limit the threats to privacy posed by new technologies.[53] In European countries there are not many initiatives in this sense, but it is conceivable that the experience of other countries might serve as an inspiration. For example in Canada, the Canadian Radio, Television and Telecommunication Commission uses some channels to educate consumers about their rights,[54] contributing to their empowerment.

Finally, besides the provisions included in the directive, the freedom to receive information was also recognized as a fundamental right. Included in Article 11 of the Charter of Fundamental Rights, the freedom to receive information may become particularly relevant for the consumer in the context of access to digital content. As we will see later in this chapter, both the fundamental freedom to receive and impart information, and the right to privacy protection have played an increasingly important role in recent case law.

3.2. *Protection from unfair terms and dispute resolution*

Accesses to justice and protection from unfair contractual terms are further important aspects of consumer law in relation to electronic communications services. Telecommunication contracts often entail unfavourable conditions for consumers, such as early termination fees, automatic renewals of contracts, or specific arbitration terms. Although consumer actions are a useful tool to test the fairness of business practices in telecommunications contracts, consumers often have difficulties in gaining access to justice.[55]

In this regard, the EU adopted specific legislative measures. Article 34 of Directive 2009/136/EC requires Member States to ensure that 'transparent, non-discriminatory, simple and inexpensive out-of-court procedures are available for dealing with unresolved disputes between consumers and undertakings'. This will help to facilitate dispute resolution between consumers and providers of electronic communications services. As we will see in Chapter 7 on access to justice, cheap and effective alternative dispute mechanisms to judicial procedures are an important component to enhance consumer redress.

[53] Self-regulation measures to develop a consumer bill of rights or industry codes of practice that go beyond the regulatory framework can further improve consumer welfare.

[54] OECD Report, *Enhancing Competition in Telecommunications: Protecting and Empowering Consumers, Ministerial Background Report* (n 47), pp. 15–43.

[55] See, for more details on access to justice of consumers, ch. 7.

Another key measure is Directive 93/13/EEC,[56] which aims to protect consumers from unfair terms and is therefore also directly relevant in electronic communications services. On this, the ECJ has taken a protective approach, granting to consumers a high level of protection against unbalanced contracts. This is for example illustrated in *Mostaza Claro v Centro Móvil*,[57] a Spanish case in 2006, revolving around a consumer action against a mobile-telephone company. In this case, an arbitration term had been inserted in the contract, which restricted the consumer's access to justice. A Spanish court found that the arbitration clause constituted an unfair contractual term in relation to a Spanish law that implemented Directive 93/13/EEC, and was, therefore, not applicable. However, as the consumer did not mention this issue in the arbitral procedure, the Spanish court asked the ECJ for a preliminary ruling, with regard to whether it could declare the arbitral clause void on its own initiative. The ECJ held that: 'The nature and importance of the public interest underlying the protection which the Directive confers on consumers justify (...) the national court being required to assess of its own motion whether a contractual term is unfair, compensating in this way for the imbalance which exists between the consumer and the seller or supplier'.[58] This case thus clarified that the national courts are *obliged* to actively intervene *ex officio* to investigate and address unfair clauses, to ensure a high level of consumer protection.

3.3. *Data protection as a human right*

Advanced technologies and innovative communications services have raised public concern regarding the protection of personal data and, more generally, the safeguarding of consumers' privacy. A vast amount of personal information can be collected by service providers, putting consumers at risk of misuse.[59]

[56] Directive 93/13/EEC of 5 April 1993 on unfair terms in consumer contracts, OJ L 95, 21.4.1993, pp. 29–34.

[57] Case C-168/05, *Elisa María Mostaza Claro v Centro Móvil Milenium SL* [2006] ECR I-10421; see more information on further recent case law regarding this issue in ch. 7 of this book.

[58] Case C-168/05, *Elisa María Mostaza Claro v Centro Móvil Milenium SL* [2006] ECR I-10421, para 38. For a detailed analysis, see C. Liebscher 'Case C-168/05, *Elisa María Mostaza Claro v Centro Móvil Milenium SL*, judgment of the Court of Justice (First Chamber) of October 2006 ECR I-10421', (2008) 45 *CML Rev.*, pp. 545–57.

[59] See e.g. the introductory note 5 of the Directive 2002/58/EC on privacy and electronic communication, of 12 July 2002.

Given the potentially serious consequences of personal information abuses, the right to privacy is protected at the human rights level. A right to privacy can be found both in Article 8 of the European Convention on Human Rights, and in Articles 7 and 8 of the Charter of Fundamental Rights.[60] Moreover, Article 16 TFEU (ex Article 286 EC) guarantees that '(e)veryone has the right to the protection of personal data concerning them'.

Besides the above provisions, the right to privacy has been protected in a concrete manner in Directive 2002/58/EC, concerning the processing of personal data and the protection of privacy which complemented the Data Protection Directive 95/46/EC. Subsequently, the new 'Citizens' Rights' Directive[61] (2009) mentioned previously amended the former Directive 2002/58/EC and improved consumer protection in terms of privacy, placing important obligations on operators in this regard. The new directive, for example, changes Article 1(1), which now states that this Act 'provides for the harmonization of the national provisions required to ensure an equivalent level of protection of fundamental rights and freedoms, and in particular the right to privacy and confidentiality, with respect to the processing of personal data in the electronic communication sector'. Personal data here refers to any information that can be traced to an individual. In turn, 'processing of personal data' is defined as any operation which is performed upon personal data, such as collection, recording, organization, storage, use, or disclosure.

According to Article 3, the directive now applies 'to the processing of personal data in connection with the provision of publicly available electronic communications services in public communications networks in the Community, including public communications networks supporting data collection and identification devices'. This covers the security of networks and services, the confidentiality of communications, access to stored data, processing of traffic, location of data, and unsolicited commercial communications.

Furthermore, Article 4, entitled 'Security of processing', obliges providers to take the appropriate technical and organizational measures to ensure that personal data can be accessed only by authorized personnel, for legally authorized purposes. Moreover, they have to protect personal data against destruction, accidental loss, or alteration, and unauthorized or unlawful storage, processing, access, or disclosure. Finally, providers need to ensure the implementation of a security policy with respect to the processing of personal data. Article 4(3)

[60] For a detailed discussion on the role of fundamental rights in contract and e-commerce, see C. Mak, 'Fundamental Rights and the European Regulation of iConsumer Contracts', (2008) 31 *J. Consumer Policy*, pp. 425–39.

[61] Directive 2009/136/EC, OJ L 337/11, 18.12.2009.

now includes an obligation on service providers to notify a personal data breach without undue delay to the competent national authority, and to individuals if the personal data breach is likely to adversely affect their privacy. In particular, providers have to describe the breach and provide a contact point for information, and recommend measures to mitigate the possible adverse effects of the personal data breach. This ensures that consumers are informed promptly about privacy threats resulting in their personal data being lost or otherwise compromised. They can thereby take precautions to minimize the possible economic loss or social harm that could result from such a security breach.

Article 5(1), a key provision on confidentiality, remains unchanged and requires Member States to ensure the confidentiality of communications and the related traffic data through appropriate legislation. In particular, they have to prohibit interception or surveillance of communications and the related traffic data by persons other than users. There are, however, a number of exceptions to the confidentiality obligation. For example, the storage of data is permitted with the consent of the affected person or where it is justified by national defence measures or for technical reasons, business practices, or billing purposes.

Article 13 concerns 'unsolicited communications', prohibiting automated calling and communication systems or electronic mail for direct marketing purposes, without the prior consent of subscribers or users. However, if a person obtains from its customers their contact emails, the person is allowed to use this contact for marketing purposes under specific conditions, in particular the consumer must be given the possibility to object to such publicity on the occasion of each message (Article 13(2)). Importantly, Article 13(6) stipulates that any 'person adversely affected by infringements of national provisions adopted pursuant to this Article, may bring legal proceedings in respect of such infringements'. This provision thereby reinforces the application of legal actions against infringers of data protection, which might become an important tool in the fight against unsolicited commercial communications in the EU.

Finally, Article 15(a) of the new directive further improves enforcement mechanisms currently in place, requiring Member States to establish rules on dissuasive penalties applicable to infringements.

3.4. *Balancing fundamental rights*

As discussed in the previous subsection, privacy rights have been recognized as human rights. Although clearly beneficial for consumer protection, this may lead to some dilemmas, as privacy rights might turn out to clash with other fundamental rights. This and the following subsection will examine this point.

An important case in this sense was *Promusicae*, decided in 2008 by the ECJ, which founded its judgment directly on the Charter of Fundamental Rights.[62] In this case the Court had to balance conflicting fundamental rights: the right to privacy on the one hand and the rights to the protection of property and to an effective remedy on the other.

Promusicae, an organization of producers and publishers of musical and audiovisual recordings, asked the Spanish Court to oblige Telefónica to disclose the identities of the customers to whom it provided Internet access. Promusicae alleged that some customers were illegally sharing files in which Promusicae's members held the exploitation rights.[63] The national court referred a question to the ECJ for a preliminary ruling, asking whether Community law, read also in the light of the Charter, must be interpreted as requiring Member States to lay down an obligation to communicate personal data, in order to ensure the effective protection of copyright in the civil proceedings.[64]

The ECJ started by examining Directive 2002/58, which provides at Article 5(1) that Member States must ensure the confidentiality of communications by means of a public communications network and publicly available electronic communications services, and of the related traffic data. An exception is provided by Article 15(1) of the same directive, which allows Member States to adopt measures that may restrict the scope of the obligation to ensure personal data confidentiality imposed on them by Article 5, where this is inter alia necessary to safeguard national or public security or to the detection and prosecution of criminal offences. The ECJ considered in this regard that while Directive 2002/58 does not preclude the possibility of Member States to establish an obligation to disclose personal data in the context of civil proceedings, they are not obliged to adopt such legislative measures. Thus, in the present case, the ECJ held that no obligation of disclosure existed.[65]

When it came to fundamental rights, Promusicae invoked Articles 17 and 47 of the Charter, concerning the protection of the right to property and to

[62] Case C-275/06, *Productores de Música de España (Promusicae) v Telefónica de España SAU* [2008] ECR I-271.

[63] Case C-275/06, *Promusicae v Telefónica* [2008] ECR I-271, paras 29–31.

[64] See also the analysis of the case in X. Groussot, 'Rock the KaZa: Another Clash of Fundamental Rights, Case C-275/06, *Productores de Musica de Espana (Promusicae)* v *Telefonica de Espana SAU*, Judgment of the Court (Grand Chamber) of 29 January 2008', (2008) 45 *CML Rev.*, pp. 1745–66.

[65] Case C-275/06, *Promusicae v Telefónica* [2008] ECR I-271, paras 50–5.

an effective remedy. The ECJ admitted that these rights were general principles of Community law, but stated that they must be balanced with the fundamental right to a private life in Article 7 of the Charter. Recital 2 in the preamble to Directive 2002/58 states that the fundamental rights provided by the Charter, in particular Article 7 on private life and Article 8 on the protection of private data, have to be respected.[66] Therefore, the right to privacy has to be balanced against the right to intellectual property. In balancing these different rights, the ECJ referred to Directive 2002/58 itself, which gives concrete indications of when data can be disclosed, as well as to other relevant directives and Member States' provisions transposing those directives.

The Court went on to hold that Member States had, in particular, to ensure a fair balance between fundamental rights when transposing relevant directives. Moreover, the ECJ stated that 'the authorities and courts of the Member States must not only interpret their national law consistent with relevant directives, but also make sure that they do not rely on an interpretation of them which would be in conflict with those fundamental rights'.[67] Finally, the ECJ concluded that under Community law Member States are not obliged to impose the disclosure of personal data in order to ensure the protection of copyrights in the context of civil proceedings.

This case shows the important role that the Charter of Fundamental Rights can play in the ECJ's jurisprudence.[68] Moreover, it suggests that the Court is taking an activist stance to ensure privacy protection in the EU. For consumers, this ruling can be considered a positive outcome. However, a high degree of privacy protection may raise new challenges in the EU market, as it risks promoting abusive behaviour and fuelling piracy. The debate on how to combat piracy, while at the same preserving privacy is still open, and new instruments still have to be found to address this dilemma.

3.5. *The* Scarlet Extended *case*

In the recent *Scarlet Extended* case,[69] the ECJ reiterated the position taken in the *Promusicae case* and went further in clarifying the meaning of other fundamental rights in the telecommunications sector. The case dealt, inter

[66] Case C-275/06, *Promusicae v Telefónica* [2008] ECR I-271, paras 63–5.

[67] Case C-275/06, *Promusicae v Telefónica* [2008] ECR I-271, para. 70.

[68] For further discussion on the role of fundamental rights in contracts and e-commerce see Mak, 'Fundamental Rights and the European Regulation of iConsumer Contracts' (n 60), pp. 435–6.

[69] Case C-70/10, *Scarlet Extended SA v Société belge des auteurs, compositeurs et éditeurs SCRL (SABAM)* 24 November 2011, report not yet published.

alia, with the question of whether the obligation on ISPs to monitor and block content infringing copyrights violates the consumers' fundamental rights.

This case concerned the dispute between Scarlet Extended SA, an Internet service provider, and SABAM, a management company responsible for authorizing the use of copyright-protected musical works by third parties. When SABAM established that users of Scarlet's services were downloading works in SABAM's catalogue by means of file-sharing software, it sought a court order requiring Scarlet to bring such infringements to an end. In response, Scarlet claimed that such an obligation to monitor communications on its network is incompatible with the directive on electronic commerce and with fundamental rights.

The Court affirmed that the imposition on ISPs to conduct a general monitoring task of Internet traffic is prohibited by Article 15(1) of Directive 2000/31 on electronic commerce. Moreover, while recognizing that the right to intellectual property is protected by Article 17(2) of the Charter, the Court clarified that this right is not absolute. On this, it stated that there is 'nothing whatsoever in the wording of that provision or in the Court's case law to suggest that that right is inviolable and must for that reason be absolutely protected'.[70]

Furthermore, referring to the *Promusicae* case, the Court held that the rights of copyright holders, which are IP rights protected by Article 17(2) of the Charter, have to be balanced with other fundamental rights.[71] In particular, a fair balance has to be struck between the protection of intellectual property rights and the freedom to conduct a business enjoyed by operators (such as providing Internet services), pursuant to Article 16 of the Charter. The Court established that, in this case, the injunction requiring the ISP to install a complete filtering system 'would result in a serious infringement of the freedom of the ISP concerned to conduct its business since it would require that ISP to install a complicated, costly, permanent computer system at its own expense, which would also be contrary to the conditions laid down in Article 3(1) of Directive 2004/48, which requires that measures to ensure the respect of intellectual property rights should not be unnecessarily complicated or costly'.[72] Importantly, according to the Court, this injunction would infringe fundamental rights of consumers; in particular Article 8, regarding

[70] Case C-70/10, *Scarlet Extended SA v Société belge des auteurs, compositeurs et éditeurs SCRL (SABAM)* 24 November 2011, report not yet published, para. 43.

[71] Case C-70/10, *Scarlet Extended SA v Société belge des auteurs, compositeurs et éditeurs SCRL (SABAM)* 24 November 2011, report not yet published, paras 43–4.

[72] Case C-70/10, *Scarlet Extended SA v Société belge des auteurs, compositeurs et éditeurs SCRL (SABAM)* 24 November 2011, report not yet published, para. 48.

the protection of personal data, and Article 11 on the freedom to receive or impart information. First, requiring installation of a filtering system would infringe the right to data protection, as it would involve a systematic analysis of all content and the collection and identification of users' IP addresses. Secondly, a filtering system could potentially undermine freedom of information since it might not distinguish adequately between unlawful content and lawful content. This may lead to the blocking of lawful communication.[73] Therefore, the Court concluded that requiring Internet service providers to install a filtering system to prevent IP-infringement 'would not be respecting the requirement that a fair balance be struck between the right to intellectual property, on the one hand, and the freedom to conduct business, the right to protection of personal data and the freedom to receive or impart information, on the other'.

This case is interesting as it exemplifies how several fundamental rights may come into play in telecommunication-related cases. Moreover, it represents a landmark as the ECJ confirmed for the first time the fundamental freedom of consumers to receive or impart information in this context. This may well have an important impact on Internet-related regulation in Member States.

In a very similar case from 2012, *SABAM v Netlog*,[74] the ECJ confirmed the decision taken in the *Scarlet Extended* case. The Court applied a similar reasoning regarding the balancing of intellectual property rights versus other fundamental rights, including protection of personal data and the freedom to receive information. In this case, the Court had to decide again on whether an online social network provider, Netlog, could be forced to install a general filtering system—under SABAM's request. In this case too, the Court ruled that such a request would not allow a fair balance between the fundamental rights already mentioned in *Scarlet Extended*.

4. Consumer Participation

The Citizens' Rights' Directive 2009/136/EC, discussed in previous sections, imposes an obligation on Member States to integrate consumer consultation and representation mechanisms into their systems regarding electronic communications services. This development will be discussed in more detail,

[73] Case C-70/10, *Scarlet Extended SA v Société belge des auteurs, compositeurs et éditeurs SCRL (SABAM)* 24 November 2011, report not yet published, paras. 51–2.

[74] Case C-360/10, *Belgische Vereniging van Auteurs, Componisten en Uitgevers CVBA (SABAM) v Netlog NV* 16 February 2012, not yet reported.

assessing institutions, such as a consumer panel on electronic communications, which would further develop and strengthen this trend in the EU.

Moreover, the Lisbon Treaty introduces the possibility of a 'Citizens' Initiative' that might enhance the capability of consumers and interest groups to become more involved in EU policy.

How can such new tools, which are sometimes developed in other contexts, be applied to consumer law? The following subsections assess these mechanisms, and examine how and whether they may enhance consumer participation in the legislative process.

4.1. *Participation and representation of consumer interests*

In increasingly complex communication markets, it is important that consumer interests are understood by regulators when framing regulation and policy initiatives. Participation of consumers in regulatory debates is an important way to influence policy-making, which, in turn, can be achieved through consumer advisory bodies outside or within the regulator.

The original Directive 2002/22/EC mentioned previously, on universal service and users' rights relating to electronic communications (Universal Service Directive), required consultation of national regulatory authorities in this field with interested parties. According to Article 33(1) of this directive, Member States had to ensure that national regulatory authorities take account of the views of end-users, consumers, and the undertakings that provide electronic communications services.

Despite this provision, for consumer organizations the difficulty often lies in making their voice sufficiently heard.[75]

In this regard, as we have seen, the above-mentioned directive was later modified by the 'Citizens' Rights' Directive 2009/136/EC. The new legal framework acknowledges the central role of consumer participation in policy-making, as it includes an essential new provision under Article 33(1), which expressly requires that consumer interests are taken into account.[76] The new directive states that 'Member States shall ensure that national regulatory authorities

[75] On the difficulties of establishing political power for consumers, see F. Trentman & M. Bevir (eds), *Governance, Citizens, and Consumers: Agency and Resistance in Contemporary Politics* (Basingstoke: Palgrave Macmillan, 2007); see also: I. Ramsey, *Consumer Law and Policy: Text and Materials on Regulating Consumer Markets* (Oxford: Hart Publishing: 2007), p. 31.

[76] Directive 2009/136/EC of 25 November 2009 amending Directive 2002/22/EC and Directive 2002/58/EC and Regulation (EC) No 2006/2004 on cooperation between national authorities responsible for the enforcement of consumer protection laws, OJ L 337/11, 18.12.2009.

establish a consultation mechanism ensuring that in their decisions [...] concerning publicly available electronic communications services, *due consideration is given to consumer interests*' (emphasis added). During the political debate leading to the adoption of the Citizens' Rights Directive, this new provision has largely remained uncontested, and was therefore recognized by the EU institutions and the Member States as a key provision to strengthen consumer participation in the legislative process.

This directive reflects a trend in the European Union to seek public consultations on legislative initiatives, paying particular importance to consumer issues. A precedent (and possibly a source of inspiration and influence) may have been the 'Communications Consumer Panel' of the telecommunication regulator Ofcom in the UK. This Consumer Panel has had a significant effect in enhancing consumer interests in the electronic communications sector and its suggestions have been incorporated in policy actions.[77]

While the new 'Citizens' Rights' Directive does not go as far as to require the establishment of such an institution, it has the potential to promote involvement of consumer groups, to directly influence national regulatory agencies towards a consumer-focused approach in this field. The UK's Communication Consumer Panel provides an example of one way to ensure that consumer interests are taken into account at national level in the field of electronic communications. Therefore, the next subsection explores this model in more detail, besides other existing approaches at the EU level.

4.2. *The Communications Consumer Panel and EU consultations*

The Communications Consumer Panel was established within the new Office of Communications in the UK in 2003. It is based upon the Communications Act 2003 as an independent policy advisory body on consumer interests in telecommunications, broadcasting, and spectrum markets.[78] The Communications Consumer Panel is composed of members with expertise in consumer issues in the electronic communications sector, representing different geographical areas of the UK.[79] The Panel advises the regulator Ofcom on consumer and citizen interests in electronic communications, working with policy-makers and industry stakeholders.

[77] See more at: <http://www.communicationsconsumerpanel.org.uk/>.

[78] See also H. Beuchler, 'Länderbericht Vereinigtes Königreich', in Keßler & Micklitz (eds), *Kundenschutz auf liberalisierten Märkten* (n 2), p. 365.

[79] For more information see the website of the Communications Consumer Panel: <http://www.communicationsconsumerpanel.org.uk/>.

The UK experience has illustrated, in particular, three channels through which the Panel can promote consumers' interests. First, the Panel participates in the decision-making process with the regulator before political or regulatory measures are taken. This increases consumers' involvement in regulatory processes, giving them an early opportunity to influence the debate. Secondly, the consumer panel is active in bilateral meetings with consumer stakeholders, and creates a consumer forum on electronic communications, bringing together different consumer organizations. Thirdly, the Panel is a promoter of new consumer instruments that may influence policy-makers. For example, in 2006 the Panel developed the so-called 'Consumer Interest Toolkit', which can control and effectively increase consumer considerations in policy-making. The Toolkit consists of a series of questions that regulators should ask themselves to ensure that consumer interests are appropriately considered throughout the organization or in a particular policy area. Such an instrument thus serves a double purpose: it forces regulators to build consumer concerns into their systems, and allows them to assess whether they have identified and implemented consumer interests in their policy.[80] A review in 2008 showed that this tool had influenced Ofcom's decision-making, and had been successful in improving consumer interests within the UK regulator. In particular, Ofcom has evaluated its policies with this tool and has consequently adapted its regulative measures.[81]

The Communication Consumer Panel could be an effective model for other Member States and for the EU in order to achieve a coherent consumer interest policy. In the EU a number of consumer consultative groups already exist. In 2004 the European Commission established FIN-USE as an independent expert consumer forum. Its mandate is to strengthen the role of consumers and small businesses in the EU financial services sector.[82] FIN-USE provides opinion and recommendations to the European Commission on initiatives influencing financial services users to improve policy-making in this field. Furthermore, it identifies core financial services issues.

[80] Communications Consumer Panel, *Capturing the Consumer Interest. A Toolkit for Regulators and Government*, February 2006; see the website of Communications Consumer Panel: <http://www.communicationsconsumerpanel.org.uk/downloads/Policy/Consumer%20InterestToolkit/Publications/capturing_the_consumer_interest%20a%20toolkit%20for%20regulators%20etc.pdf>.

[81] For more information see the website of the Communications Consumer Panel: <http://www.communicationsconsumerpanel.org.uk/>.

[82] See the FIN-USE website: <http://ec.europa.eu/internal_market/fin-use_forum/index_en.htm>.

Another long-established institution of this kind is the European Consumer Consultative Group (ECCG), established by the European Commission in 1973. The ECCG, which during its operations developed sub-groups in several fields, such as for competition policy,[83] was established precisely to address insufficient participation and representation of consumers in EU law-making.[84] The ECCG meets four times a year and is mainly composed of one representative of national consumer organizations per country, and one member from each European consumer organization (BEUC and ANEC).[85]

Following a review which highlighted the need to improve efficiency and openness, the ECCG was reformed by the Commission, by means of Decision 2009/705/EC. Article 2 of this latter re-stated the objectives of the ECCG, affirming that this serves, inter alia, for general discussions on issues related to consumer interests, and advises the Commission on issues relevant to EU consumer policy. The reformed ECCG will assist in representing general consumer interests, enabling an informative dialogue with the Commission and thereby integrating the consumer's voice in EU policies. For example, following its remit, in 2011 the ECCG provided advice to the Commission regarding some issues in contract law.[86]

This formal establishment of a consultation requirement and consumer advisory groups shows the willingness of the EU to promote participation of all interest groups in law-making procedures. Although this will certainly provide information to law-makers on consumer-related issues, it is not clear how powerful this influence will be. One factor which could be helpful in this regard is a regular review procedure by the EU institutions, showing if and how the ECCG recommendations were taken into account. This would provide more transparency and accountability, enhancing the practical value of the consultation tools.

Further consolidation of these instruments, ultimately benefiting participation, could also be obtained by the creation of specialized sub-groups similar to the UK Communication Consumer Panel, which could provide detailed advice in technical consumer law areas, such as in electronic

83 See e.g. the Commission Decision of 14 September 2009 setting up a European Consumer Consultative Group, OJ L 244, 16/09/2009, pp. 21–4.

84 On legislative participation of consumers in financial services see J. Mendes, *Participation in Rule-Making, A Rights-Based Approach*, Studies in European Law (Oxford: OUP, 2011), pp. 302–3; on interest representation see also J. Greenwood, *Interest Representation in the European Union* (Basingstoke: Palgrave Macmillan, 2011).

85 <http://ec.europa.eu/consumers/empowerment/eccg_en.htm>.

86 <http://ec.europa.eu/consumers/empowerment/minutes/minutes_28012011_en.pdf>.

communications law. This would make it more likely that both consumer and citizens' interests are better taken into account by national regulators.

To summarize, the required consultation mechanism proposed in the 'Citizens' Rights' Directive is a clear indication of a commitment of the EU to a broader, more politically involved, consumer concept. For the electronic communications sector in particular, the establishment of an independent consumer panel would further enhance consumer representation in regulatory decisions.

4.3. *Participation and the citizens' initiative after Lisbon*

The Lisbon Treaty introduces a novel form of public participation in the European policy-making process,[87] by defining, quite uniquely, a new right: the right of 'citizens' initiative'.[88] Stated as a general right of citizens, this could become of direct interest to consumers, and may in particular allow interest groups to influence telecommunication regulation.

The key provision in this regard is Article 11 TEU stating that 'one million citizens who are nationals of a significant number of member states may take the initiative of inviting the European Commission, within the framework of its powers, to submit any appropriate proposal'. This grants to EU citizens the right to ask the Commission to propose legislation on a particular issue, such as consumer protection, if they collect at least one million signatures from a large number of Member States.

The details of this 'citizens' initiative' procedure had to be defined by the Council and the European Parliament by the ordinary legislative procedure. Therefore, in March 2010, the European Commission prepared a proposal for a regulation of the European Parliament and of the Council on the citizens' initiative.[89] The EU regulation on the citizens' initiative was eventually adopted on 16 February 2011 and entered into force on 1 April 2012.[90]

According to this regulation, a European citizens' initiative would require the European Commission to submit a legislative proposal if it lies in its

[87] See P. Craig, *The Lisbon Treaty. Law, Politics and Treaty Reform* (Oxford: OUP, 2010), p. 77; J. Mendes, 'Participation and the Role of Law after Lisbon: A Legal View on Article 11 TEU', (2011) 48 *CML Rev.* 1849–78.

[88] See the Commission's website: <http://ec.europa.eu/dgs/secretariat_general/citizens_initiative/index_en.htm>.

[89] Proposal for a Regulation of the European Parliament and of the Council on the citizens' initiative by the European Commission, COM(2010) 119 final, 31.3.2010.

[90] EU Regulation No 211/2011 on the citizens' initiative, OJ L 65/1, 11.3.2011.

competence. Such an initiative has to be made by one million EU citizens that have to cover at least seven Member States. In addition, a minimum number of signatories is needed in each of those Member States, which is determined in an annex to the aforementioned regulation.[91]

Currently, the EU includes about 500 million consumers, of whom approximately 375 million are eligible voters.[92] The gathering of one million signatures in the EU thus seems a relatively accessible target. To start such an initiative, at least seven EU citizens of voting age, who are residents of at least seven different Member States, have to form a 'citizens' committee' (Article 3).[93] Organizations are not allowed to manage a citizens' initiative, but they can promote such an initiative on condition that this is done in a transparent way.[94]

However, the regulation on the citizens' initiative also sets important constraints for the procedure: first, the signatures must be collected from at least one quarter of Member States (Article 7(1)), which means they must come from at least seven countries. Secondly, a minimum varying number of signatories is required in each of them.[95] Thirdly, the initiative may only regard 'matters where citizens consider that a legal act of the Union is required for the purpose of implementing the Treaties' (Article 1). Thus, the initiative must be within the scope of the existing, general EU legal framework. Finally, once such an act is proposed by the Commission, it has still to get through a lengthy legislative process and requires sufficient political support in order to be adopted. However, this initiative procedure provides a welcome alternative way to create a more democratic dialogue.

There are already some relevant open initiatives that were registered in 2012. One initiative, for example, aims to invite the Commission to propose legislation 'implementing the human right to water and sanitation as recognized by the United Nations, and promoting the provision of water and sanitation

[91] Commission Delegated EU Regulation No 268/2012 amending Annex I of Regulation (EU) No 211/2011 on the citizens' initiative OJ L 89/1, 27.3.2012.

[92] For the number of eligible voters, see the European Parliament's website: <http://www.europarl.europa.eu/>.

[93] The committee member must be of the age to be entitled to vote in elections to the European Parliament (Art. 3(1) Citizens' Initiative Regulation).

[94] See the European Commission information website: <http://ec.europa.eu/citizens-initiative/public/basic-facts>.

[95] <http://ec.europa.eu/citizens-initiative/public/signatories>.

as essential public services for all'.[96] Another initiative, dealing with responsible waste management, is also related to sustainable consumption behaviour of households.[97]

Interestingly, an initiative has also been registered in 2012 specifically impinging on the telecommunications sector. This initiative proposes a 'Single Communication Tariff Act', which would create a 'European common market for all mobile phone customers' and eliminate roaming fees across the Union.

Although it is too early to predict the long-term impact of the citizens' initiative, it will provide consumers with new possibilities to steer the EU policy towards more consumer-citizens-oriented objectives.

5. Conclusions

This chapter has discussed some aspects of the EU electronic communications law and policy, considering their relative impacts on consumer protection. Initially, the EU legislative framework was mainly focused on economic competition objectives, while consumer protection per se had a much lesser role. However, this seems to be gradually changing now, as the new legislation pays growing attention to consumer-citizens aspects, and aims at empowering consumers.

An example of this is provided by the new 'Citizens' Rights' Directive 2009/136/EC, which aims to protect consumers and promotes market transparency, as can be seen in its provisions ensuring clearer comparative information and strengthening consumers' rights. At the same time, the directive focuses on the consumer-citizens perspective, improving access to electronic communications services for the disabled, elderly, and financially-disfavoured.

Fundamental rights can play an important role regarding the freedom to receive and impart information and the protection of privacy. As we have

[96] This initiative is also supported by the European Federation of Public Service Unions (EPSU), the European Anti-Poverty Network, and European Environmental Bureau; see: <http://www.right2water.eu/news/media-advisory-first-european-citizens%E2%80%99-initiative-water-launched-april-1st>.

[97] See the European Commission's website regarding open initiatives: <http://ec.europa.eu/citizens-initiative/public/initiatives/ongoing/details/2012/000009>.

seen, both the Charter and the ECJ have recognized these freedoms and rights as binding fundamental rights. However, as shown by the *Promusicae* case, privacy protection may conflict with other fundamental rights such as the right to property, and thus needs to be balanced—something which will require new legal solutions.

This chapter concluded by considering Article 11 of the Lisbon Treaty for its provisions on direct participation in the EU legislative process and the 'Citizens' Rights' Directive for its consultative requirements. Both may produce important effects on consumer law, bringing policy- and law-makers closer to social issues and to citizens' needs.

7

Consumers' Access to Justice and Procedural Rights

1. Introduction[1]

Access to justice is commonly recognized as a core human right. At the same time, it is a right that has proved difficult to realize,[2] particularly in consumer law. Consumers often have difficulties in obtaining redress in order to receive compensation, especially in a cross-border context. They face various barriers in exercising their rights, including a lack of knowledge of the legal systems and limited funding. Furthermore, a recent surge in supranational mass damages cases has indicated an urgent need for simple, cheap, and collective ways of enforcement.

As a policy response, there has been a gradual shift from a substance-focused to a more procedural-oriented perspective to consumer law. A growing number of Member States have incorporated collective redress mechanisms into their national systems as a way of dealing with the multiplication of consumer claims. Furthermore, a similar trend has begun to emerge in the EU context, where collective redress measures are currently evaluated as a tool to improve access to justice and alternative dispute resolution has gained prominence within the priorities of EU consumer policy.[3]

[1] This chapter draws on previous work by the author, published in: I. Benöhr, 'Consumer Dispute Resolution after the Lisbon Treaty' (2013), 36(1) *J. Consumer Policy*, pp. 87–110. DOI: 10.1007/s10603-012-9202-0.

[2] A recent study by the EU Agency for Fundamental Rights (FRA) has revealed that common barriers to access to justice in Member States are: long procedures, high legal costs, and restrictive rules on who may take a case to court; see the EU Agency for Fundamental Rights' Report, *Access to Justice in Europe: An Overview of Challenges and Opportunities* (2011).

[3] See: <http://ec.europa.eu/consumers/redress_cons/collective_redress_en.htm>.

Despite their merit, collective enforcement mechanisms have also raised some controversy. On the one hand, they have sometimes led to excessive compensation claims, as illustrated by US-style class actions.[4] On the other, the first experiences in some EU Member States have shown that they may have a rather limited impact in practice. Therefore, the design and effectiveness of such mechanisms have to be carefully evaluated.

In the light of the above development a number of questions arise: what are the main obstacles to consumer access to justice? Can collective redress mechanisms improve effective redress and what alternative procedures could facilitate consumer dispute resolution?

This chapter aims to evaluate how the formal right of access to justice can be transformed into effective enforcement procedures. To do so, it first analyzes the issue of consumer access to justice as a fundamental right in the EU, comparing collective redress models and major cases in the Member States, to evaluate their cross-border implication. Secondly, it examines how the new competences in the Lisbon Treaty regarding civil procedure may facilitate consumer redress, evaluating alternative dispute resolution schemes and collective redress mechanisms. Finally, it puts forward financing models, such as a collective action fund and contingency fees, which may increase the affordability of judicial actions.

2. Access to Justice as a Human Right

At a global level, access to justice has been clearly recognized as a human right.[5] This right generally includes 'the right to a fair trial, the right to have one's case decided within a reasonable time, and the right to a remedy, such as compensation'.[6] At an international level, the right to access to justice is provided in Articles 2 and 14 of the International Covenant on Civil and

[4] See C. Hodges, *The Reform of Class and Representative Actions in European Legal Systems: A New Framework for Collective Redress in Europe* (Oxford: Hart Publishing, 2008); D. Hensler, C. Hodges, & M. Tulibacka, *The Globalization of Class Actions, The Annals*, Special edition, vol 622 (Thousand Oaks: CA, SAGE Publications, 2009).

[5] E. Storskrubb & J. Ziller, 'Access to Justice in European Comparative Law', in F. Francioni (ed.), *Access to Justice as a Human Right* (Oxford: Hart Publishing, 2007), p. 177; A. Ward, 'Access to Justice', in S. Peers & A. Ward (eds), *The EU Charter of Fundamental Rights, Politics, Law and Policy, (Essays in European Law)* (Oxford: Hart Publishing, 2004), p. 247.

[6] See the EU Agency for Fundamental Rights' Report, *Access to Justice in Europe: An Overview of Challenges and Opportunities* (n 2), p. 14.

Political Rights and in the 2011 UN Guiding Principles on Business and Human Rights.[7]

At the European level, access to justice has been acknowledged as a fundamental right, through the procedural right to an individual hearing and to a remedy in the European Convention on Human Rights (Articles 6 and 13 ECHR). Furthermore, Article 47 of the EU Charter of Fundamental Rights, entitled 'Right to an effective remedy and to a fair trial', states that everyone has 'the right to an effective remedy before a tribunal' and is 'entitled to a fair and public hearing within a reasonable time by an independent and impartial tribunal previously established by law'. Moreover, 'Everyone shall have the possibility of being advised, defended and represented'. This Article also expressly stipulates that legal aid should be provided to those who lack sufficient resources, if this is required to ensure effective access to justice. In addition, the fundamental right to an effective remedy has been affirmed by the recent ECJ case law including in the particular field of consumer protection.[8]

Despite this formal recognition, consumers still face major barriers to enforcing their rights in practice. This has created a civil justice gap that undermines the credibility of the EU legal system and impedes efficient functioning of the internal market.[9]

2.1. *Access to justice barriers*

Already in the late 1970s, the access to justice scholars Mauro Cappelletti and Bryan Garth evaluated complaints mechanisms to render law procedures more effective.[10] As a result, they identified three key obstacles: cost, organizational problems, and lack of adequate procedures.[11] However, today, almost 40 years later, cost barriers and inefficient procedures are still upheld as the main problems for access to justice for consumers in the current European system.[12]

[7] See the Report of J. Ruggie, *Guiding Principles on Business and Human Rights: Implementing the United Nations 'Protect, Respect and Remedy' Framework*, 2001 (see also: <http://www.business-humanrights.org>).

[8] See the European Commission, *2010 Report on the Application of the EU Charter of Fundamental Rights*, 2011, p. 77 and e.g. the following case law: Joined Cases C-317/08 to C-320/08, *Alassini and others v Telecom Italia* [2010] ECR I-2213.

[9] European Commission, Eurobarometer 2006, Special Report 252, 'Consumer Protection in the Internal Market'; 44% of consumers are less confident when purchasing in another EU state.

[10] M. Cappelletti & B. Garth (eds), *Access to Justice: a World Survey* (Milan: A. Giuffre, 1978), p. 49.

[11] M. Cappelletti, 'Alternative Dispute Resolution within the Framework of the World-Wide Access-to-Justice Movement', (1993) 56 *MLR*, pp. 282–90.

[12] In the Eurobarometer survey 2006 (n 9), 73% of consumers indicated that they would not bring their complaint to court, because of the high litigation costs, the length (33%), and the procedural complexity (33%).

First, the main reason for not bringing a case is the financial risk of a legal case that can be so costly as to effectively preclude the participation of consumers or their interest groups. In the Eurobarometer survey 73 per cent of consumers indicated cost as a reason not to complain. In particular, the amount of damages claimed by consumers might be relatively low in relation to the cost of a claim. As a result, consumers with small claims often refrain from bringing an individual action.

Secondly, an organizational problem for access to justice is the lack of legal expertise.[13] Consumers perceive resolving arguments with sellers or service providers in court as difficult. Owing to procedural complexity, and the lack of information in a global market, the diffuse interests of consumers are becoming more dependent on interest groups or public bodies to enforce the law. However, consumer groups often lack funding and adequate legal knowledge in order to represent collective consumer claims. In this regard a promising Consumer Law Enforcement Forum (CLEF) project has been established in the EU that could improve the capability of consumer interest groups. This Enforcement Forum deals with the involvement and the possible roles of consumer organizations in both public enforcement, i.e. getting public authorities to engage more fully with consumer problems, and in private enforcement, i.e. bringing a case to courts via collective action.[14]

Finally, another factor that might obstruct justice is the lack of adequate redress mechanisms for damages. In fact, 74 per cent of European consumers would be more willing to defend their rights in court if they could join with other harmed consumers in the procedure.[15] However, at the transnational level this is often not possible.

Nonetheless, the data also highlighted that only a small number of consumers wish to bring a case before the courts, as a complaint is time-consuming and might be expensive.[16] This indicates the importance of effective alternative dispute resolution mechanisms for consumers in the EU.

[13] According to the Eurobarometer 2006 survey (n 9), 41% of consumers were not satisfied with the handling of the complaint. Further, around 50% of unsatisfied consumers do not complain against a company because of a lack of resources or legal expertise.

[14] See: <http://www.clef-project.eu/cms/index.php>.

[15] Consumers remain passive in complaints, because they have the impression that they are not heard and often do not know where and how to complain.

[16] Taking sellers or providers to court occupies the second lowest position in the Eurobarometer survey (an EU average of 17%).

In conclusion, at present, access to justice remains difficult for consumers, which indicates a need for novel procedural solutions at cross-border level. Accordingly, before exploring new redress schemes the following section assesses both the effectiveness of existing EU redress mechanisms and out-of-court procedures.

2.2. *Existing redress mechanisms in the EU*

A set of access to justice instruments has already been put in place to facilitate consumer redress. In 1993 the European Commission published a Green Paper on Consumer Access to Justice in order to improve redress mechanisms and out-of-court procedures,[17] and since 1995 consumer access to justice through efficient redress has been given high priority in the Commission's policy.[18]

With the entry into force of the Treaty of Amsterdam in 1999, 'judicial cooperation in civil matters' became a new EU policy, to improve the efficiency of the European civil justice system.[19] Accordingly, three priority actions have been decided: better access to justice, mutual recognition of judicial decisions, and convergence of procedural law. For consumer law, the output of this new policy field was the adoption of common minimum rules on legal aid in 2003, to improve access to justice[20] and a European Small Claims Procedure Regulation in 2007.[21] While the latter regulation reduces the length and cost of procedure, gaps in coverage, cost, and complexities still pose a barrier to access to justice.[22]

In 2004, a Regulation on Consumer Protection Cooperation was adopted, to improve the public enforcement of consumer law. This permits designated national authorities to request actions on an infringement by an authority in another Member State.[23]

[17] Commission Green Paper on Access of Consumers to Justice and the Settlement of Consumer Disputes in the Single Market, COM(93) 576.

[18] In 1996, the Commission focused on alternative dispute resolution and presented an action plan to improve consumer access to justice and extrajudicial conciliation, COM(96) 13, 14.02.1996.

[19] E. Storskrubb, *Civil Procedure and EU Law: A Policy Area Uncovered* (Oxford: OUP, 2008).

[20] Directive 2003/8/EC, OJ L 26, 31.01.2003, to improve access to justice in cross-border disputes by establishing minimum common rules relating to legal aid; see also subsection 4.1 of this chapter.

[21] See Regulation (EC) 861/2007 of 11 July 2007 establishing a European small claims procedure, OJ L 199/1, 31.7.2007; see more in G. Haibach (2005), 'The Commission Proposal for a Regulation Establishing a European Small Claims Procedure: An Analysis', *Eur. Rev. Private Law*, pp. 593–600.

[22] See more at the Leuven Study, *An Analysis and Evaluation of Alternative Means of Consumer Redress other than Redress through Ordinary Judicial Proceedings*, 2007, p. 10.

[23] Regulation 2006/2004 of 27 October 2004 on cooperation between national authorities responsible for the enforcement of consumer protection laws, OJ l 364, 9.12.2004.

Moreover, a particular instrument to address collective consumer redress was introduced by Directive 98/27/EC on injunctions for the protection of consumer interests (the 'Injunctions Directive'),[24] adopted in 1998.[25] This directive establishes common procedures enabling qualified organizations in one Member State (such as consumer interest groups) to bring actions for the cessation of an infringement of consumer rights in another Member State.[26] By so doing, this directive protects the collective interest of consumers in the internal market. However, it has rarely been applied, because of the intricate system it relies on, and because it does not prescribe financial compensation for the consumer for the damage suffered.[27]

Finally, the EU has strengthened alternative dispute resolution (ADR) by setting minimum-quality criteria for these schemes, and by facilitating cross-border complaints.[28] These schemes offer an expeditious and cheap alternative to court procedures. However, they often lack binding force and are not available in all EU countries and market sectors.[29] Therefore, the EU adopted new consumer ADR and online dispute resolution (ODR) rules in 2013, which aim to fill the gaps in ADR coverage at the Union level.[30]

In conclusion, the existing consumer redress mechanisms still present some procedural flaws, which undermine their effectiveness.[31] While these EU

[24] Directive 98/27/EC on injunctions for the protection of consumers' interests, OJ L 166, 11.6.1998. This directive has been modified subsequently and has been codified by Directive 2009/22/EC of 23 April 2009 on injunctions for the protection of consumers' interests, OJ L 110/30, 1.5.2009.

[25] Other EU directives also include a clause allowing consumer organizations to take enforcement actions, such as Directive 93/13/EEC on unfair contract terms and Directive 2005/29/EC on unfair business-to-consumer commercial practices.

[26] H.-W. Micklitz, *Verbraucherschutz durch Unterlassungsklagen: Umsetzung und Anwendung der Richtlinie 98/27/EG in den Mitgliedstaaten* (Baden-Baden: Nomos, 2007); P. Rott, 'The Protection of Consumers' Interests After the Implementation of the EC Injunctions Directive Into German and English Law', (2001) 24 *J. Consumer Policy*, pp. 399–439.

[27] Leuven Study (n 22), p. 273; see also the European Commission's Report concerning the application of Directive 98/27/EC Brussels, 18.11.2008 COM(2008) 756 final.

[28] ADR Recommendations 98/257/EC and 2001/310/CE; Directive 2008/52/EC of 21 May 2008 on mediation in civil and commercial matters: <http://ec.europa.eu/internal_market/finservices-retail/finnet/index_en.htm>.

[29] See the Study on ADR in the EU by Civic Consulting, 16 October 2009.

[30] See subsection 3.5 in this chapter and Regulation (EU) No 524/2013 of 21 May 2013 on online dispute resolution for consumer disputes and Directive 2013/11/EU of 21 May 2013 on alternative dispute resolution for consumer disputes.

[31] The Green Paper on Consumer Collective Redress, COM(2008) 794 final, p. 6 and Civic Consulting, Report on the Effectiveness and Efficiency of Collective Redress in the European Union, 2008, pp. 42–4.

mechanisms tend to facilitate access to justice and in particular out-of-court dispute resolution, none of them allow for collective redress for damages, which would compensate consumers for the harm or losses suffered. This might adversely affect a multitude of consumers, and raises the question of how Member States have dealt with this issue.

2.3. *Collective redress mechanisms in Member States*

A growing number of EU Member States are introducing collective redress mechanisms for consumers to respond to the sharp increases in multi-party cases.[32]

At present, the principal *common* law jurisdictions already have a category of collective action for damages, while the *civil* law jurisdictions vary in the degree of availability of such actions. At least 16 Member States include collective redress mechanisms, while others have relevant legislative proposals.[33] This marks a new trend in recognizing consumer protection as a collective procedural right.

Despite considerable differences in national collective redress procedures, three broad models can be distinguished within the EU: representative actions, group actions, and test cases.

Representative collective actions are introduced either 'by an organization, a state authority or an individual on behalf of a group of individuals, who are, however, not parties to the proceedings'.[34] Consumer associations or public bodies, such as an ombudsman, can represent the consumer interest, depending on the country. In the case of Austria, Belgium, Finland, Hungary, Italy, and the Netherlands, representative collective actions take the form of injunction procedures.[35] In other countries such as France, Greece, and Poland, the

[32] H.-W. Micklitz & A. Stadler, 'Collective Legal Actions in Europe', (2006) 17 *Eur. Bus. L. Rev.*, p. 1475.

[33] According to a 2011 study by the European Parliament collective redress schemes exist in 16 Member States: Austria, Bulgaria, Denmark, Finland, France, Germany, Greece, Hungary, Italy, Lithuania, the Netherlands, Poland, Portugal, Spain, Sweden, and UK, see the Parliament's 'Overview of existing collective redress schemes in EU Member States', IP/A/IMCO/NT/2011-16 July 2011 PE464.

[34] Leuven Study (n 22), p. 261. Representative collective procedures exist for example in Austria, France, Germany, Greece, the Netherlands, and the UK; see the Collective Redress Report (n 31), p. 6.

[35] With Directive 98/27/EC on injunctions for the protection of consumers' interests, OJ L 166, 11.6.1998, injunction procedures have become mandatory under EU law. As a result, every Member State now provides for an injunction procedure to protect the collective interests of

judge can effectively provide damages for the prejudice or moral harm caused to collective consumer interests. These damages are, however, not distributed to the individual victims, but are kept by the representative consumer body or are used by the state for public policy objectives.

In a *group action*, a delimited category of persons may bring an action to enforce their individual claims together, in one procedure, and in accordance with specific rules designed for such a purpose.[36] Group actions can be differentiated according to whether they apply a so-called 'opt-in' or 'opt-out' procedure. Opt-out procedures include all the victims of a harmful action, with the exception of those consumers who explicitly ask to be excluded.[37] In countries such as Norway and Denmark, opt-out options are complementary to the opt-in mechanisms, but are only applicable where the harm caused to the consumer is low. Conversely, other countries have only introduced an opt-in approach, which requires the explicit authorization by the harmed consumer to be included in the procedure, before the court decision has been taken. Examples of such opt-in group actions exist in Sweden and Spain, where consumers or interest groups can lead the case.

In *test cases*, one or more individuals can file a claim, which leads to a judgment that forms the basis for other claims with the same interest against the same defendant. These test cases were developed in countries such as Germany[38] and the UK,[39] and can be filed either by a consumer or by an organization.[40] Consumers whose claims fulfil the requirements of a test case can subscribe to a register maintained by the acting claimant of the test case. The peculiarity

consumers. See the European Commission's Report concerning the application of Directive 98/27/EC, COM(2008) 756 final, 18.11.2008.

[36] Member States with group actions are Bulgaria, Denmark, Lithuania, the Netherlands, Portugal, Spain, Sweden, and the UK; H.-W. Micklitz and A. Stadler, 'The Development of Collective Legal Actions in Europe, Especially in German Civil Procedure', (2006) 17 *Eur. Bus. L. Rev.*, p. 1481.

[37] In the Netherlands only authorized associations can initiate such procedures to propose a settlement, while in Denmark only the Ombudsman can apply the opt-out option.

[38] The German Capital Markets Test Case Act, in force since 1 November 2005, introduced test cases for investors who have sustained loss through false, misleading, or undisclosed information relating to public capital markets; see A. Halfmeier, P. Rott, and E. Feess, *Kollektiver Rechtsschutz im Kapitalmarktrecht, Evaluation des Kapitalanleger-Musterverfahrensgesetzes* (Frankfurt: Frankfurt School Verlag, 2010).

[39] See the Civil Procedure Rules, r. 19.15 on test claims at the webpage of the Ministry of Justice:<http://www.justice.gov.uk/civil/procrules_fin/contents/parts/part19.htm#IDA4FF5B>.

[40] Usually, a test case requires different individuals with overall similar claims against the same defendant; see Micklitz and Stadler, 'The Development of Collective Legal Actions in Europe, especially in German Civil Procedure' (n 32), p. 1478.

of such a case is that the court chooses only one claim and bases its decision on this, which binds all the registered claims. Test case procedures offer the opportunity to have legal questions relevant for a number of claims clarified by the court at once, and can thus reduce litigation costs. However, the judgment has no binding effect for the third parties that did not subscribe to the case.[41] Furthermore, the German test case procedure under the Capital Markets Model Case Act (KapMuG) has been criticized, owing to a number of shortcomings, such as complex and inefficient procedures, in particular for low-stakes claims.[42]

These facts suggest a trend in several Member States towards grouping individual claims for damages, while still following different national traditions. These legal variations (and an outright lack of collective action for damages in some countries) create legal inconsistencies, and may pose a barrier to an effective resolution of cross-border litigation. To understand the extent of these barriers, we will look at some important collective redress cases in the Member States, evaluating their cross-border aspects and implications.

2.4. *A typology of collective redress cases*

Up to 2008, approximately 326 collective redress cases took place in Member States, of which approximately 10 per cent had a cross-border implication for the EU.[43] Interestingly, a close analysis reveals that a high number of the cases actually occurred in four broad areas of consumer law, described in this section.

A large number of collective redress cases (39 per cent) concerned financial services,[44] which were further increased by the financial crisis. An example in this sector is the *Dexia* case,[45] in which private investors lodged a mass claim in 2005 in the Netherlands against Dexia for losses suffered from a financial product. After the court trial, the consumer associations and the bank reached

[41] The same, however, is true for group actions with an opt-in procedure; e.g. Leuven Study (n 22), p. 262.

[42] In order to improve the effectiveness of the KapMuG, it has been suggested to introduce opt-in mechanisms and further extend the reversal of the burden of proof for causation to the defendant; see E. Feess & A. Halfmeier (2010), 'The German Capital Markets Model Case Act (KapMuG)—A European Role Model for Increasing the Efficiency of Capital Markets? Analysis and Suggestions for Reform', *The European Journal of Finance* (2012), published online, pp. 1–20.

[43] According to the Collective Redress Study (n 31), pp. 42–4: on average, the value claimed was between €10,000 and €99,000, with some countries also including cases of more than €5 million; the average individual consumer claim represented a value between €100 and €999.

[44] Collective Redress Study (n 31), p. 41.

[45] *Dexia* decision, Amsterdam Court of Appeals, 25 January 2007, LJN:AZ 7033.

a settlement agreement, which was approved in 2007 by the Amsterdam Court of Appeal and declared binding.[46] This entitled around 300,000 investors to compensation for the shareholder losses of their share-lease contracts with Dexia. However, consumer claims with cross-border elements were excluded from the settlement indicating difficulties for individuals living outside the Netherlands to resolve the dispute. More far-reaching was the decision taken in the Dutch *Shell* case in 2009, where a US$ 352.6 million settlement agreement was approved by the Amsterdam Court, which included investors residing in 100 jurisdictions.[47] The Court therefore took jurisdiction over individuals residing outside the Netherlands. However, it remains to be seen if courts in other Member States will accept this decision.

A second category of large collective actions relates to telecommunications services (12 per cent).[48] An important example in this regard is the French mobile phone case. After the French competition board imposed a penalty for a collusive agreement among mobile phone operators in November 2005, a French consumer association created a website to help consumers calculate the individual damage they had suffered.[49] Despite this, only a very small number of consumers participated in the claim: eventually, only 0.6 per cent of the 20 million subscribers who could have been compensated subscribed to the webpage set up for complaints.[50] This may suggest that the law is poorly adapted to collective actions, and that dispute resolution could be simplified in France by allowing 'opt-out' procedures for specific types of actions.

A third area of law in which collective redress mechanisms have often been used are transport (8 per cent) and package tourism (7 per cent). A significant example of collective redress in the transport sector occurred in Sweden in 2003, following the bankruptcy of a travel agency.[51] Here, about

[46] This settlement procedure was made possible by legislation that came into effect in the Netherlands in July 2005—the Dutch Act on Collective Settlement of Mass Damages ('Wet Collectieve Afwikkeling Massaschade'—WCAM).

[47] In this case investors were compensated for losses suffered after a decrease in the value of Shell securities and for allegedly incorrect information provided by the company about its oil and gas reserves: <http://www.royaldutchshellsettlement.com>.

[48] E.g. in a Swedish electricity case, the Swedish Consumer Ombudsman filed a case for about 7000 consumers against a company which supplied electricity under a fixed price contract. The price actually charged for the new supply of electricity was considerably higher than the price previously agreed upon with the company, Oe 522-05 Court of Appeal.

[49] The association invested considerable financial means: about 21 employees and €300,000.

[50] A more successful example took place in 2004, against an overcharging telecommunication company in Portugal, which affected about 3 million consumers. The compensation to these consumers was largely in kind and non-monetary, Proc. 781/95; Comarca de Lisboa, 5° Juízo Cível, 1ª Secção.

[51] Swedish travel agency case T 1281-07 B./E., filed in March 2003 in Stockholm (T 3515-03), 01.04.2007.

700 aeroplane passengers had to buy new tickets, as the travel agency could not comply with its obligations. Five hundred of these passengers chose to be group members of a collective redress action. For the first time, after this case, a collective redress mechanism was introduced in Sweden in order to deal effectively with multi-party cases. In another case, a group of Austrian tourists had fallen ill at the same time, because of food-poisoning in a holiday resort in Turkey in 2004.[52] A consumer association brought a test case against the Austrian tour operator, and the harmed tourists received compensation. However, here effective litigation was restricted, because of the lack of a wider collective redress procedure for cross-border cases. For example, a group of Swiss tourists who were harmed at the same resort in Turkey could not be represented by the Austrian association, because their tour operator was located in another country.

Finally, collective redress mechanisms are increasingly applied in product liability cases. This has been shown in the tobacco litigation cases in some Member States, as well as in product litigation cases in the pharmaceutical sector. For instance, the majority of Group Litigation Order claims in the UK involved pharmaceutical product liability claims.[53]

These cases show that, at a national level, collective redress procedures can effectively improve dispute resolution in certain areas of law. However, they also demonstrate that although a growing number of consumers in different EU countries may have the same interests in very similar claims, shortcomings may prevail when it comes to cross-border claims.[54] Furthermore, the areas in which consumers find it most difficult to resolve mass claims (such as financial services and package tourism) are precisely those where they are likely to engage in cross-border activities.[55] This indicates that a collective redress mechanism allowing consumers from different Member States to

[52] See *Bezierksgericht für Handelssachen Wien* (BGHS), Case 17 C 1148/04d that was brought on 09.12.2004.

[53] The medicinal products actions were, however, mostly unsuccessful in the UK; see C. Hodges, 'The Civil Litigation System in England and Wales', in D. Hensler, C. Hodges, & M. Tulibacka (eds), 'The Globalisation of Class Actions', *Annals of the American Academy of Political and Social Science*, Special edition, vol 622 (Thousand Oaks, CA: SAGE Publications, 2009), pp. 109–10.

[54] In these circumstances consumers may be excluded from actions taken by a consumer organization or a public body. E.g., the Danish Ombudsman stressed that under the current regime it is difficult to represent consumers outside the country of their residence or to defend the rights of foreigners who have suffered a loss from a company located abroad; see the Danish Consumer Ombudsman website, at: <http://www.forbrug.dk/>.

[55] Green Paper on Consumer Collective Redress, European Commission, COM(2008) 794 final, p. 4.

file or settle a claim jointly could be desirable and effective to improve access to justice.

Interestingly, a large number of cases concern recently privatized markets, such as those for telecommunications or energy, which are of essential importance to consumers. This raises the question of whether it would be worth introducing sector-specific collective cross-border mechanisms, or if a general redress tool could fit all cases.

Summing up, the lack of transnational collective redress provisions may make cross-border purchases less attractive for consumers, creating a gap in consumer protection, and, moreover, resulting in an indirect obstacle to inter-Community trade. How, then, can procedural consumer rights be improved at the EU level?

3. Procedural Consumer Rights

In recent years, the European Commission has started to recognize the importance of enforcement as a central part of its policy. This trend is supported by the Lisbon Treaty, which expands and clarifies the EU competence to legislate in civil procedure, and provides new opportunities to promote a coherent redress model for consumer law. The ECJ's jurisprudence also had a major impact on the development of civil procedure rules in the EU.[56]

3.1. *Recent developments in EU law and policy*

Procedural rights and in particular collective redress mechanisms have been debated in different EU policy areas for some years now.

Collective redress mechanisms have been suggested in competition law, inspired by the ECJ's judgment in the *Courage* case.[57] The ECJ held that the full effectiveness of EC competition law would be put at risk if it were not open to any individual to claim damages. This ruling was confirmed in *Manfredi*, where the ECJ stated that '(…) any individual can claim compensation for

[56] M. Tulibacka, 'Europeanization of Civil Procedures: In Search of a Coherent Approach', (2009) 46 *CML Rev.*, pp. 1535 *et seq.*

[57] Case C-453/99, *Courage v Crehan Ltd* [2001] ECR I-6314, para. 26; see N. Reich, 'The Courage Doctrine: Encouraging or Discouraging Compensation for Antitrust Injuries?' (2005) 42, *CML Rev*, p. 35; C. Hodges, 'Competition Enforcement, Regulation and Civil Justice: What is the Case?', (2006) 43 *CML Rev.*, pp. 1381–407.

the harm suffered where there is a causal relationship between that harm and an agreement or practice prohibited under Article 81 EC'.[58]

As a result, the European Commission has considered EU collective redress mechanisms in the 2005 Green and 2008 White Papers on Damages Actions for Breach of the EC Antitrust Rules.[59] Both papers encouraged a proposal for a directive on collective redress against infringement of competition law. Political pressure, however, prevented the publication of a draft directive at the end of 2009. On 11 June 2013, the Commission eventually adopted a proposal for a directive on antitrust damages actions for breaches of EU competition law.[60]Should this directive be adopted, it may also encourage consumer actions to obtain damages in relation to breaches of competition law. This would be an important innovation, as companies infringing competition law often avoid paying any compensation to consumers.

Debates on effective judicial protection and on the right to participate in EU procedures have also resurfaced in consumer policy and in the case law. This is reflected in the EU Consumer Policy Strategy for 2007–2013,[61] which stresses that enforcement is a central part of consumer legislation. Furthermore, the EU commissioned various studies on redress mechanisms in and out of court and recently adopted new legislation on consumer ADR and ODR, which will be discussed later in this chapter.[62]

This trend is also visible in the case law. The ECJ has recognized the right to effective judicial protection of consumers[63] and the right of consumer organizations to be heard. For example, regarding this latter, the General Court affirmed in the recent *Test-Achats v European Commission* case the core role of procedural rights for consumer associations, referring in particular to

[58] Joined Cases C-295/04–298/04, *Manfredi v Lloyd Adriatico Assicurazioni SpA* [2006] ECR I-6619, para. 61.

[59] On 2 April 2008, the Commission adopted a White Paper on Damages Actions for Breach of the EC Antitrust Rules (COM(2008) 165), and on 19 December 2005, a Green Paper (COM(2005) 672).

[60] Proposal for a Directive on certain rules governing actions for damages under national law for infringements of the competition law provisions of the Member States and of the European Union, COM(2013) 404 final, 11.6.2013,

[61] Consumer Policy Strategy 2007–2013, COM(2007), 13.3.2007: <http://europa.eu/rapid/press ReleasesAction.do?reference=IP/07/320>.

[62] See the ADR and collective redress studies in the EU: <http://ec.europa.eu/consumers/redress_cons/collective_redress_en.htm#Studies>; see more on ADR in subsection 3.4 and 3.5.

[63] Key cases dealing with judicial protection of consumers will be discussed later in this chapter, e.g. Case C-168/05, *Elisa María Mostaza Claro v Centro Móvil Milenium SL* [2006] ECR I-10421; Joined Cases C-317/08 to C-320/08, *Alassini and others v Telecom Italia* [2010] ECR I-2213.

the Charter of Fundamental Rights.[64] This case was brought by Test-Achats, a Belgian consumer association, requesting the General Court to annul a clearance decision of the Commission, which declared a merger compatible with the internal market. In particular, Test-Achats claimed that the Commission breached Article 6(2) of the Merger Regulation No 139/2004,[65] because its right to participate in the procedure and to be heard had been denied. The Commission in turn argued that the applicant did not need to be heard, because the effects of the merger on the Belgian retail market would have only been secondary in nature. The General Court rejected this argument by the Commission, and its narrow interpretation, explaining that the fact that the merger may only have indirect market effects concerning consumers does not limit the applicant's right to be heard.[66]

The Court stated that in this situation the intermediate and ultimate consumers have to be heard, on the basis of Article 2(1) of Regulation No 139/2004 and in particular in reference to Article 12 TFEU, which requires that consumer protection interests must be considered in other EU policies. Interestingly, the Court also specifically referred to Article 38 of the Charter of Fundamental Rights in this context, which provides that EU policies must ensure a high level of consumer protection. The General Court held that 'the Commission cannot reject the claim of a consumer association which seeks to be heard as a third party demonstrating a sufficient interest in a merger without providing that association with an opportunity to show in what respect consumers may be concerned by the merger at issue'.[67]

By this judgment the General Court affirmed that consumer associations have the procedural right to be heard by the Commission during administrative merger investigations. This right is, however, only applicable under certain conditions: first, the merger must relate to goods or services used by final consumers; and second, an application to be heard by the Commission must have been submitted in writing by the association within the deadline.[68]

[64] Case T-224/10, *Association belge des consommateurs Test-Achats ASBL v European Commission* 12 October 2011, not yet reported.

[65] See Council Regulation (EC) No 139/2004 of 20 January 2004 on the control of concentrations between undertakings, OJ L 24, 29.01.2004.

[66] Case T-224/10, *Association belge des consommateurs Test-Achats ASBL v European Commission* 12 October 2011, not yet reported, para. 43.

[67] Case T-224/10, *Association belge des consommateurs Test-Achats ASBL v European Commssion* 12 October 2011, not yet reported, para. 44; see also Case T-256/97, *BEUC v Commission* [2000] ECR II-101, para. 77.

[68] Case T-224/10, *Association belge des consommateurs Test-Achats ASBL v European Commssion* 12 October 2011, not yet reported, para. 37.

In the present case, Test-Achats did not comply with all the required conditions, so the General Court dismissed its action. This case is significant as it highlighted the procedural rights of consumer organizations to represent the general consumer interests in administrative procedures. It is also noteworthy that the Court based its decision inter alia on Article 38 of the Charter of Fundamental Rights, thereby emphasizing the additional value of this provision for ensuring a high level of protection and procedural rights for consumers.

At the policy level, the European Commission recently assessed whether new collective consumer procedures should be adopted at the EU level. In 2008 the Commission adopted a Green Paper on Collective Consumer Redress,[69] suggesting four options to improve consumer redress: (1) no EC action; (2) cooperation between Member States; (3) a mixture of policy instruments to strengthen redress; and (4) binding or non-binding collective redress measures, or a mixture of the four options. A follow-up discussion paper[70] in 2009 provided a larger choice of policy options, including self-regulation and ADR schemes. The Commission also identified benchmarks for efficient collective redress systems.[71]

More recently, the Directorates-General for Competition, Health and Consumers, and Justice have started to focus on a more coherent approach to collective redress.[72] On 4 February 2011 the Commission issued a new consultation paper on collective redress, which aims to identify common legal principles that would fit into the EU legal system. This document shows a more open approach to an EU redress framework, considering alternative dispute resolution and litigation funding alongside collective redress mechanisms. In response to the consultation, the European Parliament adopted a resolution in February 2012, which encouraged the development of common legal principles that could offer inspiration for the different DGs to propose sector-specific collective redress measures. At the same time, the Parliament requested the Commission to assess carefully the need and legal basis for a potential future initiative.

[69] The Green Paper on Consumer Collective Redress, Brussels, COM(2008) 794, p. 7.

[70] Consultation paper: <http://ec.europa.eu/consumers/redress_cons/docs/consultation_paper 2009.pdf>.

[71] The Commission proposes 10 points, including financing of actions and the provision of satisfactory redress; see: <http://ec.europa.eu/consumers/redress_cons/collective_redress_en.htm>.

[72] 'Towards a Coherent European Approach to Collective Redress: Next Steps', Joint information note by Reding, Almunia and Dalli, European Commission, SEC (2010) 1192, 05.10.2010.

In the light of these developments the question arises as to whether the EU has sufficient competence to adopt civil procedure measures in the specific field of consumer law.

3.2. *The principle of effectiveness and EU competences*

The EU has traditionally had a narrowly circumscribed remit for legislative provisions regarding civil procedure.[73] In turn, the Member States are relatively autonomous in determining their civil justice systems.[74] The principle of national procedural autonomy was highlighted in the ECJ's early jurisprudence.[75] In *Rewe-Zentralfinanz*[76] the ECJ held that it is the role of the Member States 'to determine the procedural conditions governing actions at law intended to ensure the protection of the rights which citizens have from the direct effect of community law'. However, the ECJ also imposed two basic requirements on national procedural rules: they should be non-discriminatory and they should not make the exercise of a right impossible in practice.

Subsequently, the ECJ intervened in national civil procedures applying, among other things, *effective protection* as a guiding principle. In *von Colson* the ECJ ruled that Member States have to *guarantee real and effective judicial protection* of remedies, emphasizing the importance of the principle of effectiveness.[77] This approach was reiterated in the ECJ decisions that followed, including *Johnston*.[78] As a consequence it was argued by some scholars that 'the EU has a combination of national procedural competences and European procedural primacy'.[79]

The principle of effectiveness was eventually integrated into the Lisbon Treaty in Article 19(1) TEU, which states that 'Member States shall provide remedies sufficient to ensure effective legal protection in the fields covered by Union law'.

[73] Hodges, *The Reform of Class and Representative Actions in European Legal Systems* (n 4), p. 95.

[74] P. Craig and G. De Búrca , *EU Law: Text, Cases and Materials*, 3rd edn (Oxford: OUP, 2003), pp. 230–32.

[75] Tulibacka, 'Europeanization of Civil Procedures (n 56), pp. 1536–7.

[76] Case 33/76, *Rewe-Zentralfinanz and Rewe-Zentral AG v Landwirtschaftskammer für das Saarland* [1976] ECR 1989.

[77] See e.g. Case 14/83, *von Colson and Kamann v Land Nordrhein-Westfalen* [1984] ECR 1891, para. 23.

[78] Case C-222/84, *Johnston v Chief Constable of the Royal Ulster Constabulary* [1986] ECR 1651.

[79] E. Storskrubb, 'Civil Justice—A Newcomer and an Unstoppable Wave?' in P. Craig & G. de Búrca (eds), *The Evolution of EU Law*, 2nd edn (Oxford: OUP, 2011), p. 301.

The Lisbon Treaty broadens the competences of the EU in the field of civil procedure and may serve as a general basis for cross-border measures. While the pre-Lisbon Treaty Article 65 EC stated that measures with cross-border implications could be taken 'in so far as necessary for the proper functioning of the internal market',[80] the new Article 81(2) TFEU on judicial cooperation in civil matters provides the possibility for the EU to adopt civil procedure measures without requiring a market-making objective.[81] These measures can be on, inter alia:

(a) the mutual recognition and enforcement between Member States of judgments and of decisions in extrajudicial cases; (…)
(e) effective access to justice;
(f) the elimination of obstacles to the proper functioning of civil proceedings, if necessary by promoting the compatibility of the rules on civil procedure applicable in the Member States;
(g) the development of alternative methods of dispute settlement.

For consumer dispute resolution, Article 81(2)(e) and (g) TFEU is particularly relevant. On this basis the EU may adopt measures that facilitate collective and alternative redress mechanisms in order to promote 'effective access to justice'. This competence is nonetheless generally restricted to cross-border matters, so that Member States' procedures may remain unaffected.[82] However, the EU may adopt broader measures by relying on the specific consumer protection provision of the Lisbon Treaty. Article 169(1) TFEU (ex 153(1) EC) states that 'to ensure a high level of consumer protection, the Union shall contribute (…) to promoting their right to information, education and to organize themselves in order to safeguard their interests'.

Collective redress procedures, in or out of court, would be one way to guarantee a high level of consumer protection and facilitate consumer associations to organize themselves. In particular, Article 169(2)(b) TFEU is of relevance for collective and alternative dispute resolution, because it allows the EU to adopt consumer measures 'which support, supplement and monitor the policy pursued by the Member States'.

[80] Article 65 EC further stated, inter alia, that measure could be taken '(…) (c) eliminating obstacles to the good functioning of civil proceedings, if necessary by promoting the compatibility of the rules on civil procedure applicable in the Member States'.

[81] Tulibacka (n 56), pp. 1527–65.

[82] D. Fairgrieve and G. Howells, 'Collective Redress Procedures—European Debates', (2009) 58 *ICLQ*, p. 406.

As a large number of Member States have already introduced collective and alternative redress mechanisms for consumers into their national systems, the EU can support or complement the national redress schemes upon the basis of Article 169(2)(b) TFEU. Such a measure may allow a more coherent dispute resolution system across the EU and provide an inspiration for Member States without collective redress mechanisms.

Alternatively, Article 169(2)(a) TFEU and Article 114 TFEU (ex Article 95 EC) could be an additional basis for EU access to justice legislation. The majority of consumer protection measures have traditionally been developed on the sole basis of these provisions. However, they require a market integration objective. Thus, in order to evaluate whether Article 114 TFEU can also be applied, we have to consider whether diverging dispute resolution mechanisms in the European Member States pose a barrier to trade, and whether a relevant EU measure would improve market integration. The fact that different redress mechanisms for consumers exist in the Member States may lead to disparities and obstacles to trade, so this provision may become a potential basis for EU action.

In conclusion, since the introduction of the Lisbon Treaty the EU has broader powers to adopt civil procedure measures. In particular, Article 169 TFEU in conjunction with Article 81 TFEU can be considered as a potential basis for an EU access to justice measure for consumers. The following sections explore how these EU competences may be applied to boost affordable and effective consumer dispute resolution.

3.3. *Developing EU collective redress procedures for consumers*

In an enlarged EU market with growing exchange of similar goods and services, collective redress procedures are important for the effective functioning of a consumer dispute resolution system. These procedures present several advantages, but may also require specific safeguards.[83]

Collective action procedures could provide an incentive to participate jointly in litigation cases, as this would be a means of spreading litigation costs and risks among individuals.[84] These procedures may also increase the

[83] Cross-border collective redress proceedings can also pose new challenges for private international law that would need to be addressed by EU law. See e.g. M. Danov, 'The Brussels I Regulation: Cross-Border Collective Redress Proceedings and Judgments', (2010) 6(2) *J. Private Int'l Law*, p. 359.

[84] The Leuven Study (n 22) shows that possible savings could range between 46% and 99%, p. 63.

prospect of success for consumers. For example, a large number of individuals presenting common symptoms of an illness, or showing similarities in the harm received, may find it easier to prove the existence of the damage and the causal link with a certain product.

Secondly, these mechanisms may, to a certain extent, redress an asymmetrical balance of power between the consumer and the firm, due to the fact that the latter generally has access to greater resources and information to defend its interest.[85]

Thirdly, collective redress may contribute to procedural economy and to legal certainty.[86] For damages affecting numerous people, similar individual claims would be a major burden for the judicial system, and may lead to inconsistency in the case law. Thus, collective redress mechanisms may be a way to increase the effectiveness of the judicial procedure by saving resources, speeding up the judicial process, and increasing coherence.[87]

Finally, collective redress mechanisms can have a deterrent effect on businesses and may exert a regulatory function on the market.[88] Without this pressure, companies might be less inclined to comply with protection standards, which can lead to unfair trade practices and distort competition. Thus, collective actions may be a means of market control in cases of insufficient oversight by public bodies,[89] and can achieve a better compliance, preventing future harm to consumers.[90]

Nonetheless, these procedures have been controversial as they may entail several risks requiring safeguards to prevent excessive claims. For example,

[85] Regarding 'collective justice', see H.-W. Micklitz, 'Collective Private Enforcement of Consumer Law: The Key Questions', in W. Boom and M. Loos (eds), *Collective Enforcement of Consumer Law* (Groningen: Europa Law Publishing, 2007), p. 17.

[86] D. Rosenberg, 'Mandatory-Litigation Class Action: The Only Option for Mass Tort Cases', (2002) 115 *Harv. L. Rev.*, p. 831; according to Rosenberg collective actions are superior to individual cases, as they lead to an optimal judiciary use, avoiding repetition and contradiction in individual lawsuits; see also E. Lutfalla and V. Magnier, 'French Legal Reform: What is at Stake if Class Actions Are Introduced In France?', (2006) 73 *Defense Counsel Journal*, p. 307.

[87] See Leuven Study (n 22), p. 265; also J. Ziegel, 'Consumer Protection in Canada and the Class Action Remedy', in L. Thévenoz and N. Reich (eds), *Consumer Law* (Geneva and Baden-Baden: Schulthess/Nomos Verlag, 2006), pp. 587 *et seq*.

[88] See the Collective Redress Study (n 31), p. 10.

[89] Micklitz, 'Collective Private Enforcement of Consumer Law' (n 85), p. 17.

[90] E.g. in the US, some cases have rendered companies more responsible and diligent towards consumers, enhancing information, see W. Wagner, 'When All Else Fails: Regulating Risky Products Through Tort Litigation', (2007) 95 *Georgetown L. J.*, p. 693; T. Wilhelmsson, 'Private Law 2000: Small Stories on Morality through Liability', in T. Wilhelmsson & S. Hurri (eds), *From Dissonance to Sense* (Aldershot: Ashgate Publishing, 1998), p. 229.

it has been suggested that they might lead to an over-regulation of the market.[91] While in the US class actions were established to compensate for the government's relatively light-handed approach, the EU already has strong administrative protection for consumers, so collective actions may overload the judicial system.[92] Although these aspects need to be taken into serious consideration, recent market failures in the product safety[93] and financial sectors indicate that the public control mechanism does not always seem to function in the EU. Furthermore, the proliferation of collective redress schemes in Member States reveals a real need for these new enforcement methods.

Another risk of collective redress mechanisms is that they could lead to abusive practices. On the one hand, the representative of the group might take advantage of the situation at the expense of the consumer. Yet, this may be prevented by a compulsory judicial review of redress settlements, as is already the case in some national procedures.[94] On the other hand, collective redress might increase the financial risks for companies through high damages claims or 'settlement blackmail'. The US-style class actions are often mentioned as an excessive model not to follow in this regard.[95] However, the EU approach remains fundamentally different from the US class action system,[96] so the risk of excessive claims remains limited. This is evidenced by the experience in Member States, where these cases have not constituted unreasonable costs for businesses or led to the bankruptcy of reputable companies.[97]

The risk of abuse can also be prevented with the help of integrated safeguard measures, such as a mandatory assessment of the claim by a judge, at an early stage of the procedure, through formal 'certification'. Other forms of

[91] F.J. Säcker, *The Order of Group Actions in the Private Law System* (Munich: C.H. Beck, 2006), p. 60.

[92] Säcker, *The Order of Group Actions in the Private Law System* (n 91), p. 78.

[93] Product scandals in Europe, such as those concerning contaminated blood and BSE, lowered public opinion with regard to EU consumer protection and the traditional public regulatory system.

[94] E.g. the Dutch Act on Collective Settlement of Mass Damages requires court approval of settlements.

[95] L.A. Willet, 'U.S.-Style Class Actions in Europe: A Growing Threat', (2005) 9 *Briefly*, NLCPI.

[96] See Mulheron, *The Class Action in Common Law Legal Systems* (Oxford, Hart Publishing, 2004). Examples of differences between US and EU collective redress mechanisms include jury participation, pre-trial discovery, punitive damages, contingency fees, relaxed standing, and opt-out actions in the US, and the 'loser pays' principle and preference for opt-in procedures in the EU; Leuven Study (n 22), p. 268.

[97] Collective Redress Study (n 31), pp. 10–12; R. Mulheron, 'Some Difficulties with Group Litigation Orders—And Why A Class Action Is Superior', (2005) 24 *Civil Justice Quarterly*, p. 66.

'gatekeeper procedures' can be achieved through the 'loser pays' principle and via the mandatory representation of collective claims by consumer organizations or public bodies.[98] These safeguard measures have diminished the risk of unmeritorious claims in national systems. Thus, the argument that collective redress mechanisms per se overburden the legal system in the EU is questionable.[99]

A balanced collective redress measure that respects pre-existing legal schemes in Member States and includes safeguards against abuses can facilitate consumer dispute resolution. This would spread litigation costs and therefore lead to easier access to justice for consumers. Nonetheless, a financial risk of long and complex court cases and the 'loser-pays' principle pose further barriers to the practical application of such procedures. Thus, cheap out-of-court schemes are, in addition, an important complement, leaving judicial collective actions as a last resort to the parties.

3.4. *Alternative dispute resolution and fundamental rights*

Alternative Dispute Resolution (ADR) includes mechanisms aimed at resolving conflicts without the direct intervention of a court. Extrajudicial procedures are defined by the EU as: 'any method enabling a dispute to be resolved through the intervention of a third party that proposes or imposes a solution'.[100] These procedures may be established by public authorities, professionals in the legal sector, professional bodies, or civil society organizations.

Originally, the EU did not enjoy express power in the area of ADR. It therefore applied soft law instruments, such as recommendations, to determine minimum-quality criteria of these schemes.[101] Subsequently, the EU has adopted a directive on aspects of mediation in civil and commercial matters, which includes requirements for mediation in cross-border disputes.[102] This directive encourages judges to promote mediation, and aims at ensuring

[98] Fairgrieve and Howells, 'Collective Redress Procedures' (n 82), pp. 379–409.

[99] Collective Redress Study (n 31), p. 12.

[100] See: <europa.eu/legislation_summaries/consumers/protection_of_consumers/l32031_en.htm>.

[101] Recommendation 98/257/EC on the principles applicable to the bodies responsible for the out-of-court settlement of consumer disputes, OJ L 115, 17.04.1998, p. 31; Recommendation 2001/310/EC on the principles for out-of-court bodies involved in the consensual resolution of consumer ADR, OJ L 109, 19.4.2001, p. 56.

[102] Directive 2008/52/EC on mediation in civil and commercial matters, OJ L 136, 24.5.2008, p. 3.

a sound relationship between the mediation process and judicial proceedings, by establishing common rules.[103]

Moreover, several EU directives, such as the E-commerce Directive,[104] the Markets in Financial Instruments Directive (MiFID)[105] and the Consumer Credit Directive[106] *encourage* or *require* Member States to adopt adequate ADR schemes.

The Commission has also set up two networks to facilitate consumer access to ADR for cross-border complaints. A European Consumer Centres' Network (EEC-Net)[107] directs consumers to an appropriate ADR scheme in another Member State and promulgates a consumer claim form. For financial services, a Financial Services Complaints Network (FIN-NET) of national ADR bodies deals with out-of-court cross-border complaints in the EU.[108]

The advantage of such ADR procedures is that disputes are generally resolved more rapidly and are less costly than ordinary court procedures. They are often free for consumers or available at a modest cost and are settled within a short period of time.

However, recent studies on ADR have uncovered serious shortcomings in these procedures,[109] such as a lack of information regarding available out-of-court mechanisms, and insufficient independence of ADR schemes.[110] Although at the Member State level more than 750 ADR schemes exist there are gaps in the coverage, so that the availability to consumers varies substantially throughout the EU. They are also often voluntary, which may leave the individual consumer without sufficient means to obtain either a settlement or compliance on the part of the company.[111]

[103] See more on consumer ADR in I. Benöhr, 'Alternative Dispute Resolution for Consumers in the EU', in C. Hodges, I. Benöhr, & N. Creutzfeld-Banda (eds), *Consumer ADR in Europe* (Oxford: Hart Publishing, 2012), pp. 1–23.

[104] Directive 2000/31/EC,OJ L 178, 17.7.2000.

[105] Directive 2004/39/EC, OJ L 145/1, 30.4.2004.

[106] Directive 2008/48/EC, OJ L 133, 22.5.2008.

[107] See: <http://ec.europa.eu/consumers/redress_cons/index_en.htm>.

[108] See: <http://ec.europa.eu/internal_market/finservices-retail/finnet/index_en.htm>.

[109] Study on the use of ADR in the EU, Civic Consulting, 16 October 2009, pp. 9–11, and Annex of the EU ADR consultation for an overview of the existing ADR schemes, pp. 164–324; the Leuven Study (n 22), p. 159.

[110] In 2009, only 3% of European consumers who did not get a satisfactory reply from the trader took their case to an ADR scheme; Eurobarometer Report 282, 'Consumer attitudes towards cross-border sales and consumer protection', published March 2010, p. 20.

[111] See the ADR consultation paper by the European Commission, note 22: <http://ec.europa.eu/dgs/health_consumer/dgs_consultations/ca/docs/adr_consultation_paper_18012011_en.pdf>.

On the other hand, a compulsory use of specific ADR schemes may pose a barrier to the EU fundamental right of effective judicial protection under certain conditions. The ECJ recently had to decide on this issue in *Alassini v Telecom Italia*.[112] In this case, Italian provisions imposed the use of mediation as a mandatory condition for the admissibility of a claim before the courts, in certain disputes relating to telecoms services.

The ECJ held that the principles of equivalence and effectiveness do not preclude such legislation, provided, among other things, that the ADR procedure does not result in binding decisions or cause a substantial delay to bringing legal proceedings or involve significant additional costs.[113]

This case was also of particular constitutional importance, because the ECJ analyzed the principle of effective judicial protection from a wider human rights perspective. The ECJ stated that effective judicial protection: 'is a general principle of EU law stemming from the constitutional traditions common to the Member States, which has been enshrined in Articles 6 and 13 of the ECHR and which has also been reaffirmed by Article 47 of the Charter of Fundamental Rights of the European Union'.

However, the Court held that in accordance with previous case law, these fundamental rights are not absolute, but can be restricted by measures of general interest, provided they are proportionate.[114] In this particular case, the Italian rules imposing a duty on the parties to attempt to find an amicable dispute resolution solution pursued legitimate objectives in the general interest, because they allowed a 'quicker and less expensive settlement of disputes relating to electronic communications and a lightening of the burden on the court system'. Furthermore, the national legislation was proportionate since 'no less restrictive alternative to the implementation of a mandatory procedure exists'.[115] Therefore, the ECJ decided that the Italian rules on mandatory mediation complied with the principle of effective judicial protection and were consistent with EU law.

This case shed light on the conditions under which mandatory national ADR procedures are likely to comply with EU law. Amongst others, they should suspend 'the period for the time-barring of claims' and be available free of

[112] Joined Cases C-317/08 to C-320/08, *Alassini and others v Telecom Italia* [2010] ECR I-2213.

[113] Joined Cases C-317/08 to C-320/08, *Alassini and others v Telecom Italia* [2010] ECR I-2213, para. 67.

[114] Joined Cases C-317/08 to C-320/08, *Alassini and others v Telecom Italia* [2010] ECR I-2213, para. 63.

[115] Joined Cases C-317/08 to C-320/08, *Alassini and others v Telecom Italia* [2010] ECR I-2213, para. 65.

charge or at low costs. Moreover, electronic means should not be the only means by which the settlement procedure may be accessed and interim measures should be possible in exceptional cases.[116]

The ECJ also emphasized the significant role of the quality requirements included in the Commission's recommendations to promote consumer ADR,[117] which should be respected by Member States. Furthermore, the judgment highlighted that effective judicial protection is a general principle included in European fundamental rights, which may only be limited under specific circumstances. This case will provide some guidance for Member States on how to implement consumer ADR into their national system. At the same time, it remains to be seen to what extent the requirements established by the ECJ also apply to voluntary ADR schemes created by private parties.[118]

In a number of cases the ECJ also had to decide on the conflict between consumer protection included in Directive 93/13 on unfair terms and contractual arbitration clauses.

In *Claro v Centro Móvil*, the standard contract terms of a company included the use of an arbitration tribunal to resolve disputes, raising issues of fairness.[119] The ECJ ruled that the national court was required to assess whether a contractual arbitration clause was void, even if the consumer had not raised the issue of unfairness in the arbitration proceedings, but only in the action for annulment. This was considered as a way of compensating the imbalance of power between the consumer and the company.[120] Arbitration clauses may not always be geared towards consumer protection, as they often include a waiver to go to court. Thus, a court procedure or different ADR options such

[116] Joined Cases C-317/08 to C-320/08, *Alassini and others v Telecom Italia* [2010] ECR I-2213, paras 53–9; see also J. Davies & E. Szyszczak, 'ADR: Effective Protection of Consumer Rights?' (2010) 35(5) *Eur. L. Rev.*, pp. 695–706.

[117] The ECJ clarified the legal effect of Recommendation 98/257, stating that while recommendations are not binding and are not capable of creating rights, 'Member States should take account of them when establishing ADR procedures and national courts must take them into consideration in order to decide disputes brought before them'. Joined Cases C-317/08 to C-320/08, *Alassini and others v Telecom Italia*, [2010] ECR I-2213, para. 63; see also Case C-28/05, *Doktor and Others* [2006] ECR I-5431, para. 40.

[118] See more on consumer ADR in N. Reich, 'Legal Protection of Individual and Collective Consumer Interests', in H.-W. Micklitz, N. Reich, & P. Rott (eds.), *Understanding EU Consumer Law* (Mortsel: Intersentia, 2009).

[119] Case C-168/05, *Elisa María Mostaza Claro v Centro Móvil Milenium SL* [2006] ECR I-10421.

[120] The consumer often lacks legal knowledge and has limited power to change contractual arbitration clauses.

as mediation or ombudsman schemes might sometimes be more favourable for consumers in terms of location or procedure.[121]

A more recent judgment, *Asturcom Telecomunicaciones v Rodríguez Nogueira*,[122] concerned the enforcement of an arbitration award. In this case, an arbitration clause had been included in a mobile phone contract of a Spanish telecommunications company. The ECJ ruled that under these circumstances, a national court 'is required, where it has available to it the legal and factual elements necessary for that task, to assess of its own motion whether an arbitration clause in a contract concluded between a seller or supplier and a consumer is unfair, in so far as, under national rules of procedure, it can carry out such an assessment in similar actions of a domestic nature'.[123] Furthermore, the ECJ stressed that Article 6 of the directive on unfair terms, which provides that unfair contract terms should not be binding on the consumer, is to be regarded as having equal standing to national rules of public policy rank.[124]

As a result of these cases,[125] the national courts have to become active under certain conditions and act of their own motion to verify the potential unfairness of standard terms or to annul an arbitration award if it is based on an unfair contract clause. [126]

3.5. *The new legislation on ADR and ODR*

More recently, at the EU policy level, several actions were taken to strengthen consumer ADR.[127] The European Commission published a consultation

[121] N. Reich, 'More Clarity after Claro?' (2007) 1 *Eur. Rev. Contract Law*, pp. 42 *et seq*.

[122] Case C-40/08, *Asturcom Telecomunicaciones SL v Cristina Rodríguez Nogueira* [2009] ECR I-9579.

[123] Case C-40/08, *Asturcom Telecomunicaciones SL v Cristina Rodríguez Nogueira* [2009] ECR 2009 I-9579, para. 59.

[124] Case C-40/08, *Asturcom Telecomunicaciones SL v Cristina Rodríguez Nogueira* [2009] ECR I-9579, para. 52.

[125] See also the recent Case C-137/08, *VB Pénzügyi Lízing Zrt. v Ferenc Schneider*, 9 November 2010, report not yet published, paras 46–9 and Case C-243/08, *Pannon GSM Zrt. v Erzsébet Sustikné Győrfi* [2009] ECR I-4713; K. Sein (2011), 'Protection of Consumers against Unfair Jurisdiction and Arbitration Clauses in Jurisprudence of the European Court of Justice', (2011) vol XVIII *Juridica International*.

[126] More in B.U Graf & A.E. Appleton, 'ECJ Case C 40/08 Asturcom—EU Unfair Terms Law Confirmed as a Matter of Public Policy', (2010) 28(2) *ASA Bulletin*, p. 417.

[127] See Benöhr, 'Consumer Dispute Resolution after the Lisbon Treaty' (n 1), 87–110; for more information on consumer ADR, see also Benöhr, 'Alternative Dispute Resolution for Consumers in the EU' (n 103), pp. 1–24.

paper in 2010 on how to improve ADR,[128] highlighting the inconvenience of existing consumer ADR procedures and a lack of collective proceedings. In particular, a 2009 ADR study revealed that only 62 per cent of ADR schemes were able to deal with cross-border claims from consumers living in another Member State, so that overseas consumers were faced with additional burdens.[129] While the ECC-Net managed to resolve approximately half of cross-border consumer complaints on an amicable basis, for a large number of cases ADR schemes did not exist or were inapplicable.[130] Furthermore, cross-border cases were often linked to e-commerce transactions, which lacked a common legal framework on online redress mechanisms.[131]

As a result of the aforementioned consultation, the European Commission published two legislative proposals in November 2011: a draft directive on consumer ADR[132] and a draft regulation on consumer ODR.[133] Both proposals were based on Article 114 TFEU and intended to overcome three key shortcomings in consumer ADR: gaps in coverage of out-of-court schemes, insufficient awareness about these tools, and variation in quality.[134] In particular, the proposed draft directive on consumer ADR aimed at ensuring the quality and availability of ADR schemes for contractual disputes.[135]

In December 2012 a political agreement was reached on the two legislative proposals and on 12 March 2013 the European Parliament voted to support these proposals. Eventually, in spring 2013 the Council of the European Union adopted the final revised version of the proposed legislation on ADR

[128] See the 2010 consultation paper by the European Commission, 'On the use of Alternative Dispute Resolution as a means to resolve disputes related to commercial transactions and practices in the European Union'.

[129] E.g., unfamiliar ADR systems and hearings are inconvenient in cross-border cases; ADR Study (n 109), p. 339.

[130] ECC-Net Publication, *Cross-border Dispute Resolution Mechanisms in Europe—Practical Reflections on the Need and Availability*, 2009, pp. 10–11 and 57–8.

[131] P. Cortes, 'A European Legal Perspective on Consumer Online Dispute Resolution', (2009) 15(4) *Computer and Telecommunications L. Rev.*, pp. 90–100.

[132] European Commission, Proposal for a Directive on alternative dispute resolution for consumer disputes and amending Regulation (EC) No 2006/2004 and Directive 2009/22/EC (Directive on consumer ADR), COM(2011) 793/2, final, 29.11.2011.

[133] European Commission, Proposal for a Regulation on online dispute resolution for consumer disputes (Regulation on consumer ODR), COM(2011) 794/2, final, 29.11.2011.

[134] European Commission, Communication by the European Commission on Alternative Dispute Resolution for consumer disputes in the Single Market, COM(2011) 791, final, 29.11.2011, p. 2. See Study on the Use of Alternative Dispute Resolution in the European Union of 16 October 2009, <http://ec.europa.eu/consumers/redress_cons/adr_study.pdf>, pp. 56–63; 112–15; 120–1.

[135] See Benöhr (n 103).

and ODR.[136] As a result, Member States will now have to implement the new EU rules on consumer ADR and ODR by July 2015. Furthermore, an ODR platform will be established in January 2016.[137]

The new directive will provide for full ADR coverage, so that Member States will have to ensure that such ADR procedures exist for all consumer contractual disputes.[138] According to Article 2(1) this directive applies: 'to procedures for the out-of-court resolution of domestic and cross-border disputes concerning contractual obligations stemming from sales contracts or service contracts between a trader established in the Union and a consumer resident in the Union'. Furthermore, all ADR schemes will now have to comply with key quality standards which ensure that they work in a competent, independent, effective, fair, and transparent way.[139] The directive also requires companies to inform consumers about available ADR schemes which will raise the general awareness of these schemes. In addition, the ODR Regulation requires that an EU dispute resolution platform ('ODR platform') is established, which will help consumers and companies to submit disputes arising from online purchases.[140] This platform, which will link all the national ADR entities, consists of an interactive website available in EU official languages, offering a single, free of charge, entry point for complaints.[141]

The new ADR and ODR rules are ambitious and are welcome initiatives to strengthen consumer ADR in the European Union. The mixture of ODR Regulation and ADR Framework Directive is a promising move towards a comprehensive solution for consumers to access out-of-court schemes. At the same time, these measures build on existing ADR schemes, leaving Member States free to decide how to transpose them into national legislation.

[136] On 8 June 2013 both legislative acts were published in the Official Journal of the EU. See OJ L 165 Volume 56, 18 June 2013: Regulation (EU) No 524/2013 of 21 May 2013 on online dispute resolution for consumer disputes and amending Regulation (EC) No 2006/2004 and Directive 2009/22/EC (Regulation on consumer ODR), Directive 2013/11/EU of 21 May 2013 on alternative dispute resolution for consumer disputes and amending Regulation (EC) No 2006/2004 and Directive 2009/22/EC (Directive on consumer ADR).

[137] See the Commission's website at: <http://ec.europa.eu/consumers/redress_cons/adr_policy_work_en.htm>.

[138] However, some exceptions apply, mentioned in Art. 2(2) of the directive.

[139] See the explanation of the directive on the Commision's website and in a press release (MEMO/13/193): <http://ec.europa.eu/consumers/redress_cons/adr_policy_work_en.htm>.

[140] See n 139.

[141] See n 139.

These new rules on consumer ADR can be seen as an important step to facilitate access to justice for consumers. In particular, they will be essential to increase availability of affordable dispute resolution mechanisms for consumers and to guarantee their quality standards, enhancing consumer confidence in these schemes.

Meanwhile, binding court procedures and collective redress mechanisms remain important both as an incentive for businesses to use ADR, and for those cases where no amicable settlement is found. While ADR mechanisms offer a simple and inexpensive way to improve consumer dispute resolution, they do not eliminate the need for collective redress procedures. ADR schemes are often most effective if combined with judicial collective redress mechanisms which encourage the use of out-of-court schemes and act as a deterrent against non-compliance. However, such court procedures would require adequate funding models, ensuring that consumers can resort to them if the ADR option remains unsuccessful.

4. Litigation Funding

The availability of adequate funding schemes is a significant precondition to attaining effective judicial consumer protection, as litigation costs are often high compared to the consumer's personal finances.[142] Despite this, the subject of funding, in particular for collective actions, still remains underexplored. This section aims to fill this gap, assessing traditional and innovative financing models. While some of these models, such as legal aid and legal insurance, already exist in many Member States, they do not always fit the particular requirements to fund collective redress actions. Thus, complementary funding tools, such as contingency fees and collective action funds, are evaluated to improve the capability of consumers to access justice.

4.1. *The fundamental right to legal aid*

Public funding through legal aid is one of the classic solutions to facilitate access to justice. In 2003 the EU adopted a directive that sets minimum standards concerning legal aid for individuals who do not have sufficient

[142] Funding difficulties are one reason for the limited use of collective redress in the Member States, Leuven Study (n 22), p. 267.

resources for court proceedings.[143] This directive aims to improve access to justice in cross-border civil cases. Legal aid usually includes the services of a lawyer, exemption from the costs of the proceedings, and provides cover for additional cross-border costs, such as interpretation and travel funding.

The right to legal aid is also recognized as a human right that helps to improve access to justice and is explicitly mentioned in a number of human rights documents. Article 6(3)(c) of the European Convention on Human Rights guarantees the right to legal assistance where the defendant 'does not have sufficient means to pay for legal assistance'. This legal aid has to be provided 'free of charge when the interest of justice so requires'. In addition, Article 47 of the Charter states that 'Legal aid shall be made available to those who lack sufficient resources in so far as such aid is necessary to ensure effective access to justice'. At the policy level Commissioner Reding acknowledged legal aid as a fundamental right in 2010 and emphasized its key role for citizens' access to justice.[144]

The ECJ affirmed the importance and broad scope of legal aid as a fundamental right. In *DEB Deutsche Energiehandels- und Beratungsgesellschaft* the ECJ ruled that the principle of effective judicial protection also applies to companies seeking legal aid. In this case the application for legal aid of a company was refused by the German Government, owing to an absence of public interest.[145] The ECJ held that effective judicial protection, as enshrined in Article 47 of the Charter, must be interpreted as meaning that it is not impossible for legal persons to rely on that principle of effective judicial protection and legal aid may cover the assistance of a lawyer and dispensation from advance payment of the costs of proceeding. In its fundamental rights analysis the ECJ referred to a large extent to the ECHR provisions and related case law, to remain consistent with the ECHR in its decision-making.[146] The ECJ ruled that it is for the national court to assess

[143] Directive 2003/8/EC of 27 January 2003 to improve access to justice in cross-border disputes by establishing minimum common rules relating to legal aid for such disputes, OJ L 26, 31.01.2003.

[144] See the 2010 speech by Reding, who is Vice-President of the European Commission responsible for Justice, Fundamental Rights and Citizenship: 'Legal aid: a fundamental right for citizens to access justice' for the joint CCBE-ERA conference on the occasion of the CCBE's 50th anniversary, Brussels, 26 November 2010: <http://www.ccbe.eu/fileadmin/user_upload/document/50th_anniversary/Speech_Reding_final.pdf>.

[145] Case C-279/09, *DEB Deutsche Energiehandels- und Beratungsgesellschaft* [2010] ECR I-13849.

[146] The Charter provisions that originated from the ECHR have the same meaning and scope as those included by the ECHR; see the Commission's explanation on the application of the Charter at DG Justice: <http://ec.europa.eu/justice/fundamental-rights/charter/index_en.htm>.

whether the requirement for granting legal aid constitutes a limitation on the right of access to the courts. However, the Court provided precise directions on which points the national courts have to consider in their analysis: 'In making that assessment, the national court must take into consideration the subject-matter of the litigation; whether the applicant has a reasonable prospect of success; the importance of what is at stake for the applicant in the proceedings; the complexity of the applicable law and procedure; and the applicant's capacity to represent himself effectively.'[147]

Since 2003, many EU Member States have enacted local rules which allow some form of legal aid to fund lawsuits. In general, in the event that an individual is eligible for legal aid, he or she has to substantiate that the case has a reasonable chance of success, and that the result would be proportionate to the costs which would have to be spent on the case. The lawyers providing legal aid receive their fees from a fund or from the losing party at commercial rates provided the case is won.

Today, however, the legal aid scheme is often under pressure because of its cost and limited public resources.[148] In the UK for example, although a large part of the financial risk involved in a dispute remains with the legally aided person (who in most cases is liable to pay the costs of adversarial parties if the case is lost), the costs of legal aid have increased considerably. As a consequence, these schemes are available under strict merit conditions and only for a small number of individuals (lowest-income consumers).

Another reason why the legal aid scheme is losing popularity is the unintended consequences it may generate. In particular, the application of legal aid for the purpose of collective actions is sometimes contested, as it might raise unmeritorious claims.[149] This could have a major impact on the defendant entity, such as a loss of confidence in a public authority or company, because large-scale litigation usually receives high media attention.[150] Thus, allocation of legal aid to multi-party claims needs to be carefully assessed.[151]

[147] Case C-279/09 *DEB Deutsche Energiehandels- und Beratungsgesellschaft* [2010] ECR I-13849, para. 61.

[148] C. Hodges, S. Vogenauer, & M. Tulibacka, *The Funding and Costs of Civil Litigation. A Comparative Perspective* (Oxford: Hart Publishing, 2010), pp. 21–5; see also the Report of the Civil Justice Council in the UK, *Improved Access to Justice, Funding Options and Proportionate Costs*, 2007, Appendices, fnn 26 *et seq*.

[149] D. Collins, 'Public Funding of Class Actions and the Experience with English Group Proceedings', (2005) 31 *Manitoba L. J.*, pp. 211 *et seq*.

[150] For the discussion on damages for antitrust actions, see I. Riley and J. Peysner, 'Damages in EC Antitrust Actions: Who Pays the Piper', (2006) 31 *E.L. Rev.*, pp. 748–61.

[151] Collins, 'Public Funding of Class Actions and the Experience with English Group Proceedings' (n 149), p. 211.

This can be achieved through strict scrutiny of the reasonable prospects of success of the case by the legal aid authority. However, as shown in the case above the ECJ applies a broad definition to legal aid. This indicates that collective actions entities may qualify if they have no sufficient means and show a reasonable chance of success.

4.2. *Contingency fees*

In the contingency fee system, the lawyer usually agrees to provide legal representation, and his or her payment is only required in the event of a favourable result through a settlement or recovery. This system exists in the US, which allows various success fees that—depending on the state in question—can be limited to a certain percentage.[152]

In the EU, contingency fees are still generally regarded with suspicion. The reasons for this are often of political and moral origin. Nonetheless, the European Commission's emphasis on promoting consumer access to justice has pushed Member States to review their laws relating to the funding of litigation, with the result that contingency fee systems are increasingly available. For instance, France, Italy, Luxembourg, and Portugal authorize law firms to charge fees which are based, to some extent, upon results. Greece permits a US-style contingency fee by limiting the fee to 20 per cent of the amount recovered.

Although a contingency system is expensive, it facilitates access to justice if consumers cannot afford to pay the lawyer's fees or do not qualify for public legal aid funding. Moreover, under a contingency scheme, the lawyers often assume the financial risk of the litigation, which might move the burden away from the plaintiff and partially reduce unmeritorious cases. Lawyers may also have an additional incentive to win the case, dedicating time and funding in order to succeed, whilst becoming more specialized in consumer claims.[153] All this suggests that contingency fees could overcome the financial and legal knowledge barriers to accessing justice. Having said this, in order to prevent lawyers from taking advantage of over-payment, it might be important to legally limit contingency fees to a certain percentage rate of the awarded damages.[154]

[152] H. Kritzer, *Risks, Reputations and Rewards: Contingency Fee Legal Practice in the United States* (Stanford: Stanford University Press, 2004), pp. 258–9.

[153] In contrast, legally aided clients might be treated with less importance because of the lower compensation and might be represented by more inexperienced lawyers.

[154] For a discussion concerning contingency funding in competition cases, see Riley & Peysner, 'Damages in EC Antitrust Actions' (n 150), pp. 748–61.

However, this and the financial risk of the 'loser pays' principle may make it less attractive for law firms to engage in contingency fees and collective redress cases in the EU.

In conclusion, contingency fees can facilitate consumer access to justice and should be included in the discussion on collective redress.[155] However, this method of litigation funding often only functions well for particularly profitable cases. Thus, it should be considered as a complementary solution to legal aid and alternative funding methods described below, which are especially needed in complex or low financial value cases.

4.3. *Conditional fee agreements and human rights limitations*

In the UK, the option of a 'conditional fee agreement' was introduced to compensate for a general reduction of legal aid.[156] Under this scheme, a lawyer represents a client upon the basis that, if the case is lost, either no fee or only a reduced fee is payable by the client. These conditional fees are linked to an 'after-the-event insurance', which would pay the adversarial party's costs in the event of losing the case.[157]

A drawback of this system is that the losing parties have to pay considerable compensation for the litigation, as well as the lawyers' fees and the insurance premium. This has generated criticism of the enforceability of conditional fee agreements and has even been seen as potentially conflicting with human rights.[158] For example, in the recent case of *MGN Limited v The United Kingdom* the European Court of Human Rights ruled that the conditional fee agreement regime, in which the loser is liable for the success fees of their opponent's legal costs, breaches the applicant's right to freedom of expression.[159] It held in particular that 'the requirement that the applicant pay success fees to the claimant was disproportionate having regard to the legitimate aims sought to be achieved and exceeded even the broad margin of appreciation accorded

[155] See also Civil Justice Council, The Future Funding of Litigation—Alternative Funding Structures, *Access to Justice through the Development of Improved Funding Structures*, 2007, pp. 68 *et seq.*

[156] Section 58 of the Courts and Legal Services Act1990 in the UK.

[157] As litigants are often unable to fund the insurance premiums the solicitor sometimes funds the premium, or a loan is obtained from a bank.

[158] On average, lawyers charge between 25 and 50% of the damages awarded to the client; see the Civil Justice Council Report in the UK, *Improved Access to Justice, Funding Options and Proportionate Costs* (n 148), Appendices, fnn 26 *et seq*.

[159] ECtHR, Case *MGN Ltd v United Kingdom*, App. no. 39401/04 [2011] ECHR 66, Judgment of 18 January 2011.

to the Government in such matters'.[160] Therefore, the Court decided that there was a violation of Article 10 ECHR.

4.4. *Third-party funding and legal expenses insurance*

A new trend is the emergence of third-party funders in Australia and some EU countries, such as the UK, Germany, Austria, the Netherlands, and Ireland.[161] Third-party funding involves a third party, such as a bank, that finances the case, without having a direct interest in the case. The fees of third-party funders can be between 20 and 40 per cent, depending on the country.[162] However, third-party funding tends to apply mainly to high-value cases[163] and therefore does not offer a solution for smaller consumer claims. Given the recent appearance of third-party funders, questions arise regarding their role in controlling litigation and the need to regulate this phenomenon in order to prevent potential abuses.[164]

Another means of third-party funding in order to offset the heavy financial risks of litigation is for the claimant to subscribe to legal expenses insurance before a court claim arises. This type of funding is particularly prominent in civil law countries with predictable litigation costs, such as Germany, where tariffs exist for lawyers' fees.[165] Legal expenses insurance also exists in the UK through the so-called 'Before the Event Insurance' and is obtainable as a separate policy, such as an add-on to household and motorcar insurance policies.[166] The advantage of such a funding model is that it is cheap and relatively safe for the insurer, because it usually excludes success fees. On the other hand, legal expenses insurance has been criticized in Germany for increasing spurious lawsuits.[167] It is also questionable if this funding model is suitable for collective redress actions. Given that this type of litigation could expose the insurer to significant financial risks it may often be excluded from legal expenses insurance schemes.

[160] ECtHR, Case *MGN Ltd v United Kingdom*, App. no. 39401/04 [2011] ECHR 66, Judgment of 18 January 2011, para. 219.

[161] Hodges, Vogenauer, & Tulibacka, *The Funding and Costs of Civil Litigation* (n 148), p. 27.

[162] Hodges, Vogenauer, & Tulibacka (n 148), p. 27.

[163] Hodges, Vogenauer, & Tulibacka (n 148), pp. 30–1.

[164] Hodges, Vogenauer, & Tulibacka (n 148), pp. 30–1.

[165] Hodges, Vogenauer, & Tulibacka (n 148), p. 21; in the same book see: B. Hess and R. Hübner, 'Germany', pp. 358–9.

[166] J. Peysner, 'England and Wales', in Hodges, Vogenauer, & Tulibacka (n 148), p. 293.

[167] Hess & Hübner, 'Germany', in Hodges, Vogenauer, & Tulibacka (n 148), pp. 358–9.

4.5. *Consumer actions and class proceedings funds*

Legal actions funds are public, non-commercial funds that help plaintiffs to finance a case. They exist in various countries outside Europe, such as Canada and Hong Kong, and are often funded by public entities, or third-party financiers taking the initial liability of the case. A great variety of different funds exist, but, in general, an accepted claimant would receive an indemnity against the opponent's costs as well as payment disbursements. The consumer's lawyer would be paid by the fund or by contingency fees.

An interesting funding scheme exists in Hong Kong. The 'Consumer Legal Action Fund' (the Fund), provides financial assistance specifically for consumer legal actions. This Fund is managed by the Consumer Council in Hong Kong and helps consumers to pursue their claims in courts.[168] Both individual consumers and a group of consumers can apply for assistance for a court claim. The requirement is that the case relates to consumer transactions and involves significant public interest or injustice. Furthermore, a consumer must have exhausted all other means of resolving the dispute in question, and be unable to qualify for any form of legal aid.

The advantage of the scheme is that the consumer only has to pay a moderate fee at the beginning of the case whereas the Fund pays for all the costs and expenses. Furthermore, the consumer has no financial risks, because if the case turns out to be unsuccessful, he or she does not need to refund any payments. On the other hand, if consumers win a case they are required to pay a contribution to the Fund.[169]

Other relevant models can be found in Canada, in which a number of collective redress funds were established to promote access to justice.[170] In Quebec, a special fund serves exclusively for collective actions. This fund is financed by the reimbursements made by the collective redress claimants if they win their collective actions, and also by the residual amount of the damages. The fund also serves as a central point of information with regard to group actions, such as the publication of actions, information on how to exclude oneself from a group, or the indication of the procedure of how to obtain damages.[171]

[168] See: <http://www.hkclic.org/en/topics/consumer_complaints/channels_for_consumer_complaints/q2.shtml>.

[169] For more information see: <http://www2.consumer.org.hk/claf/briefe.pdf>.

[170] Ziegel, 'Consumer Protection in Canada and the Class Action Remedy?' (n 87), pp. 587–98.

[171] Riley & Peysner (n 150), pp. 748–61.

In addition, in 1992 a Class Proceedings Fund was established in Ontario. The objective of the fund is to give financial assistance to plaintiffs for the costs of a court case. In return, the plaintiff would have to return 10 per cent of the damages obtained in any settlement or judgment. In the event that the Fund finances the litigation, it will be liable for any costs awarded to the defendants, so that the plaintiffs will not have to support the liability risk if they lose a case. Since the introduction of class actions in Canada, a considerable number of cases have already been filed at the court.[172]

In conclusion, the development of different funding models is necessary in the EU in order to provide effective consumer access to justice. Legal aid and legal expenses insurance can be particularly useful for individual claims. Contingency fees, third-party funding, and collective redress funds are specifically relevant funding options for the application of collective actions. A trend of accepting contingency fees in certain Member States and at EU level is already becoming apparent.

5. Conclusions

Despite being recognized as a fundamental right, access to justice still remains a challenge in consumer law. In particular, the risks of high costs along with increasingly complex cross-border procedures represent barriers to the exercise of consumer rights.

This chapter has analyzed specific collective redress models, ADR procedures, and new funding schemes, highlighting the significant role these could play, in improving consumer access to justice in the face of increasingly consolidated markets.

While, at this stage, collective action procedures for consumer damages are still lacking at the EU level, they are becoming increasingly important within the Member States. However, national models vary considerably and a significant number of Member States do not provide for these collective redress mechanisms. This leads to inconsistent standards of access to justice and to legal uncertainty, which may hamper consumer protection in the ever more frequent cases of cross-border transactions. A balanced collective redress

[172] G. Watson, 'Class Actions: The Canadian Experience', (2001) 11 *Duke J. Comp. & Int'l Law*, p. 275.

measure at the EU level would instead facilitate consumer access to justice and motivate companies to use ADR mechanisms. It may also help to identify market failures, providing incentives for regulatory change and compliance. A number of financing methods have been suggested in this chapter, such as contingency fees and consumer redress funds, which can further facilitate judicial access of consumers.

The EU is currently discussing the introduction of collective redress procedures for damages, with ADR being a primary first step towards providing affordable means of redress and preventing excessive court litigation. The recently adopted EU legislation on consumer ADR and ODR will help to promote consistent quality standards and will be instrumental in making out-of-court dispute resolution widely available to consumers. Furthermore, the ECJ's recent case law has highlighted the importance of effective judicial protection, applying a fundamental rights assessment, and it has recognized ADR mechanisms as an option to facilitate consumer dispute resolution.

Despite the current focus in this regard, it remains to be seen if, at the EU policy level, binding collective redress mechanisms for damages and effective funding schemes will be established, or if they will merely be given a soft law status.

8

Conclusions

This book has provided a novel perspective on consumer law. It analyzed intersections between human rights and consumer law and has proposed a conceptual framework for EU consumer law and policy. Historically, EU consumer law has mainly been used as a tool of market integration. This book has argued that it is essential to move beyond this traditional approach, embedding consumer law in a broader social and economic context and moving it towards a closer relationship with fundamental rights.

Major questions behind this book have been: how can social justice and ethical concerns be integrated in EU consumer law? Does the strengthening of fundamental rights in the EU support a broader consumer law approach? What legal instruments can effectively protect consumers, while promoting active participation, inclusion, and confidence in the cross-border market?

Answering these questions led to the development of three themes: (1) the traditional EU consumer law approach presents limitations, which could be addressed by placing a stronger emphasis on fundamental rights, following the direction provided by recent legal provisions; (2) several legal and economic theories, originally developed in other contexts, can provide a theoretical foundation for a new legal framework centred on fundamental rights and supported by the Lisbon Treaty; and (3) the development of a model of consumer law along these lines would have important practical implications, as shown by recent cases in specific areas of consumer law.

Starting off with the first theme, the book opened with an assessment of the scope and the limitations of the current EU consumer law framework. A historic overview of EU competences and case law has demonstrated that the current full harmonization trend of consumer law in the Union is narrowly drawn. This tendency has been called into question as it may downgrade consumer protection in some countries and reduce legal diversity.

Moreover, as has been argued, the current framework is unable to respond to the new challenges of a changing global landscape. On the one hand, it is now apparent that a legal model purely focused on economic freedom is unsustainable. For example, the recent financial crisis has shown that markets can fail, exposing consumers to consequences that may negatively affect future economic development. On the other hand, over-regulation may stifle private enterprise and growth, and may lead to an excessive cost in terms of control and enforcement. An ideal solution would therefore need to strike a delicate balance between inadequate protection and over-protection.

This book argued that such a compromise still has to be achieved in the EU. Perhaps more importantly, the current framework of consumer law still lacks a social perspective, making consumer protection subordinate to market-making objectives, and failing to address recent demands of European consumer-citizens.

Despite this general situation, there are some signs of an incipient change. The Lisbon Treaty makes the Charter of Fundamental Rights binding and contains a number of new social objectives that could have a significant impact on consumer law. In turn, the Charter contains various provisions which either expressly mention consumer protection, or are relevant to improving the status of the consumer in the market, an example being the right to data protection. These provisions suggest that the Charter could evolve into an important instrument of reference, serving, among others, two central purposes: strengthening consumers' rights, and stimulating the introduction of consumer-focused EU policies.

As for the first purpose, the Charter's fundamental rights may help to guarantee fair market conditions and thus provide a basis for a high level of consumer protection. While some provisions of the Charter are shaped as legal principles or policy objectives, they might develop over time into subjective rights, especially if applied together with relevant fundamental rights—such as the right to the protection of personal data or the right to an effective remedy and to a fair trial.

On the other hand, by elevating consumer protection to the status of a fundamental right objective in its 'Solidarity' chapter, the Charter strengthens a social dimension at the EU level. By so doing it promotes objectives which transcend mere economic interests and may prepare the ground for a transformation of EU consumer law. Interestingly, the case law in some Member States has shown that constitutional principles, applied in combination with other basic rights, can lead to effective protection of the weaker contractual party. Similarly, at the EU level, the ECJ is increasingly referring to the

Charter of Fundamental Rights, which demonstrates the impact that this can have on consumer law.

Besides strengthening the role of fundamental rights in the EU, the Treaty of Lisbon introduced provisions, such as those regarding access to justice and the right of a citizens' initiative, which could have a direct impact on consumer law. For example, Article 81(2) TFEU allows the EU to adopt measures on access to justice or alternative dispute resolution even without a market-making objective. In turn, Article 11 TEU provides new ways of policy participation which might also lead to novel legal initiatives in consumer-related matters.

However, while being an important step, the innovations introduced by the Charter suffer from inherent limitations. First, the Charter provision that explicitly refers to consumer protection is short and abstract; as a consequence, it does not provide specific rights, but is only formulated as a general policy objective. Secondly, the Charter does not extend the competences of the EU as defined in the Treaties. The Member States are clearly very cautious on this point.

This suggests that the Charter is a first step towards a new framework for consumer law, but that such a system is still largely to be defined. The second theme of this book has thus been the development of a theory which could underpin a legal framework to overcome some of the current limitations. To do this, several theoretical approaches have been analyzed; among them, Sen's capability theory and Habermas' discourse approach.

Born as an economic theory, Sen's approach is centred on the concepts of capability and freedoms which, as shown in this book, find a precise application in the field of human rights and are particularly relevant for the EU consumer law context. In particular, the idea of promoting capabilities places citizens at the centre of the theoretical discourse respecting differences in contexts while not disregarding the needs of the markets—as required by the multinational system of the EU. The development of a legal framework founded on the capability approach would imply a change in European policy, away from a full-harmonization and market-centred perspective and towards an economically and socially balanced model.

As shown in this book, Sen's theory could be usefully complemented by other approaches (such as that proposed by Fredman) stressing the importance of responsibility and care as important dimensions of human rights which transcend individual welfare maximization. This could then lead to a model able to accommodate new market trends such as the growing interest in ethically produced goods.

Another complement may be provided by Habermas' discourse approach. Revolving around the concept of participation seen as a prerequisite for legitimation, this theoretical framework touches on a problem particularly felt by EU institutions (the 'legitimacy deficit'), and speaks well to the European multi-level, non-hierarchical network of institutions. The application of the discourse approach to consumer law was seen to have implications at the level of information and education to be provided to consumers, and on procedural rights. Procedural rights are strictly intertwined with human rights: the former are necessary to protect and realize the latter, but procedural rights can only be upheld if certain fundamental rights (e.g. the right to information or the right to access to justice) are ensured. The extent to which procedural rights can be strengthened in current EU consumer law, in particular, following the Aarhus Convention and the Lisbon Treaty, has thus been discussed.

The third theme of this book has been the practical implications of a new consumer law model derived from the legal framework laid out by the Lisbon Treaty, centred on fundamental rights and inspired by the above theories. The focus of this part has been on two key areas, financial services and electronic communication, and on the cross-cutting topic of access to justice.

Fundamental and constitutional rights have been shown to have an increasing role in the area of financial services. In the courts, they are invoked to strengthen the position of weaker contractual parties; in policy, they can provide a driving force for the development of new consumer strategies. As we have seen, the Charter of Fundamental Rights has provided inspiration to the new Commission's Consumer Policy Agenda. In the future, it may further promote a stronger focus on financial literacy and education of consumers, along with specific values such as non-discrimination. Moreover, as shown by the *Test-Achats* case, the Charter is playing the role of a yardstick against which to assess the validity of legislative acts. By offering such a concrete tool to protect particular rights and values, the Charter may strengthen the position of consumer organizations and favour the development of a 'litigation trend' in financial services.

The second area of consumer law considered in this book is that of electronic communication, which has provided the background for a clash between fundamental rights. As we saw in a number of cases, the fundamental right to privacy protection and the freedom to receive information can be in conflict with the right to property, calling for a difficult balance between them. In several judgments the ECJ has stressed that the fundamental rights of consumers have to be taken into account in cases regarding Internet service provisions. In particular, the fundamental right to data protection and the consumer's freedom to receive or impart information (as enshrined in Articles 8 and 11 of the Charter respectively) must be respected. These rulings illustrated the important role that fundamental rights can play in the ECJ reasoning, confirming their increasing role in consumer law.

Finally, this book discussed access to justice in consumer law. It thus considered cases of effective judicial protection and looked at regulatory innovations, demonstrating how a more efficient civil justice system can be created by improving consumers' access to justice. Although recognized as a human right, access to justice is still de facto not adequately ensured for EU consumers. However, there are signs suggesting that a change may be impending. In particular Chapter 7 discussed how collective actions, specific ADR procedures, and new funding schemes can improve consumer access to justice in increasingly consolidated markets, analyzing recent ECJ cases where some of these mechanisms and fundamental rights have played an important role. Moreover, since the introduction of the Lisbon Treaty, the EU has acquired a broader competence to adopt legislative proposals that may facilitate access to justice for consumers.

To conclude, fundamental rights play an increasing role in EU consumer law. However, this is just one trend in EU policy: the market-making component, embodied by full-harmonization policies, remains predominant and may hinder the development of a more comprehensive consumer model.

This book argued that, in order to overcome some of the limitations of such an approach, it is important to strengthen certain elements of EU consumer law and policy, namely social justice and inclusion, procedural and participatory rights, and responsibility and sustainability of consumption. The Charter and the Lisbon Treaty provide a starting point for an evolution in this sense, but their innovative potential is still to be realized. The beginnings that they provide need to be developed in an affirmative and cohesive way, which will require strong political and judicial will.

BIBLIOGRAPHY

Adinolfi, A., 'The Judicial Application of Community Law in Italy (1981–1997)', (1998) 35 *Common Market Law Review*.

Alexy, R., 'Grundrechte als subjektive Rechte und als objektive Normen', (1990) 29 *Der Staat*.

____, 'Diskurstheorie und Menschenrechte', in R. Alexy, *Recht, Vernunft, Diskurs. Studien zur Rechtsphilosophie* (Frankfurt am Main: Suhrkamp, 1995).

____, *Theorie der Grundrechte*, 3rd edn (Frankfurt am Main: Suhrkamp Verlag, 1996).

____, 'Discourse Theory and Fundamental Rights Revisited', in A.J. Menendez & E.O. Eriksen (eds), *Arguing Fundamental Rights* (Berlin: Springer, 2006), vol. 77.

Alpa, G., 'New Perspectives in the Protection of Consumers: A General Overview and some Criticisms on Financial Services', (2005) 16(4) *European Business Law Review*, pp. 719–35.

Alston, P., 'Human Rights and Basic Needs: A Critical Assessment', (1979) 12 *Human Rights Journal*.

_____ & De Schutter, O., *Monitoring Fundamental Rights in the EU: The Contribution of the Fundamental Rights Agency* (Oxford: Hart Publishing, 2005).

____ & Steiner, H.J., *International Human Rights in Context: Law, Politics, Morals: Text and Materials*, 2nd edn (Oxford: Oxford University Press, 2000).

Annas, G.J., 'The Right to Health and the Nevirapine Case in South Africa', (2002) 346 *New England Journal of Medicine*.

Anton, D. & Shelton, D., 'Procedural Human Rights and the Environment', in *Environmental Protection and Human Rights* (Cambridge: Cambridge University Press, 2011).

Arango R., 'Basic Social Rights, Constitutional Justice, and Democracy', (2003) 16 *Ratio Juris*.

Arbour, M.-E., 'Compensation for Damage Caused by Defective Drugs: European Private Law between Safety Requirements and Free-Market Values', (2004) 10 *European Law Journal*.

Badura, P., 'Das Prinzip der sozialen Grundrechte und seine Verwirklichung im Recht der Bundesrepublik Deutschland' (1975) 14 *Der Staat*.

Bamforth, N., 'The True "Horizontal Effect" of the Human Rights Act 1998', (2001) 117 *Law Quarterly Review*.

Baquero Cruz, J., 'Beyond Competition: Services of General Interest and European Community Law', in G. De Búrca (ed.), *EU Law and the Welfare State: In Search of Solidarity* (Oxford: Oxford University Press, 2005).

Barnard, C., *The Substantive Law of the EU, The Four Freedoms* (Oxford: Oxford University Press, 2007).

____, Deakin, S., & Hobbs, R., 'Capabilities and Rights: An Emerging Agenda for Social Policy?', (2001) 32 *Industrial Relations Journal*.

Barnard, D., 'In the High Court of South Africa, Case No. 4138/98: The Global Politics of Access to Low-Cost AIDS Drugs in Poor Countries', (2002) 12 *Kennedy Institute of Ethics Journal*, pp. 159–74.

Barr, M., 'Credit Where it Counts: the Community Reinvestment Act' (2005) 80 *New York University Law Review*.

Beatson J. & Friedmann, D., 'Introduction: From "Classical" to Modern Contract Law', in J. Beatson & D. Friedmann (eds), *Good Faith and Fault in Contract Law* (Oxford: Clarendon Press, 1995).

Beck, U., *Risk Society: Towards a New Modernity* (translated from the German *Risikogesellschaft*, published in 1986) (New Delhi: Sage, 2002).

Beckmann, P., Colombi Ciacchi, A., et al., 'Germany', in G. Brüggemeier, A. Colombi Ciacchi, and G. Comandé, *Fundamental Rights and Private Law in the EU* (Cambridge: Cambridge University Press, 2010).

Bell, R. & Ray, N., *EU Electronic Communications Law* (Oxford: Oxford University Press, 2004).

Benjamin, A., 'Group Action and Consumer Protection in Brazil', in T. Bourgoignie (ed.), *Group Actions and Consumer Protection* (Brussels: Bruylant, 1992).

Benöhr, I., 'Alternative Dispute Resolution for Consumers in the EU', in C. Hodges, I. Benöhr, & N. Creutzfeld-Banda (eds), *Consumer ADR in Europe* (Oxford: Hart Publishing, 2012), pp. 1–23.

——'Consumer Dispute Resolution after the Lisbon Treaty' (2013) 36(1) Journal of Consumer Policy, pp. 87–110.

____ & Micklitz, H.-W., 'Consumer Protection and Human Rights', in G. Howells, I. Ramsay, & T. Wilhelmsson (eds), *Handbook of Research on International Consumer Law* (Cheltenham: Edward Elgar Publishing, 2010).

Benoît-Rohmer, F., 'Article 38, Protection des Consommateurs', in EU Network of Independent Experts on Fundamental Rights, *Commentary on the Charter of Fundamental Rights of the European Union* (2006).

Bernard, N., 'A New Governance Approach to Economic, Social and Cultural Rights in the EU', in *Economic and Social Rights under the EU Charter of Fundamental Rights: A Legal Perspective* (Oxford-Portland Oregon: Hart Publishing, 2003).

Beuchler, H., 'Länderbericht Vereinigtes Königreich', in J. Keßler & H.-W. Micklitz (eds), *Kundenschutz auf liberalisierten Märkten—Telekommunikation—Vergleich der Konzepte, Maßnahmen und Wirkungen in Europa* (Baden-Baden: Nomos, 2008).

Bevir, M. & Trentmann, F. (eds), *Governance, Consumers and Citizens. Agency and Resistance in Contemporary Politics* (Basingstoke: Palgrave Macmillan, 2007).

Bieber, R., 'Steigerungsform der Europäischen Union: Eine Europäische Verfassung', in J. Ipsen, H.W. Rengeling, J.M. Mössner, & A. Weber, *Verfassungsrecht im Wandel* (Cologne: Festschrift zum 180 jährigen Bestehen des Carl-Heymanns-Verlags, 1995).

____, 'Grundrechtsschutz in Europa: Protection des droits fondamentaux en Europe', *Swiss Papers on European Integration* (Bern: Stämpfli, 2001).

____, De Gucht, K., Lenaerts, K., & Weiler, J.H.H. (eds), *Au nom des peoples européens – in the name of the peoples of Europe* (Baden-Baden: Nomos, 1996).

____ & Widmer, P. (eds.), *L'espace constitutionnel européen, Der europäische Verfassungsraum, The European Constitutional Area* (Zürich: Schulthess, 1995).

Bognetti, G., 'Social Rights, a Necessary Component of the Constitution? The Lesson of the Italian Case', in R. Bieber & P. Widmer, *L'Espace constitutionnel européen, Der europäische Verfassungsraum, The European Constitutional Area* (Zürich: Schulthess, 1995).

Bourgoignie, T., 'Consumer Law and the European Community: Issues and Prospects', in T. Bourgoignie & D. Trubek (eds), *Consumer Law, Common Markets and Federalism in Europe and the United States* (Vol. 3: Integration through Law Series) (Berlin: Walter de Gruyter, 1987, c1986), pp. 89–234.

____, 'European Community Consumer Law and Policy: from Rome to Amsterdam', (1998) 4 *Consumer Law Journal*.

Bronzini, G., 'The European Social Model and the Constitutional Treaty of the European Union', in Ch. Joerges, B. Stråth, & P. Wagner (eds), *The Economy as a Polity: The Political Constitution of Contemporary Capitalism* (London: Cavandish Press, 2005), pp. 183–202.

Browne, J., Deakin, S., & Wilkinson, F., 'Capabilities, Social Rights and European Market Integration', ESCR, University of Cambridge, Working Paper 253, December 2002.

____, Deakin, S., & Wilkinson, F., 'Capabilities, Social Rights and European Market Integration', in R. Salais & R. Villeneuve (ed), *Europe and the Politics of Capabilities* (Cambridge: Cambridge University Press, 2004), pp. 205–21.

Brüggemeier, A., Colombi Ciacchi, A., & Comandé, G. (eds), *Fundamental Rights and Private Law in the European Union*, (Cambridge: Cambridge University Press, 2010).

Busch, C., 'Fundamental Rights and Private Law in the EU Member States', in C. Busch and H. Schulte-Nölke, *Fundamental Rights and Private Law* (Munich: Sellier, 2011).

Butt M., Kübert J., & Schultz C.A., 'Fundamental Social Rights in Europe', Working Paper, European Parliament, DG for Research, Social Affairs Series (1999).

Calais-Auloy, J., *Consumer Legislation in France* (New York: Nostrand Reinhold, 1980).

____, *Propositions pour un nouveau droit de la consommation* (Paris, Documentation française, 1985).

Calliess, C., 'Die Europäische Grundrechts-Charta', in D. Ehlers (ed.), *Europäische Grundrechte und Grundfreiheiten* (Berlin-New York: De Gruyter Recht, 2003).

Cappelletti, M., 'Alternative Dispute Settlement Procedures within the Framework of the World-wide Access-to Justice Movement', (1993) 56 *Modern Law Review*.

____ & Garth, B. (eds), *Access to Justice: a World Survey* (Milan: A. Giuffre, 1978).

Cartwright, P., *Banks, Consumers and Regulation* (Oxford: Hart Publishing, 2004).

Charles-Le Bihan, D., 'Services d'intérêt économique général et valeurs communes', (2008) 519 *Revue du Marché commun et de l'Union européenne*.

Cherednychenko, O., 'Constitutionalization of Contract Law: Something New under the Sun?', (2004) 8 *Electronic Journal of Comparative Law*.

____, 'Fundamental Rights and Contract Law', (2006) 2 *European Review of Contract Law*.

____, *Fundamental Rights, Contract Law and the Protection of the Weaker Party: A Comparative Analysis of the Constitutionalisation of Contract Law, with Emphasis on Risky Financial Transactions* (Munich: Sellier, European Law Publisher, 2007).

Civil Justice Council, *The Future Funding of Litigation—Alternative Funding Structures, A Series of Recommendations to the Lord Chancellor to Improve Access to Justice through the Development of Improved Funding Structures* (UK: Civil Justice Council, 2007).

Collins, D., 'Public Funding of Class Actions and the Experience with English Group Proceedings', (2005) 31 *Manitoba Law Journal*.

Collins, H., 'Good Faith in European Contract Law', (1994) 14 *Oxford Journal of Legal Studies*.

____, 'European Private Law and the Cultural Identity of States', (1995) 3 *European Review of Private Law*.

____, 'European Social Policy and Contract Law', (2005) 11 *European Review of Contract Law*.

Colombi Ciacchi, A., 'Protection from Unfair Suretyships', in S. Vogenauer & S. Weatherill (eds), *The Harmonization of European Contract Law: Implications for European Private Laws, Business and Legal Practice* (Oxford: Hart Publishing, 2006).

____, 'The Constitutionalisation of European Contract Law: Judicial Convergence and Social Justice', (2006) 2 *European Review of Contract Law*, pp. 167–80.

Coppel J. & O'Neill, A., 'The European Court of Justice: Taking Rights Seriously?', (1992) 29 *Common Market Law Review*.

Craig, P., 'Constitutions, Constitutionalism and the European Union', (2001) 7 *European Law Journal*.

____, *The Lisbon Treaty Law, Politics and Treaty Reform* (Oxford: Oxford University Press, 2010).

____ & De Búrca, G., *EU Law: Text, Cases and Materials*, 3rd edn (Oxford: Oxford University Press, 2003).

____ & De Búrca, G., *EU Law: Text, Cases and Materials*, 4th edn (Oxford: Oxford University Press, 2008).

____ & De Búrca, G. (eds), *The Evolution of EU Law* (Oxford: Oxford University Press, 2011).

Cranston, M., *What are Human Rights?* (London: Bodley Head, 1973).

Cranston, M., 'Are There Any Human Rights?', (1983) 112(4), *Daedalus*.

Dahl, B., Melchior, T., Rehof, L.A., & Tamm, D. (eds), *Danish Law in a European Perspective*, 2nd edn (Copenhagen: Forlaget Thomson, 2002).

Damjanovic, D. & De Witte, B., *Welfare Integration through EU Law: The Overall Picture in the Light of the Lisbon Treaty*, EUI LAW, 2008/34 (Florence: European University Institute, 2008).

Dauner-Lieb, B., *Verbraucherschutz durch Ausbildung eines Sonderprivatrechts für Verbraucher—systemkonforme Weiterentwicklung oder Schrittmacher der Systemveränderung?* (Berlin: Duncker & Humbolt, 1983).

De Andrade, V. & Carlos, J., *Os Direitos Fundamentais na Constituição Portuguesa de 1976*, 3rd edn (Coimbra: Almedina, 2004).

De Búrca, G., 'The Drafting of the European Union Charter of Fundamental Rights', (2001) 26 *European Law Review*.

____, 'Beyond the Charter: How Enlargement has Enlarged the Human Rights Policy for the EU', (2004) 27 *Fordham International Law Journal*, pp. 679–714.

____ & De Witte, B. (eds), *Social Rights in Europe* (Oxford: Oxford University Press, 2005).

De Moraes, A., *Direitos Humanos Fundamentais, Teoria Geral*, 7th edn (Saõ Paulo: Editora Atlas S.A., 2006).

De Sadeleer, N., 'Droit fondamentaux et protection de l'environnement dans l'ordre juridique de l'UE et dans la CEDH', in C. Vedure, 'Environmental Law and Consumer Protection', (2011) *European Journal of Consumer Law*.

De Schutter, O., 'Les droits et principes sociaux dans la Charte des droits fondamentaux de l'Union européenne', in J.-Y. Carlier & O. De Schutter (eds), *La Charte des droits fondamentaux de l'Union européenne* (Brussels: Bruylant, 2002).

Deakin, S., '"Capacitas": Contract Law and the Institutional Precondition of a Market Economy', (2006) 3 *European Review of Contract Law*.

____ & Browne, J., 'Social Rights and Market Order: Adapting the Capability Approach', in T. Hervey & J. Kenner (eds), *Economic and Social Rights under the EU Charter of Fundamental Rights: A Legal Perspective* (Oxford: Hart Publishing, 2003).

Deutch, S., 'Are Consumer Rights Human Rights?', (1994) 32(3) *Osgoode Hall Law Journal*.

Didier, N., 'Evaluation of the Consumer's Financial Capacity', in ECRI (ed.), *Consumer Financial Capability: Empowering European Consumers* (Brussels: ECRI, 2006).

Donnelly, J., *Universal Human Rights in Theory and Practice*, (Ithaca: Cornell University Press, 2003).

Dougan, M., *National Remedies before the Court of Justice: Issues of Harmonization and Differentiation* (Oxford: Hart Publishing, 2005).

Douglas-Scott, S., 'The European Union and Human Rights after the Treaty of Lisbon', (2011) 11(4) *Human Rights Law Review*.

Drexl, J., *Die wirtschaftliche Selbstbestimmung des Verbrauchers. Eine Studie zum Privat- und Wirtschaftsrecht unter Berücksichtigung gemeinschaftsrechtlicher Bezüge* (Tübingen: Mohr Siebeck, 1998).

Dworkin, R., *Taking Rights Seriously* (London: Duckworth, 1977) (fourth impression 1984).

Eide, A. & Rosas, A., 'Economic, Social and Cultural Rights: A Universal Challenge', in A. Eide, C. Krause, & A. Rosas (eds), *Economic, Social and Cultural Rights: A Textbook* (Dordrecht: Martinus Nijhoff, 1995).

Elster, J, 'Forces and Mechanisms in the Constitution-Making Process', (1995) 45 *Duke Law Journal*, pp. 364–396.

Ervine, W., 'Regulating Socially Harmful Lending: Reform in the United Kingdom', in L. Thévenoz & N. Reich (eds), *Liber amicorum Bernd Stauder: Droit de la Consommation/ Konsumentenrecht/Consumer Law* (Baden-Baden/Zurich: Nomos/Schulthess, 2006).

Everson, M., 'Legal Construction of the Consumer', in F. Trentmann (ed.), *The Making of the Consumer* (Oxford-New York: Berg Publishers, 2006), pp. 99 *et seq*.

____ & Joerges, Ch., 'Consumer Citizenship in Postnational Constellations?' EUI WP Law 2006/47, Florence.

Faber, W., 'Elemente verschiedener Verbraucherbegriffe in EG-Richtlinien, zwischenstaatlichen Übereinkommen und nationalem Zivil- und Kollisionsrecht', (1998) *ZeuP*.

Fabre, C., *Social Rights under the Constitution: Government and the Decent Life* (Oxford: Oxford University Press, 2000).

Fagan, A. 'Buying Rights: Consuming Ethically and Human Rights', in J. Dine and A. Fagan (eds), *Human Rights and Capitalism: A Multidisciplinary Perspective on Globalisation* (Cheltenham: Edward Elgar Publishing, 2006).

Fairgrieve, D. & Howells, G., 'Collective Redress Procedures—European Debates', (2009) 58 *International and Comparative Law Quarterly*.

Fasquelle, D. & Meunier, P., *Le droit communautaire de la consommation: Bilan et perspectives* (Paris: Documentation Française, 2002).

Frankenberg, G., 'Why Care? The Trouble with Social Rights?', (1996) 17 *Cardozo Law Review*.

Fredman, S., 'Transformation or Dilution: Fundamental Rights in the EU Social Space', (2006) 12 *European Law Journal*, pp. 41–60.

____, *Human Rights Transformed: Positive Duties and Positive Rights* (Oxford: Oxford University Press, 2008).

Galligan, D., *Due Process and Fair Procedures: A Study of Administrative Procedures* (Oxford: Clarendon Press, 1996).

Gan, S., 'Essay: Consumer Rights: A Part of Human Rights', (2008) 1(1) *Journal of International Business Ethics*.

Gerstenberg, O. & De Búrca, G., 'The Denationalization of Constitutional Law', (2006) 47 *Harvard International Law Journal*.

Goldsmith, T., 'A Charter of Rights, Freedoms and Principles', (2001) 38 *Common Market Law Review*.

Grard, L., 'La subsidiarité et le droit communautaire de la consommation', in D. Fasquelle & P. Meunier (eds), *Le droit communautaire de la consummation: bilan et perspectives* (Paris: la documentation française, coll. CEDECE, 2002).

Greenwood, J., *Interest Representation in the European Union* (Basingstoke: Palgrave Macmillan, 2011).

Groussot, X., 'Rock the KaZa: Another Clash of Fundamental Rights, Case C-275/06, *Productores de Musica de Espana (Promusicae) v Telefonica de Espana SAU*, Judgment of the Court (Grand Chamber) of 28 January 2008', (2008) 45 *Common Market Law Review*, pp. 1745–66.

Grundmann, S., 'Information, Party Autonomy and Economic Agents in European Contract Law', (2002) 39 *Common Market Law Review*.

Habermas, J., *The Theory of Communicative Action, vol. 2: Lifeworld and System: A Critique of Functionalist Reason* (translated by T. McCarthy) (Boston MA: Beacon Press, 1987).

____, 'Reconciliation through the Public Use of Reason, Remarks on John Rawls' Political Liberalism' and J. Rawls, 'Reply to Habermas', (1995) 92 *The Journal of Philosophy*.

____, *Between Facts and Norms* (Cambridge: Polity Press, 1996).

____, 'Making Sense of the EU: Toward a Cosmopolitan Europe', (2003) vol. 14, *Journal of Democracy*, pp. 86–100.

Haibach, G., 'The Commission Proposal for a Regulation Establishing a European Small Claims Procedure: an Analysis', (2005) 13 *European Review of Private Law*, pp. 293–601.

Hanson, J.D. & Kuysar, D.A., 'Taking Behavioralism Seriously: Some Evidence of Market Manipulation', (1999) 112 *Harvard Law Review*.

Harding, C., Kohl U., & Salmon, N., *Human Rights in the Market Place: The Exploitation of Rights Protection by Economic Actors* (Aldershot: Ashgate, 2008).

Harland, D., 'The United Nations Guidelines for Consumer Protection', (1987) 10 *Journal of Consumer Policy*.

____, 'Implementing the Principles of the United Nations Guidelines for Consumer Protection', (1991) 33 *Journal of the Indian Law Institute*.

Hartlief, T., 'Freedom and Protection in Contemporary Contract Law', (2004) 27 *Journal of Consumer Policy*, pp. 253–67.

Harvey, B.W & Parry, D.L., *The Law of Consumer Protection and Fair Trading*, 5th edn (London: Butterworths, 1996).

Haupt, H.-G., *Konsum und Handel: Europa im 19. und 20. Jahrhundert* (Göttingen: Vandenhoeck und Ruprecht Verlag, 2003).

Helberger, N., 'Making Place for the eConsumer in Consumer Law', (2008) 31 *Journal of Consumer Policy*, pp. 385–91.

Hensler, D., Hodges, C., & Tulibacka, M., *The Globalization of Class Actions, The Annals*, Special edition, vol 622 (Thousand Oaks, CA: SAGE Publications, 2009).

Hervey, T.K., 'The Right to Health in European Union Law', in T.K. Hervey & J. Kenner (eds), *Economic and Social Rights under the EU Charter of Fundamental Rights: A Legal Perspective* (Oxford/Portland Oregon: Hart Publishing, 2003), pp. 193–222.

Hesselink, M., 'The Horizontal Effect of Social Rights in European Contract Law, in *Europa e diritto privato* (Milan: Giuffré Editore, 2003), pp. 1–18.

____, 'Capacity and Capability in European Contract Law', Amsterdam Centre for Law & Economics Working Paper, no. 2005–09.

____, 'Are we Human Beings or Mere Consumers?' (2006) 12(38) *European Voice*.

____, 'European Contract Law: A Matter of Consumer Protection, Citizenship, or Justice', (2007) 15 *European Review of Private Law*.

____, 'A Spontaneous Order for Europe?', in H.-W. Micklitz & F. Cafaggi (eds), *European Private Law after the Common Frame of Reference* (Cheltenham: Edward Elgar, 2010), pp. 123–45.

Hodges, C., *European Regulation of Consumer Product Safety* (Oxford: Oxford University Press, 2003).

____, 'Competition Enforcement, Regulation and Civil Justice: What is the Case?' (2006) 43 *Common Market Law Review*, pp. 1381–407.

____, *The Reform of Class and Representative Actions in European Legal Systems: A New Framework for Collective Redress in Europe* (Oxford: Hart Publishing, 2008).

____, 'The Civil Litigation System in England and Wales', in D. Hensler, C. Hodges, & M. Tulibacka (eds), 'The Globalisation of Class Actions', *Annals of the American Academy of Political and Social Science*, Special edition, vol 622 (Thousand Oaks, CA: SAGE Publications, 2009).

____, Vogenauer, S., & Tulibacka, M., *The Funding and Costs of Civil Litigation. A Comparative Perspective* (Oxford: Hart Publishing, 2010).

House Of Lords: European Union Committee, 13th Report of Session 2005–06, Proposed EU Consumer-Credit Harmonization Directive: Interim Report with Evidence, HL Paper 37.

____, Impact Assessment on the Lisbon Treaty: European Union Committee, The Treaty of Lisbon: an Impact Assessment, 10th Report of Session 2007–08, 2008.

Howells, G., 'Whose Responsibility to Plan for Future Changes in Circumstances—Debtor, Creditor or the State?', in T. Wilhelmsson & S. Hurri (eds), *From Dissonance to Sense: Welfare State Expectations, Privatization and Private Law* (Aldershot: Ashgate Publishing, 1999).

____, 'The Potential and Limits of Consumer Empowerment by Information', (2005) 32 *Journal of Law and Society*, pp. 349–70.

____, 'Is the General Product Safety Directive a Maximum Harmonization Directive?', in L. Thévenoz & N. Reich (eds), *Liber amicorum Bernd Stauder, Droit de la Consommation* (Baden-Baden: Nomos/Geneva: Schulthess, 2006).

____ & Weatherill, S., *Consumer Protection Law*, 2nd edn (Aldershot: Ashgate, 2005).

____ & Wilhelmsson, T., 'EC Consumer Law', in G. Howells (ed.), *European Business Law* (Aldershot: Dartmouth, 1996).

____ & Wilhelmsson, T., *EC Consumer Law* (Aldershot: Ashgate, 1997).

____ & Wilhelmsson, T., 'Private Law in the EU: Harmonized or Fragmented Europeanization?', (2002) 10 *European Review of Private Law*.

____ & Wilhelmsson, T., 'EC Consumer Law: Has it Come of Age?', (2003) 4 *European Law Review*.

Hunt, M., 'The Horizontal Effect of the Human Rights Act', (1998) 4 *Public Law*.

Incardona, R. & Poncibò, C., 'The Average Consumer, the Unfair Commercial Practices Directive, and the Cognitive Revolution', (2007) 30 *Journal of Consumer Policy*.

Joerges, Ch., 'The Impact of European Integration on Private Law: Reductionist Perceptions, True Conflicts and a New Constitutional Perspective', (1997) 3(4) *European Law Journal*, pp. 378–406.

____, 'Interactive Adjudication in the Europeanization Process? A Demanding Perspective and a Modest Example', (2000) 8 *European Review of Private Law*, pp. 1–16.

____, 'On the Legitimacy of Europeanizing Europe's Private Law', EUI WP 2003/3, Florence.

____, 'On the Legitimacy of Europeanizing Private Law: Considerations on a Justice-making Law for the EU Multi-level System', (2003) 7 *Electronic Journal of Comparative Law*.

____, 'What is Left of the European Economic Constitution?—A Melancholic Polemic', EUI Working Papers, Law No 2004/13.

____ & Rödl, F., '"Social Market Economy" as Europe's Social Model?', in L. Magnusson & B. Stråth (eds), *A European Social Citizenship?: Preconditions for Future Policies from a Historical Perspective* (Brussels: Peter Lang, 2004).

Kandil F., 'Economic Efficiency and Social Justice: A Prudential Approach for Public Actions', in Ch. Joerges, B. Stråth, & P. Wagner (eds), *The Economy as a Polity: The Political Constitution of Contemporary Capitalism* (London: UCL Press, 2005).

Kelly-Louw, M., Nehf J., & Rott, P. (eds), *The Future of Consumer Credit Regulation, Creative Approaches to Emerging Problems (Markets and the Law)* (Aldershot: Ashgate Publishing, 2008).

Kemper, R. *Verbraucherschutzinstrumente* (Baden-Baden: Nomos Verlagsgesellschaft, 1994).

Kempson, E., Collard, S., & Moore, N., 'Measuring Financial Capability: An Exploratory Study for the Financial Services Authority', in ECRI, *Consumer Financial Capability: Empowering European Consumers* (Brussels: ECRI, 2006).

Kenner, J., 'Economic and Social Rights in the EU Legal Order', in T. Hervey & J. Kenner (eds), *Economic and Social Rights under the EU Charter of Fundamental Rights: A Legal Perspective* (Oxford-Portland, OR: Hart Publishing, 2003).

Keßler, J. & Micklitz, H.-W. (eds), *Kundenschutz auf liberalisierten Märkten–Telekommunikation—Vergleich der Konzepte, Maßnahmen und Wirkungen in Europa* (Baden-Baden: Nomos, 2008).

Kiss, A., 'Environmental and Consumer Protection', in S. Peers & A. Ward (eds), *The EU Charter of Fundamental Rights: Politics, Law and Policy* (Oxford: Hart Publishing, 2004).

Kötz, H. & Flessner, A., *European Contract Law Vol. 1: Formation, Validity, and Content of Contracts; Contract and Third Parties, vol. 1* (Oxford: Clarendon Press, 1998).

Krämer, L., *EEC Consumer Law Vol. 1* (Brussels: Story Scientia, Centre de droit de la Consommation, Louvain–la-Neuve, 1986).

____, 'The European Union, Consumption and Consumer Law', in L. Thévenoz & N. Reich (eds), *Liber amicorum Bernd Stauder; Droit de la consommation, Konsumentenrecht, Consumer Law* (Geneva: Schulthess, 2006).

Krings, G., *Grund und Grenzen grundrechtlicher Schutzansprüche: Die subjektiv-rechtliche Rekonstruktion der grundrechtlichen Schutzpflichten und ihre Auswirkung auf die verfassungsrechtliche Fundierung des Verbrauchervertragsrechts* (Berlin: Duncker & Humblot, 2003).

Kritzer, M., *Risks, Reputations and Rewards: Contingency Fee Legal Practice in the United States* (Stanford CA: Stanford University Press, 2004).

Larouche, P., *Competition Law and Regulation in European Telecommunications* (Oxford-Portland, OR: Hart Publishing, 2000).

Leibfried, S. & Zürn, M., (eds), 'A New Perspective on the State: Reconfiguring the National Constellation', in S. Leibfried & M. Zürn (eds), *Transformations of the State?* (Cambridge: Cambridge University Press, 2005).

Leskinen, J. & Raijas, A, 'Consumer Financial Capability—a Life Cycle Approach', in ECRI, *Consumer Financial Capability: Empowering European Consumers* (Brussels: ECRI, 2006).

Letowska, E., 'The Constitutional Aspect of Consumer Protection in Poland', in L. Thévenoz & N. Reich (eds), *Liber amicorum Bernd Stauder: Droit de la Consommation—Konsumentenrecht—Consumer Law* (Baden-Baden/Zurich: Nomos/Schulthess, 2006).

Liebscher, C., 'Case C-168/05, *Elisa Maria Mostaza Claro v Centro Movil Milenium SL*, judgment of the Court of Justice (First Chamber) of October 2006 ECR I-10421', (2008) 45 *Common Market Law Review*, pp. 545–57.

Lissowska, M., 'Overview of Behavioural Economics Elements in the OECD Consumer Policy Toolkit', (2011) 34 *Journal of Consumer Policy*, pp. 393–8.

Loos, M., 'Consumer Sales Law in the Proposal for a Consumer Rights Directive', (2000) 1 *European Review of Private Law*, pp. 15–55.

Lutfalla, E. and Magnier, V., 'French Legal Reform: What is at Stake if Class Actions Are Introduced In France?', (2006) 73 *Defense Counsel Journal*.

Lyon–Caen, A., 'Fundamental Social Rights as Benchmarks in the Construction of Europe', in L. Betten & D. Macdevitt (eds), *The Protection of Fundamental Social Rights in the European Union* (The Hague: Kluwer, 1996).

Maduro, M.P., 'L'équilibre insaisissable entre la liberté économique et les droits sociaux dans l'Union européenne', in P. Alston, *L'Union européenne et les droits de l'homme* (Brussels: Bruylant, 2001), pp. 465–89.

Mahlmann, M., 'Die Grundrechtscharta der Europäischen Union', (2000) 9 *Zeitschrift für Europäische Studien*.

Maillo, J., 'Article 86 EC: Services of General Interest and EC Competition Law', in G. Amato & C.-D. Ehlermann (eds), *EC Competition Law: A Critical Assessment* (Oxford: Hart Publishing, 2007), pp. 591 *et seq*.

Mak, C., 'Fundamental Rights and the European Regulation of iConsumer Contracts', (2008) 31 *Journal of Consumer Policy*, pp. 425–39.

Mak, V., 'Two levels, one standard? The multi-level regulation of consumer protection in Europe' in J. Devenney and M. Kenny (eds), *European Consumer Protection: Theory and Practice* (Cambridge: CUP, 2012), pp. 21 *et seq*.

Marauhn, T., *Rekonstruktion sozialer Grundrechte als Normkategorie—zugleich eine Kritik der konventionellen Gegenüberstellung von Grundrechten und Staatszielbestimmungen*, (Frankfurt am Main: Habilitation manuscript, 2000).

Markesinis, B., 'Privacy, Freedom of Expression and the Horizontal Effect of the Human Rights Bill: Lessons from Germany', (1999) 115 *Law Quarterly Review*.

Marleix, P., 'Que peuvent espérer en 1981 les consommateurs', *Les cahiers de l'AFOC* (May 1981).

Mattei, U., 'Hard Code Now!', (2002) 2 *Global Jurist Frontiers*.

Mattei, U. & Nicola, F., 'A "Social Dimension" in European Private Law? The Call for Setting a Progressive Agenda', (2007) 7(1) *Global Jurist Frontiers*.

Mcgoldrick, D., 'The Charter and UN Human Rights Treaties', in S. Peers & A. Ward (eds), *The European Union Charter of Fundamental Rights* (Oxford-Portland OR: Hart Publishing, 2004).

Mcgregor, S., 'Sustainable Consumer Empowerment through Critical Consumer Education: a Typology of Consumer Education Approaches, (2005) 29 *International Journal of Consumer Studies*.

Mendes, J., 'Participation and the Role of Law after Lisbon: A Legal View on Article 11 TEU', (2011) 48 *Common Market Law Review*, pp. 1849–77.

Menendez, A., 'Some Elements of a Theory of European Fundamental Rights', in A. Menendez, & E.O. Eriksen (eds), *Arguing Fundamental Rights*, Vol. 77 (Dordrecht: Springer, 2006).

Micheletti, M. & Follesdal, A., 'Shopping for Human Rights. An Introduction to the Special Issue', (2007) 30 *Journal of Consumer Policy*, pp. 167–75.

Micklitz, H.-W., 'Consumer Rights', in A. Cassese, A. Clapham, & J.H.H. Weiler (eds), *Human Rights and the European Community: The Substantive Law* (Baden-Baden: Nomos, 1991).

____, 'De la nécessité d'une nouvelle conception pour le développement du droit de la consommation dans la Communauté européenne', in *Liber amicorum Jean Calais-Auloy, Études du Droit de la Consommation* (Paris: Dalloz, 2004).

____, 'Collective Private Enforcement of Consumer Law: the Key Questions', in W. Boom & M. Loos (eds), *Collective Enforcement of Consumer Law* (Groningen: Europa Law Publishing, 2007).

____, *Verbraucherschutz durch Unterlassungsklagen: Umsetzung und Anwendung der Richtlinie 98/27/EG in den Mitgliedstaaten* (Baden-Baden: Nomos, 2007).

____, 'Universal Services: Nucleus for a Social European Private Law' EUI Working Papers, Law 2009/12, Florence.

____, 'European Consumer Law', in E. Jones, A. Menon & S. Weatherill (eds.) *The Oxford Handbook of the European Union* (Oxford: Oxford University Press, 2012).

____ & Caffaggi, F., *New Frontiers of Consumer Protection. The Interplay between Private and Public Enforcement* (Mortsel: Intersentia, 2009).

Micklitz, H.-W. & Reich, N., 'Crónica de una Muerte Anunciada: The Commission Proposal for a "Directive on Consumer Rights"', (2009) 46 *Common Market Law Review*, pp. 471–519.

____, Reich, N., & Weatherill, S., 'EU Treaty Revision and Consumer Protection', (2004) 27 *Journal of Consumer Policy*, pp. 367–99.

____, Reisch, L., & Hagen, K., 'An Introduction to the Special Issue on Behavioural Economics, Consumer Policy and Consumer Law', *Journal of Consumer Policy*, (2011) 34, pp. 271–76.

____ & Stadler, A., 'The Development of Collective Legal Actions in Europe, Especially in German Civil Procedure', (2006) 17 *European Business Law Review*.

____ & Weatherill, S., 'Consumer Policy in the European Community: Before and After Maastricht', (1993) 16 *Journal of Consumer Policy*, pp. 285–321.

Mulheron, R., *The Class Action in Common Law Legal Systems* (Oxford, Hart Publishing, 2004).

____, 'Some Difficulties With Group Litigation Orders—And Why A Class Action Is Superior', (2005) 24 *Civil Justice Quarterly*.

Müller, J.P., 'Koordination des Grundrechtschutzes in Europa–Einleitungsreferat', (2005) *Zeitschrift für Schweizerisches Recht*.

Nemeth, K. & Ortner, H., 'The Proposal for a New Directive concerning Credit for Consumers', (2003) 4 *German Law Journal*, pp. 801–13.

Nicola, F. & Mattei, U., 'A Social Dimension in European Private Law? The Call for Setting a Progressive Agenda', (2006) 41 *New England Law Review*, pp. 1–66.

Nicolini, G., 'A Regulatory Perspective on Consumer Financial Capability', in European Credit Research Institute, *Consumer Financial Capability: Empowering European Consumers* (Brussels: ECRI, 2006).

Niemi-Kiesiläinen, J., 'Collective or Individual? Construction of Debtors and Creditors in Consumer Bankruptcy', in J. Niemi-Kiesiläinen, I. Ramsay, and W. Whitford (eds), *Consumer Bankruptcy in Global Perspective* (Oxford: Hart Publishing, 2003), pp. 41–60.

____, Ramsay, I., & Whitford, W. (eds), *Introduction: Consumer Bankruptcy in Global Perspective* (Oxford: Hart Publishing, 2003), pp. 1–16.

Nihoul, P. & Rodford, P., *EU Electronic Communications Law: Competition and Regulation in the European Telecommunications Market* (Oxford: Oxford University Press, 2004).

Nussbaum, M., 'Capabilities and Human Rights', (1997) 66 *Fordham Law Review*, p. 273.

OECD, *Improving Financial Literacy: Analysis of Issues and Policies* (Paris: OECD, 2005).

____, Report from the Directorate for Science, Technology and Industry Committee for Information, Computer and Communications Policy, *Enhancing Competition in Telecommunications: Protecting and Empowering Consumers, Ministerial Background Report* (Paris: OECD, 2008).

____, Financial Literacy and Consumer Protection: Overlooked Aspects of the Crisis, OECD Recommendation on Good Practices on Financial Education and Awareness Relating to Credit (Paris: OECD, 2009).

——, 'The Changing Consumer and Market Landscape', in OECD Consumer Policy Toolkit, (Paris: OECD, 2010).

Ogus, A. I., 'Law and Spontaneous Order: Hayek's Contribution to Legal Theory', (1989) 16(4) *Journal of Law and Society*.

Osman, F. (ed.), *Vers un Code de la Consommation* (Brussels: Emile Bruylant, 1998).

Pallemaerts, M., *Proceduralizing Environmental Rights: The Aarhus Convention on Access to Information, Public Participation in Decision Making and Access to Justice in Environmental Matters in a Human Rights Context* (United Nations Environment Programme for the Geneva Environment Network, 2004).

Pearson, G., 'Financial Literacy and the Creation of the Financial Citizen', in M. Kelly-Louw, J. Nehf, & P. Rott (eds), *The Future of Consumer Credit Regulation, Creative Approaches to Emerging Problems (Markets and the Law)* (Aldershot: Ashgate Publishing, 2008).

Pernice, I., 'Multi-level Constitutionalism and the Treaty of Amsterdam: Constitution-Making Revisited?', (1999) 36 *Common Market Law Review*.

____, Franz, M., & Stephan, C.W., 'Renewing the European Social Contract: The Challenge of Institutional Reform and Enlargement in the Light of Multilevel Constitutionalism', (2001) 12 *Kings College Law Journal*.

____ & Kanitz, R., 'Fundamental Rights and Multilevel Constitutionalism in Europe', WHI-Paper 7/2004 Humboldt-Universität zu Berlin.

Perrez, F.X., *Key Questions concerning the Human Rights and Environment Debate. An Introduction* (United Nations Environment Programme for the Geneva Environment Network, July 2004).

Picard, E., 'Citizenship, Fundamental Rights, and Public Services', in M. Freedland & S. Sciarra (eds), *Public Services and Citizenship in the European Union* (Oxford: Oxford University Press, 1998).

Poillot, E., *Droit européen de la consommation et uniformisation du droit des contrats* (Paris: LGDJ, 2006).

Prosser, T., *The Limits of Competition Law: Markets and Public Services* (Oxford: Oxford University Press, 2005).

Ramsay, I., 'Consumer Redress and Access to Justice', in C. Rickett & T. Telfer (eds), *International Perspectives on Consumers' Access to Justice* (Cambridge: Cambridge University Press, 2003).

____, 'Consumer Law, Regulatory Capitalism and the "New Learning" in Regulation', (2006) 28 *Sydney Law Review*.

____, *Consumer Law and Policy: Text and Materials on Regulating Consumer Markets* (Oxford: Hart Publishing, 2007).

Ramsay, I., *Consumer Law and Policy: Text and Materials on Regulating Consumer Markets* (Oxford: Hart Publishing, 2012).

Rawls, J., *A Theory of Justice* (Cambridge, MA: Harvard University Press, 1971).

Reich, N., 'Protection for Consumers' Economic Interests by the EC', (1992) 14 *Sydney Law Review*.

____, 'From Contract Law to Trade Practices Law: Protection of Consumers' Economic Interests by the EC', in T. Wilhelmsson (ed), *Perspectives of Critical Contract Law* (Aldershot: Ashgate Publishing, 1993).

____, *Bürgerrechte in der EU: subjektive Rechte von Unionsbürgern und Drittstaats angehörigen unter besonderer Berücksichtigung der Rechtslage nach der Rechtsprechung des EuGH und dem Vertrag von Amsterdam* (Baden-Baden: Nomos, 1999).

____, 'Verbraucherpolitik und Verbraucherschutz im Vertrag von Amsterdam', (1999) *Verbraucher und Recht*.

____, 'The Courage Doctrine: Encouraging or Discouraging Compensation for Antitrust Injuries?', (2005) 42 *Common Market Law Review*.

____, 'A European Concept of Consumer Rights: Some Reflections on Rethinking Community Consumer Law', in *Liber Amicorum Bernd Stauder*, *Consumer Law* (Baden-Baden: Nomos, 2006).

____, 'More Clarity after "Claro"?' (2007) 3(1) *European Review of Contract Law*, pp. 41–61.

____, 'Crises or Future of European Consumer Law', (2009) *The Yearbook of European Consumer Law*.

____ & Leahy, D., *Internal Market and Diffuse Interests* (Brussels: Story Scientia, 1990).

____ & Micklitz, H.-W., *Consumer Legislation in the EC Countries: A Comparative Analysis* (New York: Van Nostrand, 1980).

____ & Micklitz, H.-W., *Europäisches Verbraucherrecht* (Baden-Baden: Nomos, 2003).

Reifner, U., 'Social Banking, Ansätze und Erfahrungen über die Integration sozialer Zielsetzungen in Privatwirtschaft und Finanzdienstleistungen', in L. Schuster (ed.), *Die gesellschaftliche Verantwortung von Banken* (Berlin: Erich Schmidt Verlag, 1997).

____, 'The Lost Penny, Social Contract Law and Market Economy', in T. Wilhelmsson & S. Hurri (eds), *From Dissonance to Sense: Welfare State Expectations, Privatization and Private Law* (Aldershot: Ashgate Publishing, 1999).

____, 'Personal Bankruptcy Law and Inclusive Contract Law', in J. Niemi-Kiesiläinen, I. Ramsay, & W. Whitford (eds), *Consumer Bankruptcy in Global Perspective* (Oxford: Hart Publishing, 2003).

____, *Ausgewählte Auszüge aus Normen und Begründung aus der Sicht des Verbraucherschutzes des Geänderten Vorschlags für eine Richtlinie über Verbraucherkreditverträge und zur Änderung der Richtlinie 93/13/EWG des Rates, 7.10.2005 COM (2005) 483* (Hamburg: Institut für Finanzdienstleistung e.V., 2005).

____, 'Verantwortungsvolle Kreditvergabe im europäischen Recht', in L. Thévenoz & N. Reich (eds), *Liber amicorum Bernd Stauder: Droit de la Consommation/ Konsumentenrecht/Consumer Law* (Baden-Baden/Zurich: Nomos/Schulthess, 2006), pp. 383–403.

Reimann, M., 'Product Liability in a Global Context: the Hollow Victory of the European Model', (2003) 11 *European Review of Private Law*.

Renucci, J.-F., *Droit européen des droits de l'homme*, 3rd edn (Paris: LGDJ, 2002).

Réseau U.E. d'experts indépendants en matière de droits fondamentaux, *Rapport sur la situation des droits fondamentaux dans l'Union européenne en 2003*, January 2004.

Réseau Financement Alternatif, *Financial Services Provision and Prevention of Financial Exclusion* (2008)..

Rickett, C. & Telfer, T. (eds), 'Consumers' Access to Justice: An Introduction', in *International Perspective on Consumers' Access to Justice* (Cambridge: Cambridge University Press, 2003).

Riedel, E., 'Verbraucherschutz, Artikel 38', in J. Meyer, *Kommentar zur Charta der Grundrechte der Europäischen Union* (Baden-Baden: Nomos, 2003).

Riley, A. & Peysner, J., 'Damages in EC Antitrust Actions: Who Pays the Piper', (2006) 31 *European Law Review*, pp. 748–61.

Robbers, G., *Menschenrecht auf Sicherheit—Aspekte der Geschichte, Begründung und Wirkung einer Grundrechtsfunktion* (Baden-Baden: Nomos, 1987).

Rosenberg, D., 'Mandatory-Litigation Class Action: The Only Option for Mass Tort Cases' (2002) 115 *Harvard Law Review*.

Ross, M., 'Promoting Solidarity: From Public Services to a European Model of Competition?', (2007) 44 *Common Market Law Review*.

Rott, P., 'The Protection of Consumers' Interests After the Implementation of the EC Injunctions Directive Into German and English Law', (2001) 24 *Journal of Consumer Policy*, pp. 399–439.

____, 'Heininger und die Folgen für das Widerrufsrecht', (2002) *Verbraucher und Recht*.

____, 'Consumer and Services of General Interest: Is EC Consumer Law the Future?', (2007) 30 *Journal of Consumer Policy*.

____, 'Consumer Credit', in H.-W. Micklitz, N. Reich, & P. Rott, *Understanding EU Consumer Law* (Antwerp: Intersentia, 2009), pp. 177–212.

Ryder, N., 'Out with the Old and in with the New? A Critical Analysis of Contemporary Policy towards the Development of Credit Union in Great Britain', (2005) *Journal of Business Law*.

Säcker, F.J., *The Order of Group actions in the Private Law System* (Munich: C.H. Beck, 2006).

Sadurski, W., '"Solange, Chapter 3": Constitutional Courts in Central Europe—Democracy—European Union', (2008) 14(1) *European Law Journal*, pp. 1–35.

Salais R. & Villeneuve, R., *Europe and the Politics of Capabilities* (Cambridge, Cambridge University Press, 2004).

—— & Villeneuve, R., 'Introduction: Europe and the Politics of Capabilities', in R. Salais & R. Villeneuve (eds), *Europe and the Politics of Capabilities* (Cambridge: Cambridge University Press, 2004).

Sauter, W., 'Services of General Economic Interest and Universal Service in EU Law', (2008) 33 *European Law Review*, pp. 167–93.

Scharpf, F.W., 'Democratic Policy in Europe', (1996) 2 *European Law Journal*, pp. 136–55.

____, 'The European Social Model: Coping with the Challenges of Diversity', (2002) 40 *Journal of Common Market Studies*.

Schmid, C.U., 'The Instrumentalist Conception of the Acquis Communautaire in Consumer Law and its Implications on a European Contract Law Code', (2005) 1(2) *European Review of Contract Law*, pp. 211–27.

Schulte-Nölke, H., Twigg-Flesner, C., & Ebers, M. (eds), *EC Consumer Law Compendium: The Consumer Acquis and its transposition in the Member States* (Munich: Sellier, 2008).

Schuster, L. (ed.), *Die gesellschaftliche Verantwortung der Banken* (Berlin: Erich Schmidt Verlag, 1997).

Sen, A., 'Well-being, Agency and Freedom: The Dewey Lectures 1984', (1985) 82 *Journal of Philosophy*.

____, *On Ethics and Economics* (Oxford: Basil Blackwell, 1987).

____, 'Capability and Well-Being', in M.C. Nussbaum & A. Sen (eds), *The Quality of Life* (Oxford: Clarendon Press, 1993).

____, *Development as Freedom* (Oxford: Oxford University Press, 1999).

____, *Commodities and Capabilities* (New Delhi: Oxford University Press, 1999).

____, 'Elements of a Theory of Human Rights', (2004) 32 *Philosophy & Public Affairs*.

____, *The Idea of Justice* (London: Penguin Books, 2009).

____, Arrow, K.J., & Suzumura, K., 'Social Choice Re-examined', Vol. 1, Proceedings of the IEA Conference held at Schloss Hernstein, Berndorf (Vienna, 1997).

Shaw, J., 'The Emergence of Post-national Constitutionalism in the European Union', (1999) 6 *Journal of European Public Policy*.

Simitis, K., *Verbraucherschutz—Schlagwort oder Rechtsprinzip?* (Baden-Baden: Nomos-Verlagsgesellschaft, 1976).

Stehr, N., Henning C., & Weiler B. (eds), *The Moralization of the Market* (New Jersey: Transaction Publishers, 2006).

Stiglitz, J., *Globalization and its Discontents* (London: Penguin Books, 2002).

Storskrubb, E., *Civil Procedure and EU Law: A Policy Area Uncovered* (Oxford: Oxford University Press, 2008).

____, 'Civil Justice—A Newcomer and an Unstoppable Wave?', in P. Craig & G. De Búrca (eds.), *The Evolution of EU Law*, 2nd edn (Oxford: Oxford University Press, 2011), pp. 299–322.

____ & Ziller, J., 'Access to Justice in European Comparative Law', in F. Francioni (ed.), *Access to Justice as a Human Right* (Oxford: Oxford University Press, 2007).

Study Group on Social Justice in European Private Law, 'Social Justice in European Contract Law: A Manifesto', (2004) 10 *European Law Journal*, pp. 653–674.

Stuyck, J., 'European Consumer Law after the Treaty of Amsterdam: Consumer Policy in or Beyond the Internal Market?', (2000) 37 *Common Market Law Review*.

Sunstein, C. (ed.), *Behavioural Law and Economics* (Cambridge: Cambridge University Press, 2000).

Supiot, A., (ed) *Au-delà de l'emploi: Transformations du travail et devenir du droit du travail en Europe* (Report for the European Commission) (Paris: Flammarion, 1999).

Tabb, C., 'The Historical Evolution of the Bankruptcy Discharge', (1991) 65 *American Bankruptcy Law Journal.*

Teubner, G., 'Legal Irritants: Good Faith in British Law or How Unifying Law Ends up in New Divergences', (1998) 61 *Modern Law Review.*

Tonner, K., 'Sustainable Consumption, Consumer Policy and the Law', in C. Verdure (ed.), 'Environmental Law and Consumer Protection', 2011 (1) *European Journal of Consumer Law.*

Trentmann, F., 'Knowing Consumer-Histories, Identities, Practices', in F. Trentmann (ed.), *The Making of the Consumer* (Oxford: New York: Berg Publishers, 2006).

____ & Bevir, M., (eds), *Governance, Citizens, and Consumers: Agency and Resistance in Contemporary Politics* (Basingstoke: Palgrave Macmillan, 2007).

Truchet, V., 'Le concept du consommateur informé en droit européen', in R. Bieber (ed), *Swiss Papers on European Integration*, (Bern-Zurich: Stämpfli-Schulthess, 2000).

Trumbull, G., *Consumer Capitalism: Politics, Product Markets, and Firm Strategy in France and Germany* (Ithaca-London: Cornell University Press, 2006).

Tweedy, J. & Hunt, A., 'The Future of the Welfare State and Social Rights: Reflections on Habermas', (1994) 21 *Journal of Law and Society.*

Unberath, H. & Johnston, A., 'The Double-Headed Approach of the ECJ concerning Consumer Protection', (2007) 44 *Common Market Law Review*, pp. 1237–84.

Van Gerven, W., 'Harmonization of Private law: Do we Need it?', (2004) 41 *Common Market Law Review.*

____, *The European Union: A Polity of States and Peoples* (Oxford: Hart Publishing, 2005).

Vasak, K., *Human Rights: A Thirty-Year Struggle: the Sustained Efforts to Give Force of Law to the Universal Declaration of Human Rights, UNESCO Courier 30:11* (Paris: United Nations Educational, Scientific, and Cultural Organisation, November 1977).

Von Bogdandy, A. & Bast, J., 'The EU's Vertical Order of Competences: the Current Law and Proposals for its Reform', (2002) 39 *Common Market Law Review.*

Von Danwitz, T., 'The Charter of Fundamental Rights of the EU: Between Political Symbolism and Legal Realism', (2001) 29 *Denver Journal of International Law and Policy.*

Von Hayek, F., *Law, Legislation and Liberty, Volume 1: Rules and Order* (London: Routledge and Kegan Paul, 1973).

____, *Law, Legislation and Liberty, Volume 2: The Mirage of Social Justice* (London: Routledge and Kegan Paul, 1976).

____, *Law, Legislation and Liberty, Vol. 3: The Political Order of a Free People* (Chicago/London: Chicago Press and Routledge & Kegan Paul, 1979).

Wagner, W., 'When All Else Fails: Regulating Risky Products through Tort Litigation', (2007) 95 *Georgetown Law Journal.*

Ward, A., 'Access to Justice', in S. Peers & A. Ward (eds), *The EU Charter of Fundamental Rights* (Oxford: Hart Publishing, 2004).

Watson, G., 'Class Actions: The Canadian Experience', (2001) 11 *Duke Journal of Comparative & International Law*.

Weatherill, S., 'The Commission's Options for Developing EC Consumer Protection and Contract Law: Assessing the Constitutional Basis', (2002) 13 *European Business Law Review*.

____, 'Pre-emption, Harmonization and the Distribution of Competences', in C. Barnard & J. Scott (eds), *The Law of the Single European Market* (Oxford: Hart, 2002).

____, 'Competence Creep and Competence Control', (2004) 23 *Yearbook of European Law*.

____, 'Why Object to the Harmonization of Private Law by the EC?', (2004) 12 *European Review of Private Law*.

____, *EU Consumer Law and Policy* (Cheltenham: Edward Elgar Publishing, 2005).

____, 'The Constitutional Competence of the EU to Deliver Social Justice', (2006) 2 *European Review of Contract Law*.

____, 'The Limits of Legislative Harmonization Ten Years after *Tobacco Advertising*: How the Court's Case Law has become a "Drafting Guide",' (2011) 12(3) *German Law Journal*, pp. 827–64 .

____, 'From Economic Rights to Fundamental Rights', in S. De Vries, U. Bernitz, & S. Weatherill, *The Protection of Fundamental Rights in the EU After Lisbon* (Oxford: Hart Publishing, 2013).

Weiler, J.H.H, 'The Transformation of Europe', (1991) 100 *Yale Law Journal*, pp. 2403 *et seq.*

____, *The Constitution of Europe* (Cambridge: Cambridge University Press, 1999).

____, 'To be a European Citizen, Eros and Civilization', in J.H.H. Weiler, *The Constitution of Europe, Do the New Clothes Have an Emperor? And other Essays on European Integration* (Cambridge: Cambridge University Press, 1999).

____, & Lockhart, N., 'Taking Rights Seriously: The European Court and its Fundamental Rights Jurisprudence', (1995) 32 *Common Market Law Review*, pp. 51–94.

Weiss, M., 'The Politics of the EU Charter of Fundamental Rights', in B. Hepple (ed.), *Social and Labour Rights in a Global Context* (Cambridge: Cambridge University Press, 2002), pp. 73–94.

Westphal, M., 'The EU Financial Services Policy and its Effect on Consumer Law', in M. Kelly-Louw, J. Nehf, & P. Rott (eds), *The Future of Consumer Credit Regulation, Creative Approaches to Emerging Problems (Markets and the Law)* (Aldershot: Ashgate Publishing, 2008), pp. 69–87.

Wiedenbaum, M., 'The Case Against the United Nations Guidelines for Consumer Protection', (1987) 10 *Journal of Consumer Policy*.

Wilhelmsson, T., *Social Contract Law and European Integration* (Aldershot: Dartmouth Publishing Group, 1995).

____, 'Private Law 2000: Small Stories on Morality through Liability', in T. Wilhelmsson & S. Hurri (eds), *From Dissonance to Sense: Welfare State Expectations, Privatisation and Private Law* (Aldershot: Ashgate Publishing, 1999).

____, 'The Legal, the Cultural and the Political—Conclusions from Different Perspectives on Harmonization of European Contract Law', (2002) 13 *European Business Law Review*.

____, 'Services of General Interest and European Private Law', in C. Rickett & T. Telfer (eds), *International Perspectives on Consumers' Access to Justice* (Cambridge: Cambridge University Press, 2003), pp. 149–66.

____, 'The Average European Consumer: A Legal Fiction', in T. Wilhelmsson, E. Paunio, and A. Pohjolainen (eds) *Private Law and the Many Cultures of Europe* (Alphen aan den Rijn: Kluwer Law International, 2007), pp. 243–68.

____, 'The Ethical Pluralism of Late Modern Europe and Codification of European Contract Law', in J. Smits, *The Need for a European Contract Law: Empirical and Legal Perspectives* (Groningen: Europa Law Publishing, 2005), pp. 121–52.

____, 'Full Harmonization of Consumer Contract Law?', (2008) 16 *Zeitschrift für Europäisches Privatrecht*.

____, Tuominen, S., & Tuomola, H. (eds), *Consumer Law in the Information Society* (The Hague: Kluwer Law, 2000).

Willet, L.A., 'U.S.-Style Class Actions in Europe: A Growing Threat', (2005) 9 *Briefly*, National Legal Centre for the Public Interest.

Williams C. & Windebank, J., 'The "Excluded Consumer": A Neglected Aspect of Social Exclusion', (2002) 30 *Policy and Politics*.

Wils, W., 'EU Antitrust Enforcement Powers and Procedural Rights and Guarantees: The Interplay Between EU Law, National Law, the Charter of Fundamental Rights of the EU and the European Convention on Human Rights', (2011) 34(2) *World Competition: Law and Economics Review*.

Wilson, T., 'Responsible Lending or Restrictive Lending Practices? Balancing Concerns regarding Over-indebtedness with Addressing Financial Exclusion', in M. Kelly-Louw, J. Nehf, & P. Rott (eds), *The Future of Consumer Credit Regulation: Creative Approaches to Emerging Problems, (Markets and the Law)* (Aldershot: Ashgate Publishing, 2008), pp. 91–106.

Winn, J.K. (ed.), *Consumer Protection in the Age of the 'Information Economy' (Markets and the Law)* (Aldershot: Ashgate Publishing, 2006).

Zarsky, T., 'Law and Online Social Networks: Mapping the Challenges and Promises of User-generated Information Flows', (2008) 18 *Fordham Intellectual Property, Media and Entertainment Law Journal*, pp. 741–83.

Ziegel, J., 'Consumer Protection in Canada and the Class Action Remedy, in L. Thévenoz & N. Reich (eds), *Consumer Law: Liber Amicorum Bernd Stauder* (Geneva/ Baden-Baden: Schulthess/Nomos Verlag, 2006).

INDEX

The manufacturer's authorised representative in the EU for product
safety is Oxford University Press España S.A. of El Parque Empresarial
San Fernando de Henares, Avenida de Castilla, 2 - 28830 Madrid
(www.oup.es/en or product.safety@oup.com). OUP España S.A. also acts
as importer into Spain of products made by the manufacturer.
Printed and bound by CPI Group (UK) Ltd, Croydon, CR0 4YY
14/09/2026
02216304-0005